ENVIRONMENTAL MANAGEMENT

The field of environmental management (EM) involves a broad and evolving repertoire of practices. The field originated around 1970 in response to new policy, regulation and public concern about environmental issues. EM has undergone many changes and improvements since then, progressing from a reactive, compliance-based focus towards, in leading cases, practices reflecting strong commitment to sustainability. And yet, EM remains, for the most part, ill-equipped to deal with the complex and highly uncertain implications of the ecological crisis.

Environmental Management offers a rigorous critique of conventional EM and explores alternative ideas, frameworks and approaches that are currently considered "fringe", but which have the potential to transform the practice of EM. This book goes beyond narrow definitions and considers questions regarding the purpose, roles, scope and potential of environmental management. EM is situated and contextualized within the evolving and expanding realm of environment and sustainability literature. The book argues that new approaches to EM need to be more flexible, imaginative and better equipped to address future environmental problems of a scale and severity previously unforeseen.

This book will be of great interest to students and scholars of environmental management, environmental planning, resource management, and environmental assessment.

Peter R. Mulvihill is Professor in the Faculty of Environmental Studies, York University, Canada.

S. Harris Ali is Professor in the Faculty of Environmental Studies and the Graduate Program Director of Sociology, York University, Canada.

"This very timely, detailed and provocative book provides a much-needed critical perspective on environmental management and alternative approaches to future practice. It opens up the intellectual space for debate and fruitful thinking through the integration of insights ranging from disaster management to black swan thinking —assessing and reorienting these into cogent principles for alternative EM."
—*John Sinclair, Professor, Natural Resources Institute, University of Manitoba, Canada*

"I have been waiting for a book like this. An up-to-date and comprehensive overview of the field of environmental management; one with the right balance of theory, practice and connections to the real world. Key concepts and ideas are well defined in terms that are clear and intelligent. This book understands the very ephemeral nature of environmental management; a realm responsive and reactive to shifting natural, social and economic conditions shaped by politics, the public, and the realities of our world's changing environment. An excellent work for senior undergraduate or graduate courses in environmental management, policy and history."
—*Kevin Hanna, Director, Centre for Environmental Assessment Research, The University of British Columbia, Canada*

"In this engaging and informative text, Mulvihill and Ali present a comprehensive overview of emerging debates in environmental management. Their rigorous analysis of the field's history, nuanced examination of socio-ecological approaches, and timely call for a re-orientation in environmental thinking will appeal to emerging scholars and established practitioners alike."
—*Roza Tchoukaleyska, Assistant Professor, Environmental Studies, Grenfell Campus, Memorial University, Canada*

"This thoughtful and thought-provoking book can help transform environmental management to more effectively anticipate and respond to contemporary and emerging environmental crises and challenges. It provides a systematic overview of current practice, draws upon an array of pertinent theory and research, and refines and integrates a host of alternative frameworks, concepts and models."
—*David P. Lawrence, Ph.D., Lawrence Environmental, USA*

ENVIRONMENTAL MANAGEMENT

Critical thinking and emerging practices

Peter R. Mulvihill and S. Harris Ali

Routledge
Taylor & Francis Group
LONDON AND NEW YORK

earthscan
from Routledge

First published 2017
by Routledge
2 Park Square, Milton Park, Abingdon, Oxon OX14 4RN

and by Routledge
711 Third Avenue, New York, NY 10017

Routledge is an imprint of the Taylor & Francis Group, an informa business

© 2017 Peter R. Mulvihill & S. Harris Ali

The right of Peter R. Mulvihill & S. Harris Ali to be identified as authors of this work has been asserted by them in accordance with sections 77 and 78 of the Copyright, Designs and Patents Act 1988.

All rights reserved. No part of this book may be reprinted or reproduced or utilized in any form or by any electronic, mechanical, or other means, now known or hereafter invented, including photocopying and recording, or in any information storage or retrieval system, without permission in writing from the publishers.

Trademark notice: Product or corporate names may be trademarks or registered trademarks, and are used only for identification and explanation without intent to infringe.

British Library Cataloguing-in-Publication Data
A catalogue record for this book is available from the British Library

Library of Congress Cataloging-in-Publication Data
Names: Mulvihill, Peter R., author. | Ali, S. Harris, author.
Title: Environmental management : critical thinking and emerging practices / Peter R. Mulvihill & S. Harris Ali.
Description: New York, NY : Routledge, 2016.
Identifiers: LCCN 2016027216| ISBN 9781138899933 (hb) | ISBN 9781138899964 (pb) | ISBN 9781315707570 (ebk)
Subjects: LCSH: Environmental management. | Environmental management—Methodology.
Classification: LCC GE300 .M85 2016 | DDC 363.7—dc23
LC record available at https://lccn.loc.gov/2016027216

ISBN: 978-1-138-89993-3 (hbk)
ISBN: 978-1-138-89996-4 (pbk)
ISBN: 978-1-315-70757-0 (ebk)

Typeset in Bembo and Stone Sans
by Florence Production Ltd, Stoodleigh, Devon, UK

CONTENTS

List of Illustrations   vii
Acknowledgments   viii
List of Abbreviations   ix

1 Introduction   1

2 Context: Challenges Facing Environmental Management   7

3 Drivers of Change: Key Forces Influencing New Directions in Environmental Management   23

4 Conventional Environmental Management: Origins, Evolution, Characteristics and Critique   29

5 Current State of Alternative Environmental Management: Theory, Practice, Limitations and Gaps   39

6 Critical Social Science and the Ecological Crisis   44

7 The Critical Analysis of Climate Change as a Case in Study   63

8 Disaster Studies and the Ecological Crisis   77

9 A Socio-Ecological Approach to the Ecological Crisis   95

10 Towards a Philosophical Reorientation in Environmental Management I: Post-Normal Science Thinking   115

11 Towards a Philosophical Reorientation in Environmental Management II: Black Swan Thinking 131

12 Experimental Applications of Emerging, Alternative Environmental Management 149

13 Conclusion and Prospects for Alternative Environmental Management 157

Index *161*

ILLUSTRATIONS

Figures

9.1	The Epidemiological Triangle	107
9.2	The Socio-Ecological Matrix	109
10.1	The Relationship between Decision Stakes and Systems Uncertainties	122

Box

8.1	The Hazards Identification and Risk Assessment (HIRA) Protocol	81

ACKNOWLEDGMENTS

We wish to thank the team at Routledge–Earthscan for their invaluable editorial help.

Thanks to Dean Ray for assisting with sections of the manuscript preparation.

Thanks to five anonymous reviewers for their thoughtful and helpful comments.

To the numerous environmental management practitioners as well as the environmental and disaster sociologists who we have learned from over the years, many thanks for sharing your insights.

Special thanks to our families for their love and support.

ABBREVIATIONS

ANT	Actor Network Theory
Corp	United States Army Corp of Engineers
CSR	corporate social responsibility
EIA	environmental impact assessment
EM	environmental management
EMS	environmental management system
ENGO	environmental non-government organization
IFRC	International Federation of Red Cross and Red Crescent Societies
IPCC	Intergovernmental Panel on Climate Change
ISO	Inter Organization for Standardization
LED	light-emitting diode
NSF	National Science Foundation
NEP	New Ecological Paradigm
NGO	non-government organization
RM	resource management
UN	United Nations
UNISDR	United Nations International Strategy for Disaster Reduction
WCED	World Commission on Environment and Development

1
INTRODUCTION

Organization and Purpose

The aim of this book is twofold: to examine the theory and practice of environmental management (EM) from a critical perspective, and to explore emerging directions that may improve EM and shape more sustainable futures. Our intent is not to examine environmental management in a comprehensive or exhaustive way – that would be beyond the scope of this monograph. The discussion is more selective, focusing on a limited number of themes, issues and prospects. Our motivation is straightforward. In our experience teaching courses that address environmental management, we have identified a key shortcoming in the literature: most of it can be described as conventional or mainstream (or else overly technical), and relatively little of it could be described as critical or alternative. The alternative literature that could inform new approaches to environmental management lurks largely unnoticed in places that have been generally regarded to be outside of the field as conventionally defined. In practice, important insights, ideas and experiences that could influence the field of EM can originate from anywhere across the spectrum of the natural or social sciences, arts or humanities, rather than primarily or only from "environmental" literature, theory and practice. Ideas that may seem peripheral at present may turn out to be influential or even transformative. It is therefore necessary to explore EM in a critical, provocative manner, and ask new, difficult questions about its purpose and its future directions.

In the more mainstream literature on environmental management, it is rare to find EM discussed explicitly or in a focused manner – more often, it is subsumed under other headings and treated superficially and uncritically. As Barrow (2006: 164) observes: "Environmental management is sometimes little more than a catchphrase". It tends to appear as a secondary topic alongside more elaborate discussions of, for example, environmental planning, integrated resource management (RM), watershed management, or adaptive management (which are also relatively new streams of literature). Likewise, it is difficult, though possible, to find critical or contextualized definitions of environmental management. Too often, narrow definitions are proposed, setting aside important questions regarding the purpose, roles, scope and potential of environmental management. It is not sufficient to only discuss, as is common enough in the mainstream literature, "principles" or criteria for good practice. It is also necessary to situate and contextualize environmental management within the evolving and expanding realm of environment and sustainability literature. Finally, it is necessary to continually re-examine and revisit standard assumptions about EM.

What is environmental management? Where did it come from? How has it evolved? These fundamental questions are addressed in Chapter 3 (Drivers of Change: Key Forces Influencing New Directions in EM) and Chapter 4 (Conventional Environmental Management: Origins, Evolution, Characteristics and Critique). Before that, in Chapter 2 (Context: Challenges Facing Environmental Management), we discuss the context which necessitated the introduction of formal EM some four decades ago, and which continues to demand not only continual improvement in EM practice, but arguably a radical reorientation of the field. Indeed, this is a major theme of our book: slow, incremental improvements in conventional environmental management will not be sufficient. Dramatic improvements are needed to leap-frog to a new era in which sustainability is an explicit and overarching goal and more of EM's potential is realized as a force of positive change.

The first four chapters of this book set the stage for our discussion of alternative approaches to environmental management, which then unfolds in Chapter 5 (Current State of Alternative EM: Theory, Practice, Limitations and Gaps), Chapter 6 (Critical Social Science and the Ecological Crisis), Chapter 7 (The Critical Analysis of Climate Change as a Case in Study), Chapter 8 (Disaster Studies and the Ecological Crisis), Chapter 9 (A Socio-Ecological Approach to the Ecological Crisis), Chapters 10 and 11 (Towards a Philosophical Approach to the Ecological Crisis, Parts I and II). We conclude with Chapters 12 and 13, a discussion of principles, opportunities and prospects for alternative environmental management.

Throughout the book, we distinguish generally between two approaches to environmental management: "conventional" and "alternative" (or "emerging"). Our intent is not to suggest that a simple bifurcated world of environmental management exists, either conventional or alternative. Rather, it is to suggest that a tension between conventional and emerging approaches has always existed and has shaped the evolution of environmental management. In the chapters that follow, we discuss a range of approaches, from the most conventional to the more progressive and beyond into what may be on the horizon. In our exploration of streams of literature that have been under-recognized in terms of their potential relevance to EM, we pay particular attention to the field of critical social science and, more precisely, the fledgling subfield of environmental sociology, including disaster studies.

In writing this book, our goal is to add to the existing literature on environmental management, but from new and different angles. This book is not intended to be one that will be easy for everyone to agree with. We believe that the field of environmental management is currently in a pattern of slow improvement or incremental progress. We hope to offer provocative arguments and alternatives that may resonate with others who are not satisfied with the current situation and state of the art. We hope that this book will complement existing literature on environmental management and serve as a counterpoint to the more mainstream works that currently dominate the field. We contend that EM, to a great extent, lacks a solid or coherent theoretical foundation, and we discuss concepts and theories that may help fill ongoing gaps.

We are currently at an interesting point in time as we reflect on possibilities for EM to be better informed by critical social science and environmental sociology. Environmental or ecological issues have traditionally been a minor theme in mainstream sociology, but they are commanding increasing attention. The longstanding anthropocentrism of the social sciences is giving way to a more integrated perspective and there is increasing engagement with socio-ecological matters. Environmental issues, once framed more narrowly, are now framed much more broadly. At the same time, new "types" of environmental problems – most notably climate change – challenge our fundamental beliefs about the effectiveness of management measures and solutions. This shift and reorientation creates possibilities for new theoretical and practical directions in EM; alternatives may emerge from a much wider array of sources than ever before. We explore these possibilities in detail in Chapters 6 to 11.

Defining Environmental Management?

Definitional challenges and dilemmas are common across the broad field of environmental and sustainability literature. This should not be surprising, since literature that can be categorized as explicitly "environmental" has existed for less than 50 years, and has undergone rapid development and diversification. There is still little or no agreement on how to define key environmental terms, many of which are used loosely or interchangeably. Environmental management is even vaguer than most environmental terms. It was not coined or trumpeted with fanfare, as, for example, "sustainable development", or "corporate social responsibility". Instead, it quietly gained currency as a more explicitly "environmental" version of antecedents such as forest management, natural resource management or pest management. It is, to a great extent, a generic and unglamorous term, although its role and consequences are potentially far-reaching.

Environmental management is commonly perceived as a systematic and coordinated approach to addressing environmental issues, risks and problems. It is related to, but to some extent distinct from other processes such as environmental policy, regulation, standards, assessment or auditing. It is often thought of as primarily a corporate function, the domain of industry. It is often confused with, or reduced to "environmental management system", although the former is much broader than the latter. In addition, it is sometimes confused with "development" or "resource management". It is not uncommon, in some contexts, to see activities such as mining, agriculture or forestry referred to, erroneously, as environmental management, thus equating extraction with management. This trivializes and undermines the true purpose of EM as a force of change and not as an enabling agent for business as usual practices. The term "environment" in EM has clear implications; whereas resource management has often been interpreted as management for the purposes of sustained exploitation, EM goes beyond that in suggesting that the environment itself must be sustained. This is an important, though not always recognized distinction.

Let's consider a selection of definitions drawn from literature pertaining to environmental management:

a) "Environmental management is the means of controlling or guiding human–environment interactions to protect and enhance human health and welfare and environmental quality" (Randolph, 2004: 3).
b) "Environmental management is a system of administrative functions that are used to (i) develop; (ii) implement; and (iii) monitor the *environmental strategy* of a business" (Antweiler, 2014: 2).
c) "Environmental management seeks to steer the development process to take advantage of opportunities, try to avoid hazards, mitigate problems, and prepare people for unavoidable difficulties by improving adaptability and resilience" (Erickson and King, 1999; International Network for Environmental Management website: www.inem.org, accessed January 2005, cited from Barrow, 2006: 5).
d) "Environmental management is a process concerned with human–environment interactions, and seeks to identify: what is environmentally desirable; what are the physical, economic, social and technological constraints to achieving that; and what are the most feasible options . . ." (El-Kholy, 2001: 15, cited from Barrow, 2006: 5).
e) "The control of all human activities which have significant impact upon the environment" (Barrow, 2006: 6).
f) "Management of the environmental performance of organizations, bodies and companies" (Sharratt, 1995, cited from Barrow, 2006: 6).

A spectrum of definitions is noted above, ranging from broader conceptions of the purpose of EM (Randolph, Erickson-King, El-Kholy and Barrow) to considerably narrower (Antweiler as well as Sharratt frame EM in organizational terms rather than societal in scope). The scope of EM may be confined to corporate activities, or more broadly to encompass a range of human activities, or most expansively to address the totality of all human/environment interactions – a virtually infinite realm. "Management" is variously described as guidance, steering, controlling, protecting, avoiding, mitigating or otherwise. When defined in restrictive terms or reduced to the point where it is interchangeable with EMS, it may be easier to visualize as a limited, finite function or responsibility, but it becomes less meaningful and inclusive. And it must be acknowledged that the term "management" has connotations that are problematic – it sounds technical and top-down, a vestige of a bygone era in which the ethos and tyranny of "command and control" were more common. This kind of terminological baggage is unavoidable as long as the operative term "management" retains its currency. The term "environmental governance" has gained considerable momentum in the last decade and its relationship with EM is not entirely clear, although it may be argued that EM should be thought of increasingly as a component of governance. We will return to this debate throughout the book, but this brings us to a more general point about environmental terminology. Most, if not all, environmental terms are evolving and contested, as should be expected in such a new field. "Sustainability", for example, remains a highly controversial term, even after 30 years of mainstream use. It has been critiqued on many levels and to some it remains vague, inaccessible or, even worse, heavily compromised. Many others, however, find that sustainability is a useful and compelling term. This underlines two points: we need to be as clear as possible about the meaning of terms and use them with precision, and we need to continually improve and refine environmental terminology, adding greater meaning and nuance.

It is also important to note that, notwithstanding the selection of quotes above, definitions of environmental management are not plentiful; indeed, there is a strong tendency for them to be absent in the literature. A recent book titled *Manual of Environmental Management* (Belcham, 2015) provides an excellent example of this pattern. Despite the title of this 300-page volume, environmental management is never, at any point, defined explicitly. The book contains many definitions of key concepts under the categories of environmental policy, law, sustainability, environmenteal management system (EMS), reporting, assessment, auditing, etc., but a definition of environmental management is not offered. This is reflective of a strong tendency in the literature pertaining to environmental management; it is generally assumed that the term is so understandable and accessible that it requires no definition and no explicit discussion. It is assumed that only the more specific terms under the broad umbrella of environmental management need to be defined. Environmental management thus remains largely amorphous and difficult to pin down. In Chapter 6 of Belcham's book, *Environmental Management and Assessment Tools*, the central term (EM) is undefined and simply assumed, while there is an explicit discussion and definition of environmental impact assessment (EIA), environmental risk assessment, environmental auditing, EMS and other terms. Once again, this is characteristic of the general literature; definition and explicit discussion of environmental management is suspended or overlooked, while topics such as EIA and EMS are used as avatars for the more general subject. This misses an important point; it is also important to examine the concept of environmental management with explicitness and precision. Moreover, it reinforces a common fallacy that tools or processes such as EMS or EIA are sufficient to ensure that the goals of environmental management will be achieved. In turn, this fallacy reflects overconfidence in standards, policies and techniques to achieve substantive outcomes, when in reality they are only pieces of a much more complicated puzzle.

Throughout this book we challenge limiting and restrictive conceptions of environmental management. For example, in the recent book *Elements of Environmental Management*, Antweiler offers a narrow definition and argues that environmental management should be thought of as a business activity and should not be confused with broader goals such as "management of the environment" or sustainability (p. 1). We believe the opposite is true: environmental management is a broad, collective, collaborative endeavor – it is nothing less than governance for sustainability. However, before we begin to make that case, let us consider some examples of environmental management to demonstrate that it comes in many forms. What does it look like? It is, for example, an application of herbicide or integrated pest management in a utility corridor. It is a fish ladder on a salmon-bearing river. A public information sign directing hikers away from ecologically sensitive areas in a park. A prescribed burn or replanting of trees. A beach closed to the public. A decommissioned rail bed converted to a bicycle path. The installation of solar panels or wind turbines. A training course in emergency spill response. The purchase of carbon offset credits. The installation of wildlife tunnels underneath highways. Designation of heritage trees in urban areas. Conversion of diesel engines to alternative fuels. Recyling and reuse. National, regional or local climate change reduction strategies. And, of course, much more. Environmental management is a million different things, occurring at all scales, and it is important that it is not thought of narrowly, or only as a specialized activity in the business sector. When we reduce or compartmentalize environmental management, we lose sight of its context and its essential nature and purpose, which we discuss in the next chapter.

In this chapter we have identified our purpose – a critical exploration of EM, both conventional and alternative. We have identified some key problems with existing literature pertaining to EM – the central term is seldom defined or examined, and common assumptions about the field remain largely uncontested. We have noted that the history of EM is murky, largely undocumented and seldom critiqued or analyzed. We have stated a key argument that will be elaborated throughout the book – the need for better, more powerful and alternative approaches to EM, in which it evolves towards collaborative governance for sustainability. In the next chapter, we discuss the broad and daunting array of challenges facing environmental management.

References

Antweiler, W. (2014) *Elements of Environmental Management*. Toronto: University of Toronto Press.
Barrow, C.J. (2006) *Environmental Management for Sustainable Development* (2nd ed.). London: Routledge.
Belcham, A. (2015) *Manual of Environmental Management*. Abingdon: Routledge.
Randolph, J. (2004) *Environmental Land Use Planning and Management*. Washington, DC: Island Press.

2
CONTEXT
Challenges Facing Environmental Management

We refer to the general challenge facing environmental management as *the ecological crisis*. There are many related terms that capture some of the challenges facing environmental managers, at many different scales – environmental issues or problems, environmental performance or quality, environmental incidents, accidents and disasters, etc. – but none, we argue, are as powerfully compelling and all-encompassing as "the ecological crisis". In order to do justice to the scope and magnitude of the challenges facing environmental management, we must consider environmental problems in their many forms and dimensions and in all their complexity. Otherwise, we underestimate, disaggregate and oversimplify the challenges. The challenge or goal is often referred to as "sustainability", but we prefer the term *ecological crisis*, with its more urgent connotation, its somewhat less anthropocentric meaning (sustainability of what and for whom?) and its vast, nearly imponderable implications. It is precisely our collectively weak grasp of the ecological crisis that reflects the attitudes and qualities needed for effective environmental management: humility, wariness and cautiousness are all in order. This philosophy can be thought of as a version of the "precautionary principle" in which action is to be taken on the basis of the weight of evidence rather than waiting for the point in time at which the evidence is considered to be conclusive – at which point it may be too late to respond effectively. The precautionary stance is proactive rather than reactive.

This message has, of course, been sounded for decades, ever since *Silent Spring* (Carson, 1962), *The Limits to Growth* (Meadows et al., 1972) and other seminal volumes began to point out the unfolding ecological crisis. More recent literature leaves no doubt that the crisis is as daunting as ever (e.g. Wijkman and Rockstrom, 2012; Robin et al., 2013; Worldwatch Institute, 2013; Sabin, 2013; Global Footprint Network, 2016). There is an overwhelming body of literature and evidence that the ecological crisis persists and is probably worsening. A poignant documentary film titled *Last Call* (Cerasuomo and Arvat, 2012) revisited the surviving authors of *The Limits to Growth* (Meadows et al., 1972) 40 years after their original book, in doing so showing how the core message of an impending ecological crisis was slow to sink in with policy makers and the general public. The World Commission on Environment and Development (the Brundtland Commission) popularized the term "sustainable development" in 1986 and contributed to growing consciousness. Where are we now? The good news is that the terms "sustainable development" and "sustainability" have crossed over into the mainstream. In universities, throughout the 1960s, 1970s, 1980s and 1990s, these terms were seldom heard outside of environmental studies departments, and now they are commonplace across the spectrum, the everyday language of business and engineering schools. Similarly, in government and industry circles, the theme of sustainability has been internalized and mainstreamed. In the realm of non-government organizations (NGOs), environmental and sustainability consciousness has been strongly evident even longer. But the central message of *Limits to Growth*, then and now, is still valid: awareness of the ecological crisis has been generally slow to sink in. Responses have been too little and too late, and will remain so unless there is dramatic improvement in environmental management and sustainability governance.

How deep are typical mainstream conceptions of sustainability? The spectrum of shallower and deeper ideas of sustainability is an ongoing tension, as anti-environmentalists and climate change deniers fade increasingly into irrelevance. It is now easy enough for many to recognize that sustainability is an overarching goal, but this has, in turn, created a troubling relativism as the inherent subjectivity of sustainability has become increasingly evident. In its shallower forms, sustainability can seem indistinguishable from standards of environmental quality that prevailed in the 1980s and 1990s, when it was widely acceptable for businesses and industries to aim only for legal compliance or due diligence in their operations. The moving target of deeper sustainability, meanwhile, literally implies ideal conditions such as zero emissions, zero footprints, zero impact, energy self-reliance and other similarly ambitious indicators. To be clear, it is the deeper forms of sustainability that we are concerned with in this book. When we discuss the possibilities of alternative, leading-edge environmental management, we are interested in more powerful practices that are conceived explicitly to address the ecological crisis and deep, long-term sustainability. This means that the questions we should be asking about EM are profound and, to some extent, speculative or even unanswerable given the current state of affairs.

The full magnitude of the ecological crisis is largely unknown and largely imponderable. The ecological crisis can be considered in various ways. It is the most complex and daunting collective challenge that has ever faced humankind. It is an epic risk management exercise. It is an unfolding, multifaceted disaster. For the most part, the crisis is perceived in terms of problems, events, processes and indicators that are more or less interconnected. In practice, it is thought of simultaneously in smaller picture ways (e.g. compliance with laws, certification of environmental management systems, the pursuit of performance indicators) and in bigger picture ways (e.g. sustainability of regions, the State of the World or the biosphere). We argue that the context of environmental management is best considered broadly, as a collective endeavor, global in scale, and intergenerational in its time horizon. At the same time, EM practices need to unfold more effectively at all scales.

When we argue that the ecological crisis is largely imponderable, we mean that the combination of several factors inhibits our ability to achieve a firm grasp of ecological systems. These factors include complexity, uncertainty, gaps in baseline data, shortcomings in basic science and the increasing prevalence of unnatural disasters. Any single one of these factors alone precludes the complete understanding of how ecological systems function or how we can "manage" them sustainably. Taken together, they reinforce an almost impenetrable mystery, with profound implications for environmental management. A useful starting point for considering EM, therefore, is full recognition of the severity and magnitude of the ecological crisis – a crisis that can probably never be "solved". The troubling corollary, meanwhile, is that inadequate appreciation of the ecological crisis will tend to exacerbate it. Thus, in a strange way, a sense of bewilderment and powerlessness is arguably a more appropriate mindset with which to confront the ecological crisis – at least more appropriate than the prevailing collective mindset which is characterized by misplaced overconfidence and faith in incremental approaches to EM.

There is considerable potential for confusion when ecological systems are discussed in relation to other systems (social, cultural, economic, political, etc.). It is sometimes useful to separate and differentiate these discrete systems for purposes of analysis and critique. A political system, for example, is not quite the same as a social system, and both are very different from ecological systems. And yet, the opposite can also be argued, and this point has often been made in environmental literature. Everything is connected. Humans are fundamentally part of nature, not separate from it. The traditional Cartesian way of thinking tended to separate things, while the ecological world view seeks to integrate and reconcile them. For the sake of clarity and consistency, when we discuss ecological systems in their full complexity, we are also referring to the human systems that are part of them. When we observe, for example, that ecosystems can be unpredictable, we mean not only that they may be unpredictable in the absence of human intervention, but also that they are may be even more unpredictable when there is a strong degree of human-induced change. The point we are making here is that, unless we specify otherwise throughout this book, when we refer to nature and ecosystems, we refer to them in the broadest, most inclusive sense. Likewise, when we refer to environmental management, we include all of its many aspects – social, political, cultural, economic, and potentially more.

Complexity

The literature on adaptive environmental management or governance (e.g. Holling, 1978; Folke et al., 2005) refers to complex systems as a given or omnipresent challenge. There are significant limits to knowledge with respect to how ecological systems work, how they change, how they might or might not recover from stresses, how they might be made more or less resilient, and so on. Complexity is a common theme in environmental literature, with a variety of specific meanings. One typical definition of ecological complexity, for example, is "The number of species at each trophic level and the number of trophic levels in a community" (Cunningham et al., 2005: 511). Despite the apparent straightforwardness of this definition, the broader implications of complexity are clear enough. Ecosystems are never simple or straightforward, but usually quite complicated; we are often wrong when we make assumptions about how they might behave under a variety of unpredictable circumstances. And it must be acknowledged that humankind, in general, excels at creating difficult circumstances for the biosphere, inadvertently or not.

Discussing complex systems, Lawrence notes that: "As complexity rises, precise statements lose meaning and meaningful statements lose precision" (2013: 354). The limits to ecological knowledge apply across all timescales. We struggle to understand the history of ecosystems or their condition or behavior at any given time, except in relatively simple descriptive terms – species populations, water quantity, air quality, absence of collapse, etc. We can make predictions about the impact of human activities on ecosystems, but experience has shown that in order for predictions to have credibility, they must be accompanied by qualifications about likelihood, accuracy, and sensitivity to contingencies. This was echoed by Schneider and Kay (1994: 33): "systems theory suggests that ecosystems are inherently complex, that there may be no simple answers, and that our traditional managerial approaches, which assume a world of simple rules, are wrong-headed and likely to be dangerous".

Why are ecological systems so complex and why are their futures so impervious to human understanding? Let us consider two examples from Canada. The Canadian Arctic is a vast region, or, more accurately, it is so vast that it is made up of a number of regions. Most Canadians live far south of the "treeline" – the northern limit at which trees grow (the Northern Canadian treeline). For some, the treeline is one way to approach the elusive and relative demarcation of "north" within Canada. And yet, the treeline is not a straight boundary; instead, it extends much further north in the western parts of the Canadian Arctic, curving downward as it moves east. Scientists have hypothesized that the uneven shape of the treeline is largely attributable to the long, irregular process of Ice Age retreat (Pielou, 1994; Young, 1994). If this is true, it may help to explain the surprising diversity of Canadian Arctic ecology – there are three marine eco-zones and ten terrestrial eco-zones, each distinct from the others, rendering generalizations about these systems largely meaningless.

The second, more southerly Canadian example, the Niagara Escarpment, is a linear erosional geological feature, several hundred kilometers long that begins at the Niagara Gorge (where Niagara Falls recedes slowly, in geological time), runs across Ontario and beneath Lake Huron into the United States. The escarpment, designated a Global Biosphere Reserve, is estimated to be 450 million years old and features impressive biodiversity (300 bird species, 53 mammals, 90 fish species, and 37 types of rare orchid; *Niagara Escarpment Plan*, 2003).

What do these two examples tell us about ecological complexity, or, at least, the classificatory aspects of complexity? In both the Canadian Arctic and the Niagara Escarpment cases, contemplating the process of geological time is essential to any appreciation of these phenomena. And in both cases, there is more ecological and biological diversity and variability than might be expected. This suggests strongly that a complex interrelationship between geomorphology and ecology is at the heart of any deep understanding of eco-regions. A more universal lesson might be that any understanding of ecological systems requires a nuanced, long-term consideration of the many factors that combine to shape them. Deep sustainability requires consideration of multiple time-scales as well as numerous interrelated yet subtle factors. This sensibility, though profoundly complicated and almost imponderable, is nevertheless of central importance to environmental management.

Uncertainty

Uncertainty has long been a major theme in environmental literature, in the context of management, planning, monitoring, prediction and many other subdisciplines. Earlier in the era of the modern environmental movement, in the 1970s and 1980s, uncertainties surrounded the outcomes of major issues – for example, resource depletion, acid rain or contaminated sites: how bad would the situations become, would systems recover from stress or collapse, and how might systems respond to different remedial measures? Now we grapple with risks, consequences and uncertainties of climate change and other regional and global problems. As always, we run the risk of underestimating the difficulties of addressing ecological uncertainty because of the complexity of ecological systems. If we consider, for example, the inherent unpredictability of financial markets and compare that challenge with environmental management, we are forced to acknowledge that ecological systems, by their very nature, are much more complex and unpredictable. Why? Some might argue the opposite, and point out that human-based systems are more complex and uncertain since they are social constructions, they do not follow the laws of nature and, after all, humans are highly unpredictable due to cognitive and psychological factors. All of that is true, but we need to remember that these human systems, in all of their uncertainty, are also part of ecological systems. When we consider the full implications of all of this combined, interrelated complexity, we can begin to appreciate just how complex and uncertain ecological systems may indeed be.

In less complex systems, uncertainty and risk might sometimes be reduced through research and the acquisition of knowledge and insight, or at least experts may claim that is the case. In ecological systems, however, we are often faced with irreducible uncertainties, because we are usually unable to acquire sufficient (and sufficiently relevant) scientific knowledge. In many instances scientific knowledge is far from conclusive and subject to continual revision and reinterpretation.

If scientists can devote their careers to the study of a single species or organism, and only scratch the surface in understanding a limited subject, how can we address interconnected ecological questions at more complex scales and generate useful prescriptive knowledge in the midst of the ecological crisis? Two conclusions seem inescapable: Mother Nature remains, as always, in charge, and conventional approaches to environmental management will probably never be sufficient in addressing irreducible uncertainty.

Gaps in Baseline Ecological Knowledge

Before the emergence of the modern environmental movement, which gained momentum in North America in the 1960s, "resource management" had long prevailed as a proxy or antecedent of EM. Resource managers of the past (and present) were preoccupied with matters such as resource inventories – for example, the number of trees or birds or fish that might be harvested or exploited – important, but piecemeal information. The advent of environmental laws and policies marked an important milestone, even though critics have always noted the inadequacies and shortcomings of many of these laws and policies. An important historical breakthrough was the *formalization* of environmental management, making environmental concerns more explicit, whereas before they were marginal, unrecognized or at best implicit and haphazard. We can think of this earlier era as the "dark ages" of frontier-style development, when there was no formal or explicit attention to environmental matters. Of course, nothing is ever quite that simple, and it would be overly arbitrary to suggest that environmental management emerged *sui generis* in 1969 when the United States enacted the National Environmental Protection Act. But it is clear that the formalization of environmental management, over time, has made it more consistent and standardized. It was entirely possible, and generally much easier, for environmentally unsound practices to prevail in the older days. These days, even though unsustainable development practices are still very common, it is increasingly difficult for anyone to claim ignorance of the environmental consequences of human activities.

Now that the fig leaf of environmental ignorance has been removed, there is a collective imperative for us to not only comprehend more about the biophysical world (naturalists have been doing that for centuries), but also to understand it in ecological terms at various scales. In this way, complex and integrative concepts like "environment", "ecosystems", "eco-regions" or "biosphere" have far-reaching implications. They reflect the need for a much deeper, more sophisticated, more systematic and interconnected grasp of the ecological dimensions of the planet. The need may be clear, but what is the state of knowledge? That is an enormously complicated question, but it might be generalized that knowledge of ecosystems tends to be at best tentative or preliminary, conducive to hypotheses and iterative practices. Even an exercise as ambitious as the Millennium Ecosystem Assessment (World Health Organization, 2005) raises more questions than it answers. If we only consider Western science – one way of knowing among many, but one which provides the predominant (if shaky) basis for resource use and development decisions – we quickly conclude that scientific knowledge of ecosystems is characterized universally by significant gaps and shortcomings. This should not be surprising, when we consider that basic ecological research is expensive and time-consuming and that it only began to be conducted systematically in the last few decades. Indigenous knowledge has, of course, been gathered for much longer, but it has been to date used only sparingly in mainstream decision-making.

To summarize, the state of ecological knowledge around the world is a work in progress. It is uneven. Gaps both small and large are common. Even the best efforts to establish state-of-the-art ecological knowledge have significant limitations. This leads us back to the theme of irreducible uncertainty, because, unless the state of ecological knowledge undergoes a revolutionary breakthrough, we continue to live in a context of great uncertainty about ecosystems, eco-regions and the biosphere. And no such dramatic breakthrough is likely; it is probable that the current pace of incremental, uneven progress will continue to unfold.

Unnatural Disasters

For many individuals, the ecological crisis does not resonate or register until they personally experience some of the direct impacts of the crisis. This rationale is frequently proffered as an explanation as to why people may objectively have a good deal of knowledge about many environmental problems, yet they do not change their behaviors accordingly in ways that would either mitigate or adapt to such problems – for example, climate change. The ecological crisis seems too distant and detached from their everyday experience and understandings of the world. One very strong motivating factor for behavioral change is to do things that would ensure life rather than death. For many, however, the life-and-death dimension of a given environmental problem is not brought to the fore unless they have a first-hand experience with it – for example, in dealing with the impacts of a natural disaster. The direct experience of large-scale natural disasters is almost always jarring, dramatic and unfortunately tragic. Under such circumstances, people face the most compelling of reasons to change behavior in response to such disasters – that of personal survival.

Ulrich Beck (1992) noted that environmental problems and issues would undoubtedly be subject to greater publicity, public concern and political scrutiny in the decades following his words. This is because environmental problems violate the norm of survival. For Beck, in the past, especially during the decades just after the Second World War, environmental risks were simply tolerated and rationalized as the price to be paid for the benefits of "progress." This mindset changed with the advent of the risk society where the logic of the developing welfare state based on the distribution of positives (i.e. money, jobs, benefits, educational opportunities, etc.) was increasingly being replaced by an emphasis on the distribution of negatives, as society grappled with an accumulating number of environmental risks – that is, environmental risk issues became increasingly problematic and difficult to ignore as the side-effects of the earlier period of exuberant industrialization started to catch up with society. The externalities could no longer be ignored. The need to confront environmental risks was formally institutionalized with the emergence of the modern environmental movement as a counterforce to the existing way industry and the state carried out their activities. According to Beck (1992), with this newly intensified societal and political focus on environmental risks, a new period referred to as "risk society" was ushered in. In the context of Europe, the entrenchment of the risk society was said to have become consolidated with the Chernobyl nuclear explosion in the Ukraine. This particular disaster served as the impetus for dramatic increase in environmental concern among many Northern Europeans, which set the stage for the restructuring of industry along ecologically sensitive lines (especially in Germany, the Netherlands and Scandinavian countries). However, what effect did it have in the North American or global context?

Evidence from disaster research has demonstrated that over the last quarter century there have been increases in both "natural" and "technological" disasters across the globe (Hewitt, 1997; Etkin, 2016). For example, the United Nations (UN) has noted that between 1962 and 1992 the number of disasters has increased by an average of 6 percent annually (Associated Press, 1995 cited by Bankoff, 2001: 19). Clearly, the trend has continued since that reported time and anecdotally one can likely recall many disasters over the recent past, including the BP Oil Spill in the Gulf of Mexico, various high-impact hurricanes such as Katrina and Sandy in the US, the tsunamis in South Asia in December 2004 and Japan in March 2011 (which contributed to the Fukiyama nuclear disaster in the same country). There are various specific reasons that may be identified to help account for this increase in disasters, and these will be discussed in Chapter 8, but for now it is sufficient to note that this increase is just another manifestation of the ecological crisis predicated on the basis of human intervention in nature. In this connection, perhaps the most poignant illustration of how human intervention in nature can lead to "unnatural" disasters is anthropogenic climate change.

The atmospheric accumulation of carbon dioxide and other greenhouse gases that has resulted in global climate change is a direct consequence of human decisions to utilize finite carbon-based sources of energy (i.e. fossil fuels). As such, climate change is a human-made phenomenon and the most vivid example today of an "unnatural" disaster. Furthermore, since the impacts of global change are so extensive and far-reaching, they will undoubtedly contribute to the development of other types of disasters, most notably, extreme weather events such as hurricanes, ice storms, heatwaves as well as associated disasters such as flooding, droughts, and disease pandemics – all of which would need to be considered as "unnatural" since their ultimate origin is in human decisions to intervene in nature through the intensive use of fossil fuels.

Climate change as an unnatural phenomenon is just another (though very significant) manifestation of the ecological crisis, but it brings into relief many of the aforementioned challenges faced by environmental managers. First, it reminds us that the ecological crisis is not a purely biophysical phenomenon, but a social phenomenon as well (because of the role of human decision-making in the development of disasters). Thus, humans have an important role to play in addressing the crisis. Second, climate change as an unnatural disaster brings forth the recognition of the urgency of the matter, and the need to act quickly as environmental managers – actions that are themselves problematic in light of a third set of factors. The inherent complexity of the climate change phenomenon, and associated issues related to limitations in data and shortcomings in the basic science of climate change impacts, all represent formidable barriers to effectively address this climate dimension of the ecological crisis. Many of these barriers were not fully recognized or appreciated until more recently. For instance, projections of sea-level rise due to climate change estimated only a decade ago have since been drastically revised to take into account "amplifying positive feedback loops" (Urry, 2011: 32; Derber, 2010: 35). For another example, the ability of ice sheets to reflect solar radiation, thereby keeping the surface cooler, was erroneously assumed to remain constant in climate change models. What was not taken into account was that as more of the ice melted, more water would be exposed and this water would not reflect the solar radiation as efficiently as the ice sheets. This would lead to a positive feedback situation where the melting of the polar ice caps would occur at an exponential rate (and not at a linear rate as previously thought). The implication of this was that the flooding of coastal regions would occur much more quickly and with much higher levels of melt-water, thus increasing the urgency of the situation because the time to act was drastically diminished (ibid.). This amplifying feedback loop also illustrates the complexity of the systems we are dealing with in the ecological crisis. Many disasters in the future will involve numerous other types of ecosystems (terrestrial, atmospheric, forest, water, etc.) each with their own complex interrelationships and feedback loops. The science of characterizing these types of ecosystems mechanisms is only in its infancy and certainly cannot yet provide the type of data needed for prediction and control. As such, the types of disasters we will face in the future will be largely unpredictable and therefore unmanageable through conventional means. This will force us to adopt alternative environmental management perspectives based on a different type of reasoning and a different underlying philosophy. The most notable of these would be those informed by the precautionary principle and "black swan thinking" which emphasize the need to focus on preventing disasters rather than trying to fix them after they happen – to be discussed in more detail in Chapter 11.

The Full Context of Environmental Management

What can we conclude about the context of environmental management (historical, ecological, political, social and cultural)? We can say that, some four decades into the modern environmental movement, awareness of environmental challenges and problems is increasingly universal and ubiquitous. Environmental law and policy regimes, weaker or stronger, are increasingly prevalent. Sustainability sensibility, shallower or deeper, is mainstream. Complexity, uncertainty and limits to ecological knowledge are well-established contextual themes. Extreme weather patterns and unnatural disasters appear to be the new normal. Resource and environmental problems are rampant. All of these factors create and reinforce the ecological crisis. We argue that this – the ecological crisis – is the real context of environmental management. Others may argue, not incorrectly, that the context of environmental management is legal compliance, or due diligence, or social license, or corporate social responsibility, or stewardship, or sustainable development. It is all of these things, and more – the sum of imperatives local and global, smaller and bigger pictures, an epic and collective governance challenge.

The Political Context of Environmental Management

It would be naive to ignore the political context of environmental management. Many environmental critics have noted that around the world, democratic decision-making pertaining to natural resource extraction, distribution and use continues to be significantly undermined by ongoing political factors. This is, of course, not a new social phenomenon. The history of imperialism is replete with examples of how numerous colonizing states have built their respective empires by dominating other parts of the world and exploiting their natural resources and peoples – most obviously along the Global North–Global South axis in recent times. As such, as examples from the histories of empire-building readily demonstrate, the control of natural resources (and therefore the environment) is at its core an issue of power, especially the political and economic power of elites to dominate the subaltern either through the threat of direct physical coercion or indirectly through the working of hegemonic influence. If the assertion of political and economic power has always existed, what, then, is different today and what relevance do the machinations of such power have for the nature of the contemporary ecological crisis we now face? Many argue that what is different today is the particular configuration of political and economic forces embodied in what is often referred to as neoliberalism. What exactly is neoliberalism and how does this influence the magnitude, intensity and scale of the ecological crisis and the effectiveness of current environmental management strategies to address the crisis?

At the most basic level, the doctrine of neoliberalism refers to a theory of political economic practices that is based on the premise that unlimited freedom to pursue individual entrepreneurial initiatives through protected arrangements of private property rights, free markets and free trade (Harvey, 2007) will result in prosperity – defined only in material terms with no consideration of the political question of prosperous for whom? From the neoliberal perspective, the role of the state is simply to maintain the privatized (i.e. individual) basis of the economy as opposed to any other objective such as the protection of the *collective* or society (which is defined simply as a collection of self-interested individuals). This means that the state, in effect, abdicates its traditionally defined role of protecting the security of the collective (i.e. society) by giving up those functions that serve the collective good – such as social security, public health, education functions and, most notably, the protection of the environmental commons – a process referred to as the "hollowing out of the state" (Jessop, 2004). These collective functions do not, according to this line of thinking, further the economic interests of individuals and private firms (i.e. profit maximization). Since some of these collective functions must unavoidably be recognized as being indispensable for the very survival of society, the neoliberal concession is to propose the limited provision of these types of collectively needed services through the privatization of social welfare functions. As such, the state would not itself perform these functions but would contract these out to private for-profit organizations, thereby ensuring the market basis of society.

The negative effects of neoliberalism on environmental management are numerous, but as alluded to, they all in some way impair, limit or otherwise constrain the ability of the state to protect the environment for the sake of the collective interest. It has been increasingly recognized, however, that such neoliberal limitations have essentially rendered an environmentally unsustainable condition referred to as the "tragedy of the commons" (Hardin, 1968). This is a situation where the environmental commons (e.g. air, water, soil) are exploited in such a way as to facilitate the accumulation of maximum benefits (or profits) by private firms, while at the same time, the negative costs associated with these environmentally destructive activities are shared by everyone else in the society. Under these conditions, the private firm receives a "free ride" in the sense that it does not share in a proportionate way the costs of environmental clean-up (even though they significantly contributed to the advent of the environmental problem in the first place). Taken to its logical conclusion, the environmental commons will be quickly destroyed as all private firms in a given industrial capitalist society will adopt a strategy of maximizing individual profit at the cost of the environment held in common. Consequently, the ecological functions provided by the environment to support all life on the planet will be destroyed and the ecological crisis will be taken to its logical conclusion – the end of all human and animal life.

Instead of adopting a radical, upstream-oriented approach that looks to prevent the ecological crisis at the source through the restructuring of the institutions of society, including the possibility for significant changes in how the industrial sector operates and the prevailing consumerist lifestyle, the proposed neoliberal solution is a market-oriented one that does little to effectively address the root cause of the tragedy of the commons. In this vein, a popular neoliberal-inspired approach to deal with negative environmental impacts, such as pollution, is to establish a market to pollute, often referred to as "cap and trade" schemes. Specifically, the idea is for the state to first set an upper total limit to the total amount of pollution that would be permitted. The state then issues permits to allow each private firm to pollute to a certain given level based on the size of the firm and other considerations, with the total amount of permitted pollution not exceeding the imposed overall cap. It is assumed that if an individual firm takes the initiative to curb its emissions, it will no longer need that number of permits. It can then sell its surplus permits to other firms who may want to increase the amount of pollution they generate. What this means is that private firms buy and sell what are essentially licenses to pollute. Proponents argue that such a scheme creates a "free market" for the buying and selling of pollution permits. The neoliberal market logic behind this market scheme is that the "laws" of supply and demand will "naturally" unfold in such a way as to reach a point of equilibrium whereby the environment is protected as a natural outcome of the unfolding market dynamics for pollution permits. Such a market-oriented approach to dealing with pollution leads to the consideration of only a very narrow and selective repertoire of environmental management perspectives and strategies – most notably those inspired by end-of-pipe approaches that are reactive in orientation and in line with the short-term economic timelines demanded by the profit maximization goals of the "free market".[1]

It is important to bear in mind that the tragedy of the commons is a result of political decisions made by society (or more accurately made by political elites on behalf of a democratic society, at least in theory) in relation to all types of interventions in the environment. In this context, the regulation of all environmental interventions in all stages of the life cycle of the materials and energy use from extraction to end use becomes an important consideration. Since it is the state that holds the power to regulate, environmental management must pay careful attention to the relationships among the state and industry/economic elites as this will influence the choice of environmental management strategies even considered – a particularly important consideration given that we will be proposing some alternative or fringe approaches to environmental management that may in some ways challenge the status quo relationship between state and industry (and society) under neoliberalist regimes. The state–industry relationship has been studied for some time by critical social scientists who adopt a "political economy" approach – a tradition that dates back all the way to Karl Marx's critique of industrial capitalism. Various perspectives have been put forth by political economists with respect to analyzing how the state–industry relationship has impacted negatively not only the environment but also society. In fact, many political economists have argued that under the contemporary conditions of intensified global neoliberalism, social and political factors involving power imbalances between different groups within and between societies, and the associated issues involving social injustice, corporate control and hegemony and the shrinking public sectors, have all had serious implications for regulating environmental impacts and the ability to "manage the environment" (Klein, 2014; O'Conner,1991). Indeed, one of the barriers that may arise in considering and adopting some of the alternative approaches to environmental management that we will be proposing is that there is an overwhelming regulatory emphasis on dealing with downstream environmental impacts instead of preventing the impacts from arising in the first instance. This precludes the need to consider other possible ways to institutionally orient society and the economy other than on the basis of simply unbridled profit maximization that, it must be recalled, serves as the basis of the tragedy of the commons.

Environmental regulations are quite often understood to be one of the basic foundational elements that undergird environmental management more generally.

This is because specific strategies of environmental management are usually developed and implemented in order to comply with specified environmental regulations with ostensibly the ultimate aim of protecting the environment. The development and enforcement of environmental regulations is usually understood to fall under the purview of the state since it is this body that has the authority to impose sanctions if compliance with environmental statutes is not maintained. Traditionally, with the advent of the modern environmental movement, the governance of environmental matters had come to be understood in terms of this regulatory command-and-control model. Here, regulatory policy was essentially equivalent to environmental policy and it was through such policy that the protection of the environment was to be governed. In more recent times, however, Evans (2012) has noted that environmental management and governance has evolved from a top-down, state-centric approach to a "polycentric", multi-stakeholder and multilevel perspective. This shift in approach is also reflected in a change in emphasis found in the academic realm. In their "state of the art" review of the literature, Davidson and Frickel (2004) found that earlier academic work on environmental governance was pursued mostly by political scientists who analyzed the conditions under which environmental policy was formulated or how such policy was implemented within the existent bureaucratic structures. In contrast, more recently, research emanating from environmental sociology and an expanded range of other social sciences has focused on higher levels of abstraction, including how broader national and global political economic factors influence state responses to various environmental problems and issues. Notably, researchers adopting this latter orientation have written much more extensively about issues related to the shift from environmental management based on regulation to one based on multi-stakeholder governance. For example, Garcia and Grainger observe that since the 1990s, what is understood to be "environmental management" has changed with the "worsening of the state of the resources, the intrusion of the environmental NGOs into the governmental debates and development of environmental advocacy" (2005: 36). Similarly, Hajer (1995) takes account of this shift by noting underlying changes in the discourse dealing with environmental protection – notably, as reflected through the increasing use of the term "environmental governance" as opposed to "environmental management". With this change in discourse, the spotlight was taken away from exclusively government players to a consideration of a range of non-state actors and institutions (such as the public, NGOs, and business groups) with a concomitant re-emphasis from a state-centric to a people-oriented adaptive co-management approach to environmental protection. A significant aspect of this materializing shift was that instead of focusing on managing and regulating the environment through performance-based predetermined criteria, the new emphasis on governance was on how the expanded number of interest groups could collectively and cooperatively move towards enhanced environmental protection, especially through consensus-driven processes and multi-stakeholder roundtable models (see, for example, Ali,1997, 1998).

Environmental Governance

Ironically, the neoliberal turn may have, as an unintended consequence, served as the stimulus for the transition from narrow and technically defined strategies of environmental management to broader forms of environmental governance. As alluded to above, one of the enduring effects of neoliberalism has been the "hollowing out of the state" whereby the responsibility and authority for policy decisions is increasingly being transferred from central government agencies to public and private agencies at the regional and local levels (Jessop, 2004). Although financially motivated by the neoliberal directive that state expenditure should not be used exclusively for societal and collective welfare functions, such a development has also meant that the role of the state has regressed substantially in terms of ceding power from state agencies to non-state actors. In the domain of environmental matters, this has meant the redistribution of environmental management functions to non-state organizations that, until that point, did not normally play a direct role in environmental policy decision-making and regulatory policy formation. In effect, these developments served as the opening for the inclusion of other stakeholders in environmental decision-making (Castree, 2010) in what Ulrich Beck has referred to as the advent of "subpolitics" (1992), where politics are no longer exclusively exercised through governmental, parliamentary and political parties but through alternative channels such as those related to technology, medicine, law, and the organization of work. Notably, under these changing sociopolitical conditions, the role of the government was no longer limited only to being the "steward" of the environment or "enforcer" of compliance, but to provide institutional support for environmental reform and to coordinate environmental efforts at the local and national levels while serving as a representative at the international level (Beck, 1992). This new supporting role in part stems from the shifting of authority wherein *collaborative* efforts begin to be pursued by state and non-state actors in the global, regional, national, subnational and local levels (Mol et al., 2009). In this context, the change in the nature of policy formation and decision-making was significant enough for scholars to introduce and warrant the use of a new term – "governance".

The success of governance is not conceived of in terms of a finished product, but rather, the degree of success is measured by the degree to which it fosters dialogue, debate and collaboration among all stakeholders. Particularly, stakeholders' interests lie in the overall guiding principles involving the integration of institutional rules, rules for interactions and actions to resolve problems (Evans, 2012: 1). Although today the term "management" still tends to be used interchangeably with the word "governance", it is important to recognize that the latter is more inclusive and diffuse in terms of participation and power relations. Thus, governance is a form of management that includes – and goes beyond – government action that places emphasis on the processes and procedures. In this light, the State begins to play a different role by explicitly providing institutional structures that can act as a catalyst for change (Evans, 2012). That is, governance, as a newer approach to environmental management, may open up the possibility for more serious consideration and even adaptation of the fringe approaches we will be discussing, as these types of approaches do not neatly fall within the conventional technocratic-dominated paradigm and performance-based standards of regulatory environmental management. Rather, such fringe approaches move beyond that to consider the institutional and organizational context in which these particular approaches can be embedded. Furthermore, as these fringe approaches are inherently by nature context-based, we must necessarily take into account the type of broader political economy considerations we have discussed above.

In this chapter we have discussed some of the key generic challenges facing and constraining environmental management, including complexity, uncertainty, knowledge gaps, the increasing prevalence of unnatural disasters, as well as political forces such as neoliberalism. Next, in Chapter 3, we discuss "drivers of change" – forces that are shaping new directions in EM.

Note

1. It is beyond the scope of the present discussion to go into the details of why such market-based, cap-and-trade schemes have not been effective (see Lohmann, 2006; Leonard, 2009). Here we just wish to point out how such schemes fit within the logic of neoliberalism as an example of how neoliberalism proposes "solutions" to the ecological crisis.

References

Ali, S.H. (1997) "Trust, Risk, and the Public: The Case of the Guelph Landfill Search". *Canadian Journal of Sociology*, 22 (4): 481–504.
Ali, S.H. (1998) "The Search for a Landfill Site in the Risk Society". *The Canadian Review of Sociology and Anthropology*, 36 (1): 1–19.
Bankoff, G. (2001) "Rendering the World Unsafe: 'Vulnerability' as Western Discourse". *Disasters*, 25(4): 19–35.
Beck, U. (1992) *Risk Society: Towards a New Modernity*. London: Sage.
Carson, R. (1962) *Silent Spring*. New York: Houghton Mifflin.
Castree, N. (2010) "Neoliberalism and the Biophysical Environment: A Synthesis and Evaluation of the Research". *Environment and Society: Advances in Research*, (1): 5–45.
Cerasuomo, E. and Arvat, M. (2012) *Last Call: The Untold Reasons of the Global Crisis* (documentary film).
Cunningham, W.P., Cunningham, M.A., Saigo, B.W., Bailey, R. and Shrubsole, D. (2005) *Environmental Science: A Global Concern* (Canadian ed.) Toronto: McGraw-Hill Ryerson.
Davidson, D.J. and Frickel, S. (2004) "Understanding Environmental Governance: A Critical Review". *Organization & Environment*,17: 4, 471–4,492.
Derber, C. (2010) *Greed to Green: Solving Climate Change and Remaking the Economy*. London: Paradigm Publishers.
Etkin, D. (2016) *Disaster Theory: An Interdisciplinary Approach to Concepts and Causes*. Waltham, MA: Butterworth-Heinemann.
Evans, J.P. (2012) *Environmental Governance*. New York: Routledge.
Folke, C., Hahn, T., Olsso, P. and Norberg, J. (2005) "Adaptive Governance of Socio-Ecological Systems". *Annual Review of Environment and Resources*, 30: 441–473.

Garcia, S.M. and Grainger, R. (2005) "Gloom and Doom? The Future of Marine Capture Fisheries". *Philosophical Transactions of the Royal Society: Biological Sciences*, 360(1453): 21–46.

Global Footprint Network (2016) Available at: www.footprintnetwork.org

Hajer, M. (1995) *The Politics of Environmental Discourse: Ecological Modernisation and the Policy Process*. Oxford: Clarendon Press.

Hardin, G. (1968) "The Tragedy of the Commons". *Science* 162: 3589, 1243–1248.

Harvey, D. (2007) *A Brief History of Neoliberalism*. Oxford: Oxford University Press.

Hewitt, K. (1998) "Excluded Perspectives in the Social Construction of Disaster". In E.L. Quarantelli (Ed.) *What is a Disaster? Perspectives on the Question*. New York: Routledge, pp. 75–92.

Hewitt, K. (1997) *Regions of Risk: A Geographical Introduction to Disasters*. Longman: Harrow and Essex.

Holling, C.S. (1978) *Adaptive Environmental Assessment and Management*. Chichester: Wiley.

Jessop, R. (2004) "Hollowing out the 'Nation-State' and Multilevel Governance. In P. Kennett (Ed.) *A Handbook of Comparative Social Policy*. Cheltenham: Edward Elgar, pp. 11–25.

Klein, N. (2014) *This Changes Everything: Capitalism vs. the Climate*. Toronto: Alfred A. Knopf.

Lawrence, D.P. (2013) *Environmental Impact Assessment: Practical Solutions to Recurrent Problems*. New York: John Wiley.

Leonard, A. (2009) "The Story of Cap and Trade", video documentary, produced by Free Range Studies. Available at: http://storyofstuff.org/movies/story-of-cap-and-trade/ (last accessed June 22, 2016).

Lohmann, L. (2008) "Six Arguments Against Carbon Trading". Available at: http://climateandcapitalism.com/2008/09/29/carbon-trading-the-wrong-way-to-deal-with-global-warming/ (last accessed June 22, 2016).

Marx, K. (1990) [1867]. *Capital, Volume I*. Trans. Ben Fowkes. London: Penguin Books.

Meadows, D., Meadows, D., Randers, J. and Behrens III, W.M, 1972. *The Limits to Growth*. New York: Universe Books.

Mol, A.P.J., Sonnenfeld, D.A. and Spaargaren, G. (Eds.) (2009) *The Ecological Modernisation Reader: Environmental Reform in Theory and Practice*, London and New York: Routledge.

Niagara Escarpment Plan (2003) The Niagara Escarpment Commission: Georgetown, Ontario.

O'Conner, J. (1991) "The Second Contradiction of Capitalism: Causes and Consequences". *Capitalism, Nature, Socialism*. Pamphlet 1. Santa Cruz, CA: Center for Political Ecology.

Pielou, E.C. (1994) *A Naturalist's Guide to the Arctic*. Chicago: University of Chicago Press.

Robin, L., Sorlin, S. and Warde, P. (Eds.) (2013) *The Future of Nature*. New Haven, NJ and London: Yale University Press.

Sabin, P. (2013) *The Bet: Paul Erlich, Julian Simon, and Our Gamble over Earth's Future*. New Haven, NJ and London: Yale University Press.

Schneider, E.D. and Kay, J.J. (1994) "Life as a Manifestation of the Second Law of Thermodynamics". *Mathematical and Computer Modelling*, 19(6–8): 25–48.

Urry, J. (2011) *Climate Change and Society*. Cambridge: Polity Press.

Wijkman, A. and Rockstrom, J. (2012) *Bankrupting Nature: Denying our Planetary Boundaries*. Abingdon: Routledge.

World Health Organization (2005) *Ecosystems and Human Well-Being: Health Synthesis*. Geneva, Switzerland: WHO Press.

Worldwatch Institute (2013) *State of the World 2013: Is Sustainability Still Possible?* Washington, DC: Island Press.

Young, S.B. (1994) *To the Arctic: An Introduction to the Far Northern World* New York: John Wiley.

3

DRIVERS OF CHANGE

Key Forces Influencing New Directions in Environmental Management

We concluded Chapter 2 by discussing some of the systemic barriers to effective environmental management – EM that would be equal to the task of addressing the ecological crisis. It is important to be mindful of these barriers and constraints, or else we risk ignoring significant contextual factors. Nevertheless, there is good reason, at the same time, to be optimistic about future directions in environmental management. Four factors in particular are shaping the future of environmental management, in ways that are not entirely clear but which may eventually have positive effects. The four drivers are *globalization, governance, the mainstreaming of sustainability awareness* and *the decentralization of environmental studies*. We examine these drivers, first separately and then cumulatively.

Globalization

Much has been written about the negative effects and implications of globalization. It has had undeniably mixed consequences for a wide range of regions, economies and societies. If globalization could be personified, he or she would probably be indifferent or hostile to regional uniqueness, historical values, cultural differences and social vulnerabilities. But globalization is more complex than any single characterization or personification. While greater homogeneity appears to be an inevitable consequence of globalization, so also are billions of less predictable consequences at all scales. Globalization is arguably neither essentially good nor essentially bad, but certainly unpredictable. It is an unfolding experiment with transformative results, and by the time globalization was perceptible enough to have a name, it was already irreversible. To a great extent, memories and remnants of a pre-globalized world are fading fast in the rear-view mirror.

Environmental management, in its many forms, is now practiced almost globally, aided and abetted by information and communication technologies. Consider the example of environmental impact assessment (EIA), which began formally in the United States in 1969 under the National Environmental Protection Act. EIA is now practiced around the world, and more than 100 countries have formal EIA laws and systems. Not only does the practice of EIA vary considerably from country to country, it also varies greatly within countries, with states and provinces having their own systems and requirements. In Canada, for example, provincial requirements vary in relation to regional economic considerations (economies dependent on mining, fisheries, forestry, tourism or manufacturing are all quite different and have different environmental implications). The salient point, however, is that, while the politics and practices of EIA vary everywhere, the *logic* of EIA is more or less universal. From the weakest to the most advanced and rigorous EIA jurisdictions, a common logic prevails: that the discipline of EIA should be practiced explicitly in order to help avoid, minimize, mitigate or compensate environmental impacts. This is markedly different from the looser approaches that were common prior to the formal introduction of EIA, when, for example, an engineering study examining the feasibility of a new highway might or might not address environmental considerations. Whether or not EIA makes a substantive difference is always debatable, but it is clear that the logic of the field has been largely accepted and mainstreamed across the globe. The gradual infiltration of concepts and principles, though modest at first, eventually transforms practice, for better or worse. Where once a field such as EIA did not exist, it now proliferates. This would not happen at all, or at least it would happen more slowly and more unevenly, without globalization (or, at least, internationalization) lubricating the tracks.

This is generally true, on a broader scale, with all other forms of environmental management. Globalization accelerates the spread of myriad forms of environmental management around the world – for example, as International Organization for Standardization (ISO) 14001 EMS and other certification standards are pursued by companies, as environmental regulations, protocols and standards become transboundary, as international environmental agreements are negotiated, as ethical investors pressure multinationals for improved social responsibility, and as the environmental education and training of professionals unfolds. Non-government organizations also play a strong role as they campaign successfully to internationalize environmental issues. It is now common, for example, for European environmental groups and stakeholders to intervene directly in environmental issues in North America. When the internationalization of environmental issues became increasingly prevalent in the 1980s, whether in the context of pipeline proposals in the Canadian Arctic, or in the case of forestry practices in the Amazon rainforest, it was considered novel, but now it is common. Even before climate change issues galvanized environmental advocates around the world, globalization (and, in particular, information, communication, education and advocacy processes) was already a powerful force as environmental issues leapfrogged from local to regional to international in concern. In its material dimensions, climate change is thoroughly global, and demands effective environmental management on an equally global scale.

Governance

As discussed in Chapter 2, governance has become an increasingly topical term in the context of environmental issues and sustainability challenges. While its meaning may be elusive and contested, it clearly implies a more open, collaborative and interactive approach to environmental management (Smismans, 2006) and an openness to less formal, centralized and government-controlled approaches (Saglie, 2006). Other key terms associated with governance are inclusiveness (Bulkeley and Mol, 2003), the devolution of power to local communities or upwards to transnational entities (Kettl, 2000) and an expanded role for civil society (Lemos and Agrawal, 2006; Lundqvist, 2004). It is clear that a shift from "government" to "governance" creates possibilities for more experimental and unorthodox approaches, because it allows for greater agency from civil society in environmental matters. In this sense, we argue that the prospect of alternative approaches to environmental management (the main concern of this book) is profoundly related to governance, particularly in its more innovative forms.

The emergence of environmental governance can be considered from different perspectives. From a fiscal perspective, it was never realistic or practical for governments to assume the exclusive responsibility of "managing" environmental issues. The challenge of environmental management is so complex and far-reaching that it has always overwhelmed governments, and their typically modest budget allocations for environmental matters are vastly inadequate. From an ethical perspective, it has arguably always been incumbent upon polluting and environmentally unfriendly businesses to assume greater responsibility. From the perspective of participatory democracy, it has never been tenable to limit the rights of individuals, civil society and non-government organizations to protect their environments. Perhaps most importantly, from a deep sustainability perspective, it has never been realistic to expect that traditional approaches to EM could do justice to confronting the ecological crisis. The path leading towards environmental governance has thus been inexorable, as former approaches have been proven to be ineffective and unrealistic. Now, the new challenge is for those engaged in environmental governance to demonstrate that it truly is something new and different and conducive to better outcomes.

The Mainstreaming of Sustainability Awareness

The mainstreaming of sustainability awareness is yet another factor that is changing the context of EM. Variations of the concept of environmental sustainability have been prevalent for much longer than the 1980s, when the Brundtland Commission made "sustainable development" the central idea of its influential report (World Commission on Environment and Development, 1987). Nevertheless, beginning in 1986, the terms began to gain resonance and popularity, and the Brundtland message had broad political appeal, since it seemed to promise that environmental protection and economic growth were not mutually exclusive. Two decades later, the concepts of sustainable development and sustainability had crossed over into the general public's imagination and become household terms. In government circles, laws and policies are now framed with sustainability as an overarching, albeit vague and elusive goal. Corporations issue sustainability reports and engage in dialogue with stakeholders and critics. Strategic plans of all kinds, at all levels and in all sectors, make liberal use of sustainability language in formulating objectives. Educational institutions introduce new courses, programs and departments, making explicit use of the terms. Grant applicants who neglect to address sustainability may do so at their peril. Clearly, reference to sustainability as a central concept is now omnipresent and nearly universal – it is thoroughly mainstream.

For a variety of reasons, the mainstreaming of sustainability language is largely anti-climactic for many environmental advocates. Sustainable development and sustainability have long been critiqued for their vagueness and frequent lack of substantive meaning. The penetration into mainstream parlance has been a rhetorical breakthrough, but the tension between strong and weak sustainability remains. In the two decades that it took for the mainstreaming of sustainability to happen, the ecological crisis worsened and intensified in many respects. Overall, it can be argued that little has changed. However, the mainstreaming of sustainability is notable not so much for what has happened so far, but for the potential it brings for change and transformation in the future, over a longer time frame. In other words, there is no going back – the sustainability discourse leads to the asking of increasingly difficult and deeper questions. When sustainability was a more esoteric term, it was more vulnerable to manipulation, co-optation and trivialization. Now that it is mainstream, it is debated by a much larger audience and it is not quite as easy to undermine.

The Decentralization of Environmental Education and Research

Until the late 1960s, the concept of environmental education did not exist in any formal sense, and sustainability-focused education was still decades away from emerging. The precursors of environmental education unfolded in many different forms, including geography courses, and outdoor or naturalist programs. *Environmental Studies* emerged as a new and discrete field around that time and has proliferated over the past four decades in high school and university programs. Until well into the new millennium, if universities had environmental studies programs they were typically added on to existing geography curricula, or in more progressive cases new departments or faculties were created. The salient point, however, is that environmental education remained something predominantly "new" and "additional" from the time of its introduction through its first few decades. A shift began to take place in the 2000s and it continues to unfold: the decentralization of environmental education. Environmental education still exists as a discrete field, but it is increasingly common for environmental or sustainability content to become integral to other programs – engineering, science, business, and even fine arts, to name a few. As we discussed in Chapter 1, ecological and environmental themes are increasingly prominent across the social sciences.

The decentralization of environmental education unfolded and gained momentum at the same time as the "Death of Environmentalism" debates were unfolding (Shellenberger and Nordhaus, 2004). The first generation of the environmental movement (approximately 1969–2000) had "ended", and there was palpable angst and uncertainty about what would follow. Was environmentalism really dead? What did the mainstreaming of sustainability consciousness really mean – how shallow or deep was it? Although these debates remain largely unresolved, it is clear that new forms of strategy and advocacy began to appear to accompany the older ones practiced by environmental groups such as Greenpeace, Friends of the Earth, Sierra Club and others.

The new wave of environmentalism has proven to be more dispersed and decentralized, and somewhat less polarized. Environmental advocacy evolved from being the exclusive domain of environmental non-governmental organizations (ENGOs) and environmental studies departments, and began to unfold in many other forms and places. To the first generation of environmentalists, this might seem to be a mixed blessing, but it represents in some ways a significant victory – after all, one of the original goals was to spread the message about the ecological crisis. The message has certainly spread virtually everywhere, in every sector, at every level. Environmental themes and messages were once alternative, but now it is almost impossible to read any news or sample any media without encountering numerous items about sustainability issues. The point is not so much about whether or not environmental messages have been co-opted or watered down (although they often are). It is more about the possibilities that this decentralization and proliferation create. It is a key driver of change for environmental management, along with globalization, governance and the mainstreaming of sustainability. It means that new and different forms of environmental management are more likely to evolve, in contrast to the more limited versions of earlier decades. Solutions may come from any field or sector – for example, sustainability is now an explicit focus of engineering, when not so long ago it was a concept unheard of. The decentralization and dispersion of environmental education and research will likely bring about profound changes, if not immediately then in the longer term.

In this chapter we have discussed how four interrelated drivers – globalization, governance, the mainstreaming of sustainability awareness and the decentralization of environmental studies – are altering the landscape of environmental management and creating new possibilities. The next two chapters explore different sides of the EM coin. Chapter 4 discusses conventional EM and Chapter 5 explores its more alternative and emerging forms.

References

Bulkeley, H. and Mol, A.P.J. (2003) "Participation and Environmental Governance: Concensus, Ambivalence and Debate". *Environmental Values*, 12: 143–154.

Kettl, D.F. (2000) "The Transformation of Governance: Globalization, Devolution and the Role of Government". *Public Administration Review*, 60 (6): 488–496.

Lemos, M.C. and Agrawal, A. (2006) "Environmental Governance". *Annual Review of Environmental Resources*, 31: 297–325.

Lundqvist, L.J. (2004) *Sweden and Ecological Governance*. Manchester: Manchester University Press.

Saglie, I. (2006) "Fragmented Institutions: The Problem Facing Natural Resource Management". In Y. Rydin and E. Falleth (Eds.) *Networks and Institutions in Natural Resource Management*. Cheltenham: Edward Elgar Publishing, pp. 1–14.

Shellenberger, M. and Nordhaus, T. (2004) "The Death of Environmentalism: Global Warming Politics in a Post-Environmental World". Available at: Thebreakthrough.org/images/Death_of_Environmentalism.pdf

Smismans, S. (Ed.) (2006) *Civil Society and Legitimate European Governance*. Northampton, MA: Edward Elgar Publishing.

World Commission on Environment and Development (1987) *Our Common Future*. Oxford: Oxford University Press.

4
CONVENTIONAL ENVIRONMENTAL MANAGEMENT

Origins, Evolution, Characteristics and Critique

It is often noted that what is perceived as the "modern environmental movement" began in approximately 1970 – around the time of the first Earth Day, the first laws that were explicitly environmental, and some of the seminal literature that is often cited (e.g. Carson, 1962; Meadows et al., 1972) dates to that time. Even though it is arbitrary and imprecise to assign any particular date as a definitive beginning of the modern environmental movement, many would at least agree that environmental values gained noticeable momentum around that time. It might surprise some of today's environmental activists to know that Paul Erlich, author of *The Population Bomb* (Erlich, 1968) was famous enough to have appeared on Johnny Carson's *The Tonight Show* more than twenty times in the 1970s (Sabin, 2013). The environmental movement has had many ups and downs due to the vicissitudes of public opinion and the vagaries of politics, and its future remains uncertain. But if we accept, generally speaking, that the modern environmental movement began less than 50 years ago, that leads us to an inescapable (but largely unacknowledged) fact: it is still a very young movement. It is in this context that we should consider the origins of environmental management. What we may term "conventional" or "mainstream" environmental management is an improvised work in progress, a provisional field of practice much in need of critique and improvement, and it has less than five decades of experience. As we have argued earlier, however, this reality is largely unacknowledged – it is more common for EM practitioners to assume or claim that their approaches to EM are robust and well established. In analyzing and critiquing EM, it is therefore important to first acknowledge explicitly that it is still a relatively new field.

Where did environmental management come from? What are its origins? It is impossible to establish the answers with much precision. The history of environmental management is still mostly unwritten. Its evolution has been chaotic, serendipitous and largely undocumented. Much of it has been informal and voluntary. Approaches to environmental management are described in textbooks that refer to it explicitly (e.g. Randolph, 2004; Antweiler, 2014; Barrow, 2006; Belcham, 2015), or in a wide variety of texts concerning such topics as environmental science, planning, assessment and auditing. It is addressed in a range of academic journals, although, once again, researchers must search broadly, using many different key words, to sample this literature. None of this should be surprising in such a new field. Environmental studies scarcely existed 50 years ago, and it has since grown and diversified into many subcategories. The field of "environment" remains greatly misunderstood to those who are not immersed in some aspect of it full time; its diversity and its many specialized topics are not always apparent. Common misconceptions abound – for example, "all environmental professionals are experts in climate change" or "the environment is mostly about recycling". Terms such as "environmental manager", "environmentalist", and "environmental researcher" are often conflated or used interchangeably, when in practice they may have little in common. In the context of such conceptual chaos and confusion, there are limitations to the description, analysis and critique of environmental management. At the present time, it is necessary to use multiple approaches: review of general and specialized literature; consideration of a wide variety of secondary sources; reference to stories and anecdotes; and personal experience/observation.

It is somewhat easier to probe the origins and evolution of environmental laws and policies. Environmental impact assessment, for example, in its many incarnations, began as a legal framework, and remains so to a great extent. In the early 1970s, EIA was a new law, a requirement and process to be addressed and figured out by courts, proponents, stakeholders, scientists and others. They are still trying to figure it out, but at least the EIA laws and policies provided a common reference for myriad interpretations. Environmental management, on the other hand, has been less tangible and focused than EIA, and less subject to overarching regulatory frameworks. It has been more voluntary, more decentralized, and more idiosyncratic. It has largely been left to governments and industries to invent and reinvent environmental management, in response to an evolving and variable array of laws, policies, standards, expectations and pressures.

The term "environment" evolved and crystallized as an elegant, holistic concept through which to consider the consequences of human interactions with the biosphere. "Environment" is a profound and compelling human construct, so much so that it has been embraced almost universally. Like all great ideas or complex aspirations, it is difficult to live up to. One of the more common approaches has been to combine or amalgamate pieces together, in the hope that the parts would amount to a coherent whole. The Government of Canada, for example, created its first Department of the Environment, or Environment Canada, by combining three older federal departments: The Canadian Wildlife Service; the Weather (or Atmospheric) Bureau; and Parks Canada. The logic was solid enough – the sum of the three parts might be equal to addressing the emerging and broader challenge of environmental protection, in the early days or first generation of the modern environmental movement. Similarly, when large corporations or public utilities created their first environmental departments, they usually borrowed from existing practices that were considered to be somewhat analogous. If a corporation had, for example, employees specialized in health and safety work, it might seem logical to redeploy these resources in a new, more integrated unit devoted to complying with environmental laws and regulations. The strategy to combine parts, hoping to create an environmental "whole" was neither inherently correct nor inherently incorrect. It was a practical and plausible approach at that point in the early evolution of EM. Then, as is still the case to some extent now, the people engaged in environmental work as their profession came from all backgrounds: geographers, biologists, engineers, meteorologists, cartographers, project managers, etc. In many instances, some individuals became recognized as "environmental specialists", usually because they combined a generalist orientation with a passion for environmental issues. The shift or leap to an "environmental" orientation came with recognition that an organization's responsibility was no longer limited to its own domain; it was now part of a larger picture, and its actions and impacts could extend far. The full implications of this shift are still not grasped fully and universally.

For the purposes of distinguishing between conventional and alternative environmental management, we suggest a simplified chronology consisting of three eras, from the 1970s/1980s to the current time, with a transitional era in between. We do not suggest a perfectly linear, uninterrupted evolution, but rather a gradual shift in which we can clearly note the contrast over several decades.

Evolving Eras of Environmental Management

The 1970s and 1980s

- There was an uneven perception or recognition of the ecological crisis among the general public. Compared to the present day, overall environmental awareness was much lower.
- The first formal environmental management practices began to appear in the 1970s. Compliance and due diligence-based EM approaches were predominant in industry throughout the first two decades. Lack of compliance with environmental laws was not uncommon.
- Reactive, correction-oriented EM approaches were common.
- Informal, unstandardized EM practices were common.
- The World Commission on Environment and Development highlighted the concept of sustainable development, which gradually gained currency.
- Widespread concern with environmental issues such as ozone depletion, acid rain and global biodiversity loss.

The 1990s to the Early 2000s (Transitional)

- Recognition of environmental problems or the ecological crisis became more common and mainstream among the general public.

- Debates unfolded about climate change (whether or not it was occurring or to what extent). A consensus gradually formed that climate change was a serious problem.
- Sustainability and sustainable development concepts became more mainstream.
- The formalization of EM systems and standards became common in industry.
- Corporate social responsibility emerged as an ethical framework and was adopted by many in the corporate and business sectors.
- Environmental "governance" became more topical as a possible alternative framework.

The Current Era

- In general terms, awareness and understanding of the ecological crisis is higher than in previous decades.
- Experiments with environmental governance are unfolding.
- Corporate social responsibility (CSR) is a prevalent ethos in industry. To a great extent, CSR is used interchangeably with concepts of sustainability and environmental performance.
- Sustainability is now a fully mainstream and almost ubiquitous concept.

When we consider this short history, five decades of evolving EM, we note that three main processes unfolded simultaneously: (1) the gradual growth of environmental awareness and concern accompanied by the introduction of environmental laws; (2) experiments with systematic approaches to EM; (3) a gradual shift away from command and control and towards governance. The evolution might also be considered to involve the eventual shift away from conventional approaches to EM towards alternative approaches. At present, however, conventional approaches still tend to predominate and we discuss them next.

Conventional EM

We define "conventional" environmental management as the set of approaches that were characteristic of earlier eras, most notably in the 1970s and 1980s. In retrospect, this early stage of the modern environmental movement was guided by certain underlying premises. First, there was some degree of shared confidence that environmental protection could be achieved through regulation – if laws were established and penalties were enforced, better behavior and performance would be a natural outcome, according to that school of thought. Second, according to the logic of environmental regulation, when problems were identified they might somehow be fixed if the right remedies were applied – polluting emissions could be abated, the effects of acid rain on lakes could be reversed, degraded habitats could be restored, or bird populations could recover. It was generally assumed that governments had lead roles and overall responsibility for environmental quality, and that there was a clear delineation of roles, with government and industry on "different" or "opposing" sides. Around this time, it was common for governments to develop environmental indicators and issue annual reports on the state of the environment. Later on, it became standard for corporations to issue reports on their environmental and sustainability performance. ENGOs, for their part, have a long tradition of issuing "report cards" on corporate and government environmental performance. If the general public increasingly tuned out many of these reports, it is easy to understand why – it could only endure so much depressing news, information overload, data that lacked clear meaning, and lack of connection between information and action. To summarize, conventional approaches to EM were characterized by an ethos that reflected overconfidence, complacency, patchwork solutions, and a superficial understanding of environmental problems and solutions.

Fast forward to the present, and we see a much different and more complicated picture. There is considerable doubt that environmental problems can be fixed (particularly if they are viewed as wicked problems that defy solutions). In the era of governance, it is no longer so clear that governments have the lead role in environmental management. Fewer corporations cling to outdated notions that compliance or even due diligence are sufficient; most make commitments to sustainability and social responsibility. Environmental problems, strategies and programs are increasingly globalized. At the rhetorical and strategic levels, at least, the old era of environmental management seems to be long gone.

In terms of practice, however, the imprint of the first generation of environmental management remains remarkably persistent. This brings us to a central point: the context of environmental management has transformed since the earlier era, but to a great extent the practices have evolved only incrementally. In other words, despite the advanced language of sustainability, *environmental management remains for the most part pre-sustainability*. A recent definition offered by Antweiler is generic and bureaucratic: "Environmental management is a system of administrative functions that are used to (i) develop; (ii) implement; and (iii) monitor the *environmental strategy* of a business" (2014: 2). Antweiler's definition, which is typical enough of the general literature on environmental management, does not capture or convey the broader context, as we discussed in Chapter 2 (including complexity, uncertainty and the ecological crisis). According to conventional thinking, environmental management is largely the domain of the business world, rather than a broader, more collaborative governance challenge. It is viewed primarily as a risk management function, aimed at limiting legal exposure and protecting the reputations and shareholder value of companies. As a matter of course, many companies pursue and maintain certification for their EMS (e.g. ISO 14001), or, more recently, their social responsibility practices (ISO 26000).

Let us consider some of the hallmarks or tendencies of conventional environmental management.

Reactive Orientation

A constant theme in environmental literature concerns the reactive nature of most efforts to manage or protect the environment. It was one of the key messages of *Limits to Growth* more than four decades ago (Meadows et al., 1972), and it has reappeared consistently in literally every book or report concerned with the ecological crisis, regardless of scale. The critique is simple: the general tendency has been for environmental management to take place in response to problems that become evident, by which time it may be less possible (or more difficult, complicated and expensive) to address the problems. At the root of this syndrome, there is an implicit understanding that environmental problems or resource depletions are inevitable given current patterns of development and consumptive lifestyles. The "inevitability factor" is thus an assumed subtext along with a pervasive sense of powerlessness, and provides the basis for the reactive orientation. A cycle of environmental problem/reaction/mitigation/correction has therefore evolved as the default orientation to environmental management. It is a troubling essentialist perspective, but it is persistent, and it raises questions about the psychological barriers that underlie. Do greed, over-exploitation of resources and the pursuit of short-term benefits inevitably mean worsening problems for future generations? Does the ecological crisis inspire action, or does it breed a sense of hopelessness? As always, the full story is probably much more complicated, in both negative and positive ways.

Emphasis on Correction

If environmental management is framed as a business function (which it often is), pressures for efficiencies and cost effectiveness come into play. The cost-saving imperative also plays out in the public sector, as governments weigh investments in environment and sustainability against other priorities (which many have noted correctly, is a symptom of short-term thinking). In the earlier days of the environmental movement, the full costs of problems were seldom considered, and they are still largely discounted, for reasons that have been pointed out often by environmental economists. By the 1990s, however, the more enlightened corporations were asking the general question: is it more expensive to *prevent* or *correct* environmental problems? In many cases, the clear answer was that it could often be much more expensive to correct environmental problems, particularly if some approximation of a full accounting could be done. (It is difficult to measure or quantify some costs that are considered to be indirect or less "real", such as a company's reputation.) It is now more widely accepted that investments in preventing environmental problems often turn out to be very wise. But a dilemma remains for even the most enlightened corporations: how do they decide which environmental prevention investments to make and not to make, and when? After all, most of these investments are not required, but discretionary. And how can they know if prevention investments are effective, if the outcome is that "nothing happens" (i.e. how can we possibly know that an event that might have happened was instead prevented?)? If we consider this dilemma more globally, in the public realm, what should we consider to be an adequate investment in addressing the ecological crisis and deep sustainability? There is no obvious solution to this dilemma, and that is why the characteristic or default approach remains the "correction" orientation. To a great extent, we remain stuck in a pattern in which we fail to invest adequately in preventing environmental problems, and when they do occur they are often seen as "too expensive to fix". Or, if they are subject to litigation, as many cases are, corrective action may be delayed indefinitely.

Compliance/Due Diligence/Reputation Focus

In earlier decades, it was understandable that those subject to new environmental laws and regulations (they were often referred to generically as "polluters") – would first seek to ensure that they were in compliance with applicable laws. For most companies, compliance is seen as a normal or basic part of being in business; only a minority of operators would, at any given time and under normal circumstances, willfully break laws, especially in jurisdictions that are inclined to strict enforcement. As the environmental movement unfolded, it became apparent that maintaining only a level of minimum compliance could involve considerable risk if regulators and courts decided to interpret and apply laws vigorously and if scientific evidence proved to be damning. For example, what if ecological damage, human health hazards, deaths and disasters could be attributed to corporate negligence? In complicated cases where courts might or might not decide that corporations were partly or fully liable, demonstration of due diligence might be the only effective defense – not only was the company in compliance with laws, according to the logic, it also went above and beyond by making all reasonable efforts to prevent problems from occurring. In some cases, much of the due diligence defense might be based on whether or not a company had a recognized or certified environmental management system (EMS). This, too, can be problematic – since EMSs do not guarantee good environmental performance; they only demonstrate that a system is in place. If there are gaps or deficiencies that result in poor environmental performance, this may be immediately apparent, or it may only become evident much later.

As the environmental movement unfolded from the 1970s onward, it became clear that poor performance could have an adverse effect on a company's image and reputation. It is somewhat less clear if efforts to improve image – for example, through advertising, philanthropy or reporting – are as effective as companies hope, since much of this is dismissed as greenwashing, perhaps unfairly so in some instances. Negative perceptions can, however, be enduring: for example, decades after major oil spills that receive extensive media coverage, the public tends to continue to associate particular companies with disasters.

In general, industry has adapted to the imperative of environmental protection in incremental ways. (There have always been exceptions, with some businesses far ahead of or far behind the curve.) The incremental adaptation began with compliance, then extended to due diligence and concern with reputation. More recently, it has addressed expectations of corporate social responsibility. However, much of the adaptation has come at a strategic level, and it is important to distinguish *strategy* from *substance*. The substantive dimensions of environmental management relate to action and outcomes. When we consider evidence of substantive progress towards sustainability, we might consider examples such as the decommissioning of non-renewable energy supply and replacement with advanced renewable or conservation; dramatic improvements in air or water quality; lowering carbon emissions or reversing declines in biodiversity. These examples all involve societal efforts and improved governance – they do not result only from corporate strategy because the issues are fundamentally collective, requiring broad collaboration and public policy. When a corporation reduces its waste stream, or improves its handling of hazardous materials, or makes measurable progress on other issues, it deserves credit. But such initiatives represent incremental improvements in social responsibility – they may be substantive but they fall short of addressing the more difficult imperatives of a more rapid transition towards deep sustainability. In practice, when corporate sustainability targets are not met, there are probably few, if any, consequences, although the cumulative shortfalls in sustainability performance by corporations around the world have obvious negative outcomes globally.

Other Characteristics of Conventional Environmental Management

Other hallmarks of conventional environmental management include a tendency to manage on short time-frames; a focus on single issues rather than overall environmental health or sustainability; and an implicit philosophy that sustainability is peripheral, rather than integral, to core business. Another worrisome practice is the tendency (or strategy) for companies to keep parts of their business separate for the purposes of environmental management and social responsibility. It is common practice for companies to separate *operational* and *capital* issues for the purposes of management and regulatory processes. For example, a mining company may operate a gold mine and, in doing so, use a recognized environmental management system to handle operational issues (waste, emergency response, hazardous materials, tailings, water quality, human health, etc.). However, if the same company is the proponent of a new gold mine, the issues and impacts that arise in the exploration phase may not be subject to the same environmental management practices. The *capital projects* side of the business is usually subject to other requirements – approvals, permits, licenses and environmental impact assessment – which in practice may or may not address issues adequately. In the case of EIA requirements, many proponents have avoided fuller scrutiny and accountability through a variety of strategies – for example, by splitting projects into smaller parts that are below legal or discretionary screening thresholds for EIA review. In summary, when corporations compartmentalize aspects of their business, instead of managing them collectively and cumulatively, the public interest (and the prospect of deeper sustainability) is often undermined.

The shortcomings of conventional environmental management are clear, and so are the underlying causes. The need for environmental management emerged in the 1970s, and caught many by surprise, resulting in a long game of catching up. This might partly explain the paradox that becomes apparent when we contrast some of the urgent and radical messages of environmentalism with the relatively incremental and unhurried development of environmental management. The full implications of the ecological crisis were not as widely apparent in 1970 as they are now (although they were quite clear to prescient authors such as Meadows and others). It was common for skeptics to opine that environmentalism was a passing fad and not worth worrying about; this sentiment is not altogether extinct, although it is now more rarified. Approaches to environmental management were understandably improvised. Existing practices were redeployed and patched together, whether they were adequate or not. There was, and still is, a dearth of applicable theory; hence the critique that environmental management is still largely atheoretical. Experiments with environmental law and regulation have met with mixed success. The initial promise of new environmental protection measures such as EIA faded with experience as stakeholders, proponents and practitioners succumbed to fatigue and detachment. Meanwhile, the ecological crisis continued and worsened and along with it, the need for alternatives to conventional environmental management became more evident.

Sustainability Deep Sixed: The "Bermuda Triangle" of Conventional Environmental Management

In a continuing regime of conventional environmental management, the prospect of substantive progress towards deep sustainability is dim. Deep sustainability would require the interaction of positive forces that are currently in short supply: at a minimum, advanced ecological awareness, strong political will, political and economic reform, powerful governance, breakthrough technologies and unprecedented cooperation and collaboration at many scales. In the meantime, sustainability is undermined in a variety of ways. The following represent different triangulations, any or all of which feature negative interactions – it can be argued even if as few as three negative factors prevail, a kind of "Bermuda Triangle" effect can result. Let's consider six simplified relationships or syndromes consisting of three random negative forces each:

1. Voluntary/Discretionary EM + Compliance/Due Diligence Orientation + Neoliberalism
2. Irreducible Uncertainty + Short-term economics + Reactive EM
3. Loose regulation + Organizational Patterns + Baseline Data Gaps
4. Globalization + Ecological Complexity + Irreducible Uncertainty

5. Neoliberalism + Baseline Data Gaps + Compliance/Due Diligence Orientation
6. Ecological complexity + Short-term economics + Voluntary/Discretionary EM.

Each "Bermuda Triangle" features the interaction of three negative forces. It is arguable that the presence of only one or two of these negative forces would be enough to constrain, undermine or even preclude the prospect of sustainability. Some of these negative forces are more pre-existing or omnipresent, such as ecological complexity or irreducible uncertainty. Other forces are emergent, such as globalization or neoliberalism. Still others are variable, such as reactive, compliance/due diligence-oriented environmental management. Each triangle is arbitrarily depicted as having three major interacting forces, but in reality more negative forces may prevail in any given context – the triangles are merely simplified accounts. Using the Bermuda Triangle metaphor, the prospect of sustainability is precluded, lost or "deep sixed" under any of these negative configurations. It is more likely, however, that the conditions for a "perfect storm" are increasingly present, in which potentially all of these negative forces are present to a significant extent. Nevertheless, some of the negative forces – particularly those that are symptomatic of conventional environmental management, held over from earlier in the environmental movement – can be challenged and changed. This challenge and prospect is the subject of the chapters that follow.

References

Antweiler, W. (2014) *Elements of Environmental Management*. Toronto: University of Toronto Press.
Barrow, C.J. (2006) *Environmental Management for Sustainable Development* (2nd ed.). London: Routledge.
Belcham, A. (2015) *Manual of Environmental Management*. Abingdon: Routledge.
Carson, R. (1962) *Silent Spring*. New York: Houghton Mifflin.
Erlich, P.R. (1968) *The Population Bomb*. New York: Ballantine.
Meadows, D., Meadows, D., Randers, J. and Behrens III, W.M. (1972) *The Limits to Growth*. London: Universe Books.
Randolph, J. (2004) *Environmental Land Use Planning and Management*. Washington, DC: Island Press.
Sabin, P. (2013) *The Bet: Paul Erlich, Julian Simon, and Our Gamble over Earth's Future*. New Haven, CT and London: Yale University Press.

5
CURRENT STATE OF ALTERNATIVE ENVIRONMENTAL MANAGEMENT

Theory, Practice, Limitations and Gaps

We are currently in a phase that can be characterized as a transition to more collaborative environmental management, brought about by the forces that we discussed in Chapter 3 (governance, mainstreaming of sustainability, globalization, and the decentralization of environmental research and education). If a transition to radically new forms of environmental management does take place, we will no longer think of it in disaggregated terms, in which government, civil society and industry maintain their own visions of its theory and practice. We have not reached that point yet; we are still in an era in which each of the sectors yields examples of leading and lagging practice. Let's consider examples of the current state of the art of alternative environmental management, respectively in industry, civil society and government.

Industry

As recently as the 1990s, it might have been accurate to estimate that at most 10 percent of all businesses – small, medium, large or multinational – were demonstrating measurable leadership in environment and sustainability. Interface Ltd., a large carpet tile manufacturing company, is often noted as an example of corporate leadership in sustainability and social responsibility. Interface's founder, the late Ray C. Anderson, described his journey in several books, including *Confessions of a Radical Industrialist* (2009). After setting ambitious goals in 1994, the company was able, over the next decade or so, to make dramatic reductions in greenhouse gas emissions, fossil fuel consumption, waste and water use, all while increasing sales and profitability (Anderson, 2009). The Interface story exemplifies the possibilities for the private sector to influence substantive change and progress towards sustainability, perhaps even deep sustainability. Now, as we write in 2016, the field of green business leadership and social responsibility is much more crowded and the success stories are more numerous. In the realm of smaller business (e.g. innumerable organic or sustainability oriented producers and suppliers) and not-for-profits, leadership has also been long evident. To the casual observer, it might seem that we have reached a state of green utopia – everything seems green and sustainable – but of course, that is far from true.

The pioneering green business leaders, some of them true visionaries, demonstrated passion for progressive change and the willingness to eschew traditional notions of success in favor of broader visions. Our purpose here, however, is not to celebrate green business – its leaders have been well recognized. We wish to make two points about green business. First, as is generally the case in any field or pursuit, the leaders have always been the minority, as the majority of players in industry follow their examples, at their own respective paces, some quite slowly. Second, and more importantly, if investors and shareholders always wait for concrete evidence of financial return on investment as a rationale for green business strategies, the ecological crisis will continue to worsen. The "business case" for a strong shift towards sustainability, even when it is expanded from the old single bottom line to the more inclusive triple bottom line, is largely a matter of perception and interpretation. More precisely, it requires a leap of faith and a different mindset on the part of business people and investors. In other words, environmentalism is fundamentally about intrinsic values; if we emphasize these values it is not done on the basis of any business rationale – it is because we believe it is the right thing to do, regardless of financial implications. No other motive can be as compelling as the pursuit of sustainability for intrinsic reasons. In saying this, we do not discount the importance of financial business cases. We only wish to point out that business cases are relevant in the pursuit of shallower sustainability, but become less meaningful as the journey goes deeper.

Environmentalism is, in essence, an ideology – a perspective about the world and how it should be. The ideology of environmentalism proclaims that the world is experiencing an ecological crisis and that humankind needs to make profound, fundamental changes. Likewise, the world of industry and commerce is underpinned by ideology; capitalism and free enterprise have traditionally provided the guiding vision. Can these two ideologies – environmentalism and capitalism – coexist? The main message of *Our Common Future* (WCED, 1987) some thirty years ago, was that the pillars of sustainability (economic, environmental and social) were not inherently in opposition and could be reconciled. A similar message has been reiterated often since then, particularly by governments and industries. The more critically the question is examined, however, the more problematic it becomes. An equally strong argument can be made that business and environmental values cannot be reconciled fully. In the absence of definitive evidence one way or the other, the prospect is largely a matter of personal belief. It is therefore useful to have a *pragmatic* perspective on the issue and allow the benefit of the doubt. The alternative is worse – if we truly believe that nothing sustainable can result from business, the environmental outlook becomes even gloomier. In other words, even if one is skeptical that deep sustainability can be achieved in a context of capitalism and neoliberalism, it is reasonable to hope that some progress can be made towards shallower sustainability. It can be viewed as a transitional phase that may provide a bridge to more fundamental change later on, in future generations. Of course, it is unfair to delegate the challenge of deep sustainability to future generations. Realistically, however, it is probable that the best-case scenario in terms of an ecological legacy that present generations might leave is to not preclude the *possibility or opportunity* for future generations to do things differently. Such is the rather constrained and compromised environmental path for the foreseeable future – but it is probably better that this current reality be recognized rather than ignored.

What, then, is the state of the art of alternative environmental management in industry? The leaders are making measurable and verifiable progress towards "zero" goals or, in Ray Anderson's words, the mountaintop – no waste, no net energy use, no footprint, and so on. They have moved far beyond the performance of previous decades, when it might have been enough to only have a modest recycling program. When leading companies in industry operate in transparent and accountable ways, as many increasingly do, stakeholders and regulators can monitor and track their progress through the shallower to the deeper forms of sustainability. More problematic are those who lag behind the leaders, some in close pursuit but many others far behind. The implications of the ecological crisis are clear – the gap between leaders and followers must be closed quickly.

Civil Society and ENGOs

The environmental movement can mostly attribute its origins, continued existence and momentum to the grassroots efforts of citizens and non-government organizations. Although considerable environmental leadership has also been provided by government and industry, there is no substitute for the role of citizens and civil society. The "public interest" – no matter how naive such a notion may be – lies in the pursuit of effective environmental governance. Citizens and ENGOs are therefore often skeptical or ambivalent about environmental management, which they tend to view as only one piece of a complex puzzle of governance. Many point to poor environmental management as a problem, and stronger environmental governance as a possible solution. From the public interest perspective, there is often a palpable tension between *management* and *governance* – the latter, if not quite the antithesis of the former, is nevertheless a significant departure.

Much has been written on the subject of public involvement in environmental issues, and much of the experience has been problematic from the perspectives of interveners or stakeholders. It can be generally concluded that citizens and non-government organizations are often dissatisfied or disillusioned with public involvement processes and opportunities, particularly in cases where outcomes or decisions are considered undesirable. But as experience has accumulated, the strategies of interveners have evolved also. Citizens and ENGOs still play the roles of watchdog, whistleblower, critic and advocate, but their longer term strategies revolve around influencing the transformation of industry and government. It is commonly believed that some of the less sustainable businesses or industries may be of the "sunset" variety – they will eventually fade away. Whether or not a particular industry is sunset is debatable – for example, what is the future of mining? Outdated manufacturing? Fossil fuel energy? Even as the sun sets for some industries, many more are around for the long term, and it is the transformation of the latter that provides a daunting governance challenge.

Some of the most effective input in this regard from civil society has come from organizations like The Natural Step or Ecological Footprint. The strategy of ENGOs such as these is not only to point out and critique unsustainable practices, but also to provide tools for change. In both instances, the ENGO takes what might be described as a less judgmental approach and offers rigorous data concerning progress (or lack thereof) towards measurable sustainability goals (i.e. zero net ecological impact or the smallest possible footprint). The premise is that companies and industries are usually willing to start the journey towards sustainability, without necessarily knowing the full implications of the journey, which might well eventually involve much more radical changes than they had ever envisaged. This approach, while incremental, is realistic and pragmatic, in contrast to the "change the world" message of environmentalists in earlier decades.

Governments

By virtue of their mandates, governments have prescribed roles in environmental management, with a wide variety of tools at their disposal. They may deploy any number of these tools, in different combinations; laws, regulations, policies, standards, inspection, monitoring, enforcement, licensing, permitting, approvals, enforcement, fines, strategies, plans, programs and public education are some of the tools in the repertoire. Historically, environmental departments have been relatively junior, with modest budgets (a provincial department of the environment might, for example, have a budget comparable to a district school board). Even though there are green "champions" in every walk of life, including government, it can be generally argued that governments have tended to follow, rather than lead, when it comes to environmental protection or sustainability action. This is unsurprising, since governments must seek to balance priorities and it is nearly always politically risky for them to make dramatic policy changes. By default, therefore, the role of environmental leadership has generally been left to individuals and organizations in civil society who are less constrained in advocacy – ENGOs are free to argue that environment and sustainability must be assigned top priority. Governments are further constrained in environmental matters by electoral politics; the success of Green Parties around the world has been modest so far, and governments are typically formed from more mainstream and less alternative constituencies. In general, then, it can be argued that the strong tendency will remain for governments to only reflect mainstream public values and opinions concerning environmental matters, and not to push for deeper sustainability (unless this, too, becomes the mainstream agenda). Finally, it must also be noted that in many instances government environmental policies are contradictory – for example, laws to protect the environment may be enacted, even while approvals and subsidies for many unsustainable activities continue to be issued, with ominous ecological implications.

For all of the reasons noted above (and no doubt many more reasons that we have not mentioned), it is probable that governments, in general, will remain too constrained to assume anything more than mainstream or incremental environmental leadership. The role of advocacy and leadership towards deeper sustainability will fall to civil society, and increasingly it will be framed as a governance, rather than governmental, quest. The abiding message seems clear enough: governments must do everything they can to promote effective environmental management and the pursuit of deep sustainability, but their roles will be limited. Old notions of command and control, sweeping regulation, strong enforcement and government-driven environmental plans and solutions are outdated. The more enlightened governments have moved on from old assumptions and practices and have perceived the next (and much more difficult) challenge: combining traditional government functions like regulation with emerging and still undefined roles in governance.

Conclusion

To an increasing extent, governments, industry and civil society are involved in experiments with sustainability governance, whether this is explicitly recognized or not. It can be argued that the ecological crisis, in all of its global dimensions, is the condition that is transforming traditional notions of decision-making in fundamental ways, by demanding solutions that are far beyond the capacities of governments, industries or civil society to undertake alone.

So far, we have explored environmental management in terms of its origins, context, evolution and challenges. In the next several chapters, 6 through 11, we explore theoretical foundations of emerging, alternative EM, highlighting prospects from critical social science, environmental sociology, disaster studies, post-normal science and black swan thinking.

References

Anderson, R., with White, R. (2009) *Confessions of a Radical Industrialist: Profits, People, Purpose – Doing Business by Respecting the Earth*. New York: St. Martin's Press.
Ecological Footprint (www.footprintnetwork.org).
The Natural Step (naturalstep.org).
World Commission on Environment and Development (WCED) (1987) *Our Common Future*. Oxford: Oxford University Press.

6
CRITICAL SOCIAL SCIENCE AND THE ECOLOGICAL CRISIS

It could be generally agreed that environmental management conjures up some sense of "action". This action-orientation of environmental management should not be surprising – after all, the inclusion of the term "management" directly alludes to this. A cautionary point that we would like to add at this point, though, is that despite the immense enthusiasm and interest directed almost exclusively towards the practical aspects of environmental management by many practitioners in the field, it must also be recognized that environmental management must ultimately rest on a firm theoretical foundation to be effective.[1] That is, in light of the limitations of existing conventional perspectives, if at the general and overarching level, the goal of environmental management action is, as we contend, to address the ecological crisis, then we must pay sufficient attention to the theoretical scaffolding that would justify and support new and emerging alternative approaches to environmental management. By ensuring a sound theoretical foundation we would be able to move forward by ensuring that environmental management would be equal to the formidable task of addressing the ecological crisis in its many dimensions. In particular, how could theories from social science help environmental managers address the key elements of the ecological crisis that have hitherto been largely neglected or defined as being outside the scope of technocratic and limited conceptions of environmental management? We emphasize here the need to include and incorporate more seriously the social sciences in the theoretical foundation of environmental management for many reasons. However, for the purposes at hand, one of the major benefits of certain strands of theoretical social science analyses is that they offer a decidedly *critical* perspective on the relationship between human beings and the environment. As such, a critical social science perspective will have an exceedingly important role to play in building the foundation of alternative environmental management approaches as it will help shine a light on some of the social, organizational, political, and economic basis of the limitations and problems that continue to plague conventional environmental management approaches. By identifying, understanding and putting into proper context these limitations, we would then be in a much better position to move towards the development of alternative approaches. But how can we move towards this goal? In this chapter, we suggest that the establishment of the theoretical foundation of alternative approaches to environmental management may be pursued by adopting and refining concepts and perspectives from critical social science in general and environmental sociology in particular. The chapter begins with several sections that review the historical origins and conceptual foundations of critical social science and environmental sociology respectively. We then discuss what these particular fields of study can bring to the analysis of the ecological crisis that lies at the heart of environmental management efforts. We do so by reviewing some of the current perspectives that environmental social scientists are using to approach and analyze the relationship between nature and society. We conclude with some preliminary remarks about the potential usefulness of critical social science and environmental sociology for building alternative orientations for environmental management.

Critical Social Science and the Ecological Crisis

The adoption and influence of a critical stance within modern (Western) social science has a long history dating back to at least the social and political theorists who were grappling with the societal turmoil in Europe that resulted from the French and Industrial Revolutions. In this historical context, these theorists understandably focused their attention on the many social changes that were unfolding at the time – for instance, those associated with urbanization, secularization and rationalization of society. Indeed, many of the early social theorists from both political science in the seventeenth to eighteenth centuries (e.g. Thomas Hobbes, John Locke, Jean-Jacques Rousseau, Montesque) and sociology in the nineteenth century (e.g. Karl Marx, Max Weber, Emile Durkheim) were directly and/or indirectly tackling questions pertaining to the nature of social order in the politically and socially tumultuous times emanating from the two revolutions. Today, however, the problem of social order implicates another dimension that was not perceived as being critical during the formative years of modern social science. Specifically, we are referring here to the contemporary realization that the influences of the material/ biophysical dimension on the modern social order can no longer be neglected or ignored to the extent that they were in the past – ergo the ecological crisis must now be considered as a social problem and not simply a problem defined exclusively in natural terms and therefore outside the scope of social science. In other words, as many environmental sociologists point out, modern social science can no longer bracket out the biophysical world from social analysis as was the custom through much of the historical development of social science and particularly sociology (with some exceptions in terms of the work of classical sociological thinkers such as Marx, Weber and Durkheim – see, for example, respectively, Foster, 1999; Foster and

Holleman, 2012; Catton, Jr., 2002). Rather, today, social science must rise to the challenges of incorporating a distinctively socio-ecological method of approach in their work that does justice to both nature and society, and the role they both play in contributing to the ecological crisis (Catton Jr. and Dunlap,1978a, b; Murphy, 1994; Freudenburg et al., 1995). How, then, can a critical perspective that is decidedly socio-ecological, better position us to move towards the *development* of alternative and more effective environmental management practices? And second, how can a critical socio-ecological perspective help us to *adopt* such practices once developed? To address these questions let us first consider in more detail what is meant by a "critical" stance in social science and what it means for conceptualizing both the ecological crisis and understanding the response to that crisis via the conventional environmental management orientation.

The "Critical" Approach in Social Science

The term "critical" tends to be used quite extensively in the social sciences but the more widely it is used, the more variable its meaning becomes. In this light, Davies and Zarifa (2009) note that today critical approaches tend to fall into two camps. The first is usually linked to current theories dealing with feminism and anti-racism, and focuses more generally on issues of social inequality involving the analysis of race, gender and sexual orientation. The second camp analyzes modern society from a comparative and historical vantage point, and has its roots in the Frankfurt School (also referred to as Critical Theory), which draws upon and synthesizes Marxist and Weberian thought to develop critiques of modern society (to be discussed below). The point of convergence between these two camps, whether it is the former that exposes various bases of social inequality, or the latter that holistically critiques the character of modern social life, is that they both ultimately challenge dominant understandings of society, and, as we shall see, both may be adopted to challenge dominant views of the ecological crisis as well.

Perhaps a natural entry point for a more detailed overview of the critical stance in social science is to begin with the school of thought historically associated with the formal critique of modern social structures, because it is these structures that have ultimately contributed to the onset of the ecological crisis. Critical Theory emanated from a group of social theorists associated with the Frankfurt Institute of Social Research founded during the interwar period. These theorists included Max Horkheimer, Theodore Adorno, Herbert Marcuse, Walter Benjamin, Erich Fromm and, more recently, Jurgen Habermas. These social analysts followed the Marxist social science tradition inasmuch as they were concerned with questions of how social conditions facilitate or hinder the possibility for progressive social change and the establishment of "rational" institutions on which such change could be built. Where they differed from Marx was in their analytical point of entry. Whereas the orthodox Marxist position emphasized the role of the economy, labor and production as the basis of society (what Marx refers to as the "substructure"), the critical theorists focused on what Marx referred to as the "superstructure" –

that is, the non-economic dimensions of society, such as consumption, culture, religion, ideology and politics – and it is for this reason that critical theorists have come to be known as "neo-Marxists", even though much of the superstructural analysis drew from the work of Max Weber. Critical Theorists strove to apply knowledge from the social sciences and humanities in a reflective and self-conscious way to critique how society was institutionally organized. In particular, they emphasized how cultural institutions maintained the interests and ideologies of the dominant groups within a society, thereby perpetuating the exploitative and oppressive conditions of the day. Notably, this analytical vantage point led critical theorists to investigate how these superstructural elements functioned in ways that justified or legitimized the domination of people in capitalism, especially how people came to cognitively accept their position of relative powerlessness in a passive way. In this context, they focused their critical gaze on the continued ideological influence of "modernity" (or the "Modern Age of Reason") that had begun with the Enlightenment in Europe in the mid to late eighteenth century, including the periods of the industrial and democratic revolutions.

One key influential ideological element of the Western Enlightenment tradition was the belief that continued societal progress and improvement could only be achieved through the ever-increasing development and application of reason and scientific knowledge in the service of continued economic growth. It was largely accepted that, on the basis of this Enlightenment-inspired ideal, advances in technology and industry would automatically lead the way to increased material prosperity for society (Porter, 1994). The critical theorists questioned this strongly held belief on multiple grounds, but for the purposes at hand, we will focus only on one of these – namely, the environmental critique. John Barry notes that critical theorists had long recognized and gave analytical significance to the fact that "Not only do the origins of many present environmental problems lie in the Enlightenment (particularly the Industrial Revolution), but some of the roots of 'green' critique and alternative to industrialism also lie in the various reactions to the Enlightenment" (1999: 43). This was, in fact, the stance adopted and modified by later environmental writers such as Murray Bookchin (1990, 1996) and David Pepper (1996). These scholars realized that the underlying and unquestioned assumption of the Enlightenment tradition was that human progress and improvement was premised on an ever-increasing exploitation of the natural environment on a larger and larger scale. Based on such understandings, the critical theorists developed various accounts of how the domination and exploitation of "nature" (which included not just natural resources and the environment but all things associated with the biophysicality of human beings) went hand in hand with the domination and exploitation of humans. This in turn led to a wider range of ways of thinking about how those problems pertaining to the natural environment and nature were inextricably linked to problems of social inequality and other societal phenomena. Thus, for example, critical theorists investigated the issue of how colonialism and the control of natural resources were linked to human exploitation and inequality.

The Frankfurt School environmental critique of society was perhaps best developed in the work of Max Horkheimer and Theodor Adorno. In the *Dialectic of Enlightenment*, first published in 1944, the authors contend that the Enlightenment led to the widespread acceptance of the idea that the only value the natural environment could posses was its *instrumental value*. That is, the natural world was thought to possess value only because of its capacity to be useful for human purposes or ends. For Horkheimer and Adorno (1973), the ideological dominance of this position meant that the only relationship that human beings could conceive of, with respect to the natural environment, was one that would always be tainted by instrumentalism. Further, the implication was that Western society's orientation towards the environment would be exclusively governed by productive and technically defined concerns about how best society could exploit nature (Barry, 1999: 85). Within this intellectual backdrop pertaining to the analysis of instrumentalism, a central aspect of the Frankfurt School critique was a focus on the social and psychological consequences of increasing rationalization within society.

Building on sociologist Max Weber's foundational work on "rationalization", critical theorists had a shared interest in the question of how organizations within Western capitalist societies were becoming obsessed and preoccupied with developing and pursuing the most efficient and effective means to attain predefined organizational ends. In particular, critical theorists were concerned with how such developments had the unintended side-effect of subjugating people. In analyzing the influences of rationality within and on society, critical theorists referred to the type of instrumentalism discussed above. Notably, critical theorists argued that an integral and significant characteristic of instrumental rationality was an ideology based on the domination of nature. Specifically, they posited that the calculation and efficiency upon which instrumental rationality was built, was actualized in the real world in terms of efforts to exploit and "manage" the natural environment. For critical theorists, however, although instrumental rationality was originally adopted as part of a larger strategy to dominate nature for purely the sake of pursuing economic gains that would accrue to the capitalist class, the spirit of the approach soon spread to other domains of social life. This was because the dominant class quickly realized that the instrumentalist principles so successful in the domination of nature could also be applied effectively in terms of the social control of people, particularly in relation to changing individual behaviors in not only the workplace but in the marketplace as well. Nowhere was the deployment of this strategy more evident than in the sphere of consumption where instrumental approaches were incorporated as key strategies in the expansion of the advertising industry. As such, the advertisers began to approach the selling of commodities on the basis of appeals to social lifestyle and the social and status attributes associated with the commodity instead of the past practice of emphasizing the functional usefulness of the commodity for sale (i.e. what Marx referred to as "use value"). It was in the context of this ever-increasing application of instrumental rationality to other spheres of social life that Barry observes that:

> [T]he increasing rationalization which was central to the successful technical manipulation of external nature had a tendency to "spill over" into other spheres of human life in which they were not appropriate and were dangerous. The basic problem was this: the instrumental use of nature developed institutions, modes of thinking and acting which were then "transferred" illegitimately to human social and person relations. The domination and exploitation of the natural environment leads to the domination and exploitation of humans.
>
> (1999: 85–86)

What this meant was that the Enlightenment-inspired modes of rationality that were previously adopted only in relation to human–natural environment interactions were now increasingly being applied to human social relations, and this, for critical theorists, was a very dangerous and harmful development. The application of instrumental rationality had particular significance and negative consequences when considered in the context of inequality and social class relations. Specifically, the adoption of an instrumentalist view of other human beings by the capitalist class meant that other human beings – that is, the working class – came to be subjects of ideological manipulation at the cultural level. The implication was that people could be controlled through the application of instrumental rationality vis-à-vis ideological manipulation, as we have seen with the case of advertising. The socially detrimental effect of adopting this strategy, however, was that it essentially served to divert attention away from those issues that would necessarily require a collective rather than an individual orientation, including most if not all social issues, such as homelessness, poverty and the environment (Jhally, 1997). The application of instrumental reasoning in this manner would therefore serve as a diversionary tactic, in that, the rabid pursuit of individualized consumerism would draw people's attention away from questioning the structural conditions that undergird economic and environmental exploitation as well as social inequality, thus maintaining the status quo to the benefit of the dominant class.

Emanating from a Marxist tradition, it is not surprising to learn that critical theory has a normative dimension. For example, Horkheimer was quite explicit on this point and has remarked that the goal of critical theory was the "emancipation of human beings from the circumstances that enslave them" (1982: 244). The emancipatory potential of critical theory was meant to come about by providing people with the tools to question the prevailing taken-for-granted ideology to which they unconsciously and normally ascribe. In this light, the practical aim of critical theory was to dig beneath the surface of social life and uncover the underlying assumptions that prevent people from fully grasping a true understanding of how the world works. Once identified through the social critique process, the barriers to understanding could then be explicitly addressed through political action. For critical theorists, critique could be developed by first identifying the particular ideological currents prevalent in a given society – for instance, the belief in individual freedom or the free market under capitalism, and then comparing these ideologies with the lived social reality experienced in the given society, for example, living under conditions of social inequality and exploitation. To adopt and pursue such a strategy of critique, however, requires first an understanding of how a given society has come to be ideologically and institutionally configured in the particular way that it is found at a specific point in time. Such as stance is predicated on the notion of historical specificity.[2] That is, the view that consciousness, or the sense of self and the state of mind that an individual possesses, is a product of the political economic circumstances associated with a given historical epoch. Consciousness is therefore embedded in a particular historical epoch. In this light, the question that we can ask is, what characterizes our epoch and how does that affect our cognitive outlook? We will return to these questions later in Chapter 10 where we discuss the philosophical reorientation of environmental management, but for now we can acknowledge that clearly the ecological crisis is a preeminent defining feature of our current epoch.

Sociology and the Biophysical Environment: Tracing the Roots of the Relationship

From its inception, "sociology" has been defined as the study of "society", which in turn was conceptualized as the relationships between human beings (i.e. social relations). Thus, the "environment" was often defined as that which is not human and therefore outside the scope of the discipline (Cudworth, 2003: 14). It is therefore not surprising to learn that for the most part, during the formative years of Western sociology, the consideration of the natural environment was very limited. The "founding fathers" of the discipline – Emile Durkheim, Karl Marx and Max Weber – engaged with environmental concepts on only a very few and select occasions. For example, Durkheim applied ideas from Darwin's theory of evolution in his analysis of social change (Catton, 2002); Marx adopted the idea of a "metabolic rift", referring to disruption in the natural cycling of nutrients from countryside to the city and back as part of a larger critique of industrial capitalism of his day (Foster, 1999), while Weber analyzed how culture was to some extent anchored in people's material existence (Foster and Holleman, 2012). For the most part, however, such instances were the exception rather than the rule. Historically, the process of incorporating the environment into sociological analysis was met with considerable resistance. This resistance may to some extent be attributed to the way sociology had come to be formally established as a discipline. Particularly influential in this connection were the efforts of early sociologists to define their field of study as unique and distinct from other competing disciplines such as biology, psychology and history.

The early founders of sociology tended to treat the environment as merely a passive backdrop of little relevance to their primary concern – namely, the scientific analysis of social action. This stance was particularly well developed in Emile Durkheim's methodological work, which had as its explicit aim the establishment of sociology as an empirical science. In this light, Durkheim's method of approach was to emphasize the need to explain social phenomena exclusively in terms of observable "social facts". Social facts included, for example, norms, groups and institutions which could be studied by analyzing recorded legal codes, expressed utterances and discourses, displayed symbols and gestures, including language and direct observation of social interactions. This method of approach had the effect of directing the sociological gaze towards the cultural, symbolic and discursive aspects of social life and away from the possible influences that biological and physical factors could have on social phenomena. This analytical emphasis was part of Durkheim's attempt to have sociology carve out its own place as a uniquely defined academic discipline with its own subject matter and associated methods. It was also for this reason that Durkheim argued that the discipline should concentrate exclusively on the social while rejecting any explanations of the social made through recourse to environmental, physical, biological or psychological factors.[3]

Another point of resistance to incorporating biophysical and environmental factors into sociological thought comes from the discipline's traditional and deeply rooted aversion towards the use of various types of essentialism, such as biological and geographic (or environmental) determinism, to explain social phenomena and justify an existing social order. Biological determinism (i.e. that social organization and behavior are exclusively conditioned by our biology), particularly in the form of Social Darwinism, was very influential and popular at the turn of the previous century (Buttel, 2000). Social Darwinism was an ideology based on the biological and evolutionary principles of "natural selection" and "survival of the fittest" and was used to legitimize certain types of social organization and structured inequality. For example, many of the nineteenth-century industrial elites of North American society (i.e. the so-called "robber barons" such as Andrew Carnegie and John D. Rockefeller) subscribed to Social Darwinism because it served to legitimize their position of power and justified their exploitation of others on the basis of competitive individualism and *laissez-faire* capitalism. Those in positions of power were believed to be there because they were the "fittest", and so would inevitably rise to the top because of their biologically defined capabilities alone. Applying this logic to those less well-off, Social Darwinists argued that those who were impoverished were poor because of biologically determined physical and mental weaknesses, not because of a social class structure that prevented them from achieving social mobility. Some Social Darwinists even advocated for the use of eugenics whereby those who were poor, of a different ethnic group, or handicapped, would undergo enforced sterilization so that they would not be able to have offspring. Geographic determinism had similar racist overtones. For instance, in the early twentieth century, Ellsworth Huntington (1915, 1924 cited by Freudenburg, 2008), a Yale professor, wrote an influential book in which he argued that the temperate climate of Europe was much more conducive to the development of intellectual capabilities than the climate of the tropical regions or the colder climate of the Arctic regions. This led Huntington to conclude that those who were white-skinned were basically more intelligent and better equipped to survive than those who did not have that particular skin color. Such writings, based on an essentialist ideology of environmental determinism that justified racism and inequality were simply not palatable to the early sociologists, and something to which many of these sociologists understandably reacted against. In light of this historical context, it is not surprising that even today, some sociologists react with suspicion to the very idea of incorporating the biophysical (including the natural environment) into sociological analysis.

A further barrier to the incorporation of the environment into sociological analyses involves the analytic orientation of the micro-perspectives within the discipline. Perspectives, such as symbolic interaction, phenomenology and ethnomethodology emphasize the subjective, interpretive and processual aspects of social life. They thus take into account such factors as shared meanings, definitions of the situation, role taking and so forth in their explanation of social phenomena. Such an emphasis on the "inner world" has tended to lead to the adoption of a perspective in which the biophysical tends to be downplayed and relegated to simply playing the relatively unimportant and secondary role of material backdrop to the primary matter of concern – namely, social interactions and subjectivity.

In summary, in light of sociology's attempt to define itself as a distinct field of study, an aversion to essentialist explanations, and an emphasis on the subjective, the field as a whole was not receptive to the idea of incorporating the "environment" in its explanation of social phenomena (or, conversely, understanding the environment as a sociological issue). This situation started to change, however, in more recent times.

Sociology Confronts the Ecological Crisis

Despite the historical difficulties faced, environmental sociology, as a subdiscipline, has been able to gain some traction over more recent times as it became increasingly recognized that the material basis of social life matters if one is to more fully understand the ecological crisis. This realization was perhaps first articulated by developments in the sixties when many sociologists began to turn their attention to the various social movements that were coming into existence, such as civil rights, peace, anti-nuclear, and notably, environmental. Through the studiy of social movements (which itself became a subdiscipline within sociology), the environmental problematique was beginning to make inroads into mainstream sociology, a development which was perhaps also bolstered by the advances in ecological science and the institutionalization of environmental studies and environmental sciences as formalized fields of academic study. The public awareness and sense of urgency of the ecological crisis also dramatically increased with the OPEC oil crisis of the seventies, and a new phase in the emergence of the subdiscipline of environmental sociology was ushered in.

During the late seventies, an explicit debate was developing around the need to establish a more formalized sociological approach to the environment. This debate was initiated by the claim made by William Catton Jr. and Riley Dunlap (1978a,

b) that the whole of mainstream sociology had to first reject its inherent anthropocentrism and then move to incorporate ecological understandings as a central element to its approach (Dunlap, 2008; Buttel, 2002). They argued that mainstream sociology took as a starting point, in an unquestioned manner, the assumption that humans were an exceptional species – to such an extent that humans were thought even to be exempt from those same ecological constraints that all other species had to contend with. That is, it was argued that in common with mainstream society, mainstream sociology unquestioningly shared the idea that humans have allegedly superior capabilities and qualities, including a distinctive ability to reason and use rationality, science, technology and culture. As a result, it was assumed that humans were simply not dependent on the environment, at least not to the extent to which all other living creatures were bound to nature. This ideology of human exemptionalism was clearly anthropocentric and could be construed as another manifestation of the Enlightenment legacy critiqued by critical theorists. Catton and Dunlap (1978a, b; Dunlap, 2002) claimed that mainstream sociology was not immune to this type of anthropocentric bias, particularly in light of the distinctive way the discipline had historically developed (as discussed above). To rid the discipline of this bias (i.e. the wholesale neglect of the natural environment) a corrective was required. Of particular concern for Catton and Dunlap was that subscribing to human exemptionalism (whether consciously or not) would blind mainstream sociological researchers from appreciating the social significance and social origins of the ecological crisis. As a remedy, Catton and Dunlap (1978a, b) proposed that sociologists adopt what they referred to as the New Ecological Paradigm (NEP).

The NEP was based on a series of premises that Catton and Dunlap (1980: 34) argued needed to be adopted by sociologists in doing their work so as to correct for anthropocentric and human exemptionalist biases. Specifically, the NEP held that:

1. Humans have exceptional characteristics but remain one among many in an interdependent global ecosystem.
2. Human affairs are influenced not only by social and cultural factors but also by the complex interactions in the web of nature, so that human actions can have many unintended consequences.
3. Humans are dependent on a finite biophysical environment which sets physical and biological limits to human affairs.
4. Although the inventiveness of humans, the power derived therefrom may seem for a while to extend carrying limits, ecological laws cannot be repealed.

The type of understanding that follows from the adoption of the NEP has significant implications not only for the academic discipline of sociology but for the philosophical basis of environmental management more generally. In particular, the NEP directs attention to the need to focus on the dual importance of both the social and natural in the analysis and response to the ecological crisis.

The debate around the need for sociology to adopt the NEP did not resonate widely within the discipline, but it did serve to help formalize and institutionalize the subdiscipline of environmental sociology in the decades that followed. Although the NEP may not be explicitly acknowledged within environmental sociological studies, it has influenced the approach of the subdiscipline (Buttel, 2002). Today, environmental sociology has evolved and matured to the extent that there now exists some consensus that nature and society inform and constitute each other in a reciprocal manner.

The State of Contemporary Environmental Sociology

By the 1990s environmental sociology in North American could be recognized as a small but discernible subfield of the discipline (Hannigan, 1995: 11; Cudworth, 2003: 3; Gould and Lewis, 2009: 5). The emergence of this academic subfield was supported through the American Sociological Association section on Environment and Technology which had formed in 1975. From that time on, the section has contributed significantly to the institutionalization of environmental sociology by providing an active list-serve as well through the regular distribution of a section newsletter (first through the post then later electronically). Journals such as *Environmental Sociology* also exist to provide an outlet for research work in the subdiscipline (previously the journal *Organization and Environment* also fulfilled this need, but is no longer published).[4]

Environmental sociology has, however, remained an area of research focus that exists at the fringe of the mainstream discipline. Indeed, Arthur Mol (2006) points out that this positioning of U.S. environmental sociologists at the fringe of the discipline has led to a reaction whereby U.S. environmental sociologists appear to be engaged in a constant and active quest to legitimize their subdiscipline within mainstream sociology. The development of this situation may be accounted for in number of ways. First, the continuing marginalization of environmental sociology may in no small part be due to the general historical resistance to the subject matter of environmental sociology, particularly resistance to the insistence of environmental sociologists that nature and the environmental context be considered as central to mainstream sociological analysis (discussed in length above). Second, as of yet there have been no seminal pieces which would help define and raise the recognition and awareness of environmental sociology as a subdiscipline (Hannigan, 1995: 12). Lastly, it has been noted that the absence of any solid consensus on a theoretical base for environmental sociology has created a theoretical void that has undermined the legitimacy of this specialty area (Cable and Benson, 1993).

Nevertheless, in more recent times, there do seem to be some points of fundamental convergence with respect to a common understanding in developing the analytical relationship between sociology and the analysis of environmental issues. Thus, as Arthur Mol (2006) observes, environmental sociology in the U.S. does seem to have a common identity and frame of reference that holds the subdiscipline more or less together. For instance, there now appears to be a greater disciplinary receptiveness to the very idea that environmental problems are indeed social problems.[5] Such an understanding is based on the idea that environmental problems should not be conceived as problems of concern purely for natural science, or as problems exclusively related to issues of technology and industry, ecology and biology, or to pollution control and pollution prevention (Bell, 1998: 2). There is now an accepted recognition by sociologists that environmental problems are social problems in at least two ways. First, environmental problems are problems *of* society, in the sense that the cause of many environmental problems is ultimately due to human intervention in nature via decisions we as humans make and the way we organize our society. It is in this light that Martell (1994: 7) notes that it is the requirements and practices of a given society that result in the making of those particular technological choices and developments that have pervasive environmental impacts. Such an orientation is in line with critical theory because it recognizes that certain political, economic and social practices and institutions have led to the domination of nature that have directly and indirectly contributed to destruction of the environment. That is, the perspective that environmental problems are problems *of* society is related to the critique of modern capitalist society that is predicated on economic growth, a consumer culture and a rapid urbanization, all of which contribute to the worsening of the ecological crisis. Second, once created, environmental problems threaten our existing patterns of social organization, thus environmental problems are problems *for* society as well. The particular approach and methods that environmental sociologists adopt to analyze a particular environmental problem or issue, to some extent, are influenced by which of the two perspectives of the environmental problem as a social problem they ascribe to. Such a recognition is implicit in a distinction in analytical emphasis made between "environmental sociology" and the "sociology of environmental issues".

According to Riley Dunlap (2008), the "sociology of environmental issues" refers to an orientation in which standard sociological perspectives are applied to the study of broadly "environmental" topics such as environmental attitudes, environmental activism, and environmental politics. Thus, the standard tool kit of sociological variables, such as social class, race/ethnicity, gender, age etc., as well as traditional sociological concepts such as role, inequality, power, authority, status, frame alignment, social capital, the state, globalization, networks and so on, are applied to environmentally related phenomena in the same way they would apply to the analysis of any other social phenomena. For instance, applying concepts from social movements theories such as resource mobilization theory (i.e. the thesis that social movement success is dependent on access to scare resources such as money, time and effective communication capabilities), to the analysis of environmental movement groups such as Greenpeace, represents an example of the "sociology of environmental issues". Further, the types of studies that Macnaghten and Urry (1995: 208–216) suggest for environmental sociologists – the social context of scientific knowledge about the environment and its relation to policy decisions, the role of the media in socially constructing environmental issues, and the study of how social processes such as industrialism, consumerism and globalization give rise to environmental problems and environmental attitudes, values and behaviors – all would fall within the category of "sociology of environmental issues".[6]

On the other hand, "environmental sociology" is a relatively more radical approach to the analysis of environmental cum social phenomena. This is because for Dunlap (1995: 9), "real" environmental sociology represents a major departure from mainstream sociology's exclusive focus on the social environment. That is, a "real" environmental sociology would explicitly incorporate and unabashedly incorporate "environmental variables" in studying the interaction between environment and society. What this means is that the biophysical comes to play an equally important role as the social in the analysis. It follows, therefore, that, within this context, environmental sociology comes to be defined as the study of societal–environmental interactions or relationships – a definition that Freudenburg (2008) notes has since enjoyed widespread recognition and acceptance. By expanding the definition to include the study of relationships between environment and society more broadly, many more types of environmentally related phenomena occur under the purview of environmental sociology, including the numerous and varied manifestations of the ecological crisis.

In light of the discussion above, it is clear that the key challenge for environmental sociology is to understand the human–nature relationship in all its complexity. As environmental sociologist Nathan Young (2015: 2) observes, trying to understand each type of system alone is itself a daunting task, but then to proceed to analyze how social systems interact with ecosystems (and we would add vice versa) will require a monumental effort indeed. From an analytical point of view, what is common to all the different approaches found within environmental sociology is that they all must in some way grapple with, and problematize in their own ways, the conceptual divide between nature and society, with most environmental sociologists arguing for the blurring of dichotomous categories to some degree or another (Cudworth, 2003: 30). According to Murdoch (2001), the various existing attempts to grapple with the nature–society divide may be situated along a continuum of epistemologically defined approaches to environmental questions and issues. At the one end of the spectrum there are the more conventionally "sociological" perspectives (which Dunlap (2008) would characterize as falling into the category of the "sociology of environmental issues"), while at the other end of the spectrum there are those positions that explicitly attempt to transgress disciplinary boundaries by adopting a more "ecological stance". To illustrate the differences among these, Young (2015: 198–214) reviews three perspectives on the human–environment relationship, each of which approaches the nature–society relationship differently – political ecology, panarchy theory, and theories of co-construction. Without going into detail, we can briefly summarize some of the key distinguishing features to demonstrate some of the differences in approach.

As alluded to in Chapter 2, the political ecology approach is consistent with the classical sociological tradition of political economy which emphasizes the role of the market economy and the state in society. The political economic perspectives adopt an implicitly human-centered approach that critically focuses on issues such as power, inequality and the market. To these traditional concerns of political economy, the natural environment is put forth as another central element of analysis, hence leading to an amalgam perspective referred as political ecology. The explicit goal of the political ecology perspective is to understand human impacts on the biophysical environment. In this light, environmental problems are largely conceived of in terms of the result of political failures and shortsightedness, often expressed and analyzed in terms of the shortcomings of capitalism as an economic system. Critics of the political ecology position argue that such a perspective presumes that nature is passive – that is, nature is seen to merely conform to human intervention rather than playing an active role in shaping human beings. In other words, the social, it is alleged, is given analytic priority over nature. As a corrective to this allegedly passive conception of nature, panarchy theory emphasizes the other end of the spectrum. That is, panarchy theory assigns nature a predominant role in influencing human–nature relationships and interactions.

First formulated by the ecologists Lance Gunderson and C.S. Holling (2002), panarchy theory explicitly develops a nature-centered interpretation of the world. Placing primacy on the notion and phenomenon of the ecosystem and how an ecosystem functions, these authors developed a perspective that sought to understand how ecosystems respond to disturbances (for example, a forest fire or flood) by either restoring the previously existing state of equilibrium or "flipping" to an entirely new but stable state. Much of their discussion focuses on how ecosystem changes can occur on the basis of the particular characteristics of the natural cycles embedded within ecosystems, such as those associated with time and spatial scales – that is, how quickly cycles are completed, and how long they have taken to evolve to a certain stage and whether the ecosystems are very small or large. Somewhat controversially, Gunderson and Holling claim that their characterization of natural ecosystems also applies to human societies. In particular, they contend that economic and organizational systems go through similar processes of responding to disturbances by either restoring a previous equilibrium state or through a "flip" that entails large-scale social change (for example, through a political revolution). For the most part, sociologists reject the panarchy approach on the grounds that it proffers overly simplistic explanations of very complex phenomena. Second, sociologists are wary of the possibility that the application of panarchy theory to social phenomena will result in simply a new form of environmental determinism that has already been rejected by the contemporary social sciences. That is, panarchy theory is seen as wholly inadequate because it advances a rather narrow understanding of society and neglects important considerations such as politics, culture or economic inequality, while the notion that social systems follow predetermined cycles is viewed as somewhat naive and wholly unrealistic (Young, 2015: 208). Furthermore, to deem certain processes as "natural" raises red flags among social scientists accustomed to understanding the conceptualization of such processes as being based on ideological stance and positioning rather than as a statement of fact.

Falling in the middle of the epistemologically defined continuum concerning the relationship between humans and nature are those perspectives that Young (2015: 209) refers to as "co-constructionist". These perspectives hold that the human and natural worlds are so thoroughly intertwined that they should, in fact, be considered as "co-constitutive" – that is, they produce one another. From this perspective, it makes no sense to separate out the social from the natural, as they both equally contribute to our reality. Perhaps the most prominent of these perspectives is actor-network theory (ANT) proposed by the sociologist Bruno Latour (2005). For Latour, since reality is essentially about human–nature hybrids, analysis should make a concerted effort to capture that reality by not separating the "social" from the "natural" – and this is precisely what ANT attempts to do. As a "symmetrical" approach that gives equal weight to the social and natural in analysis, ANT traces or maps out the associations between non-humans (including technologies, objects, environmental phenomena) and humans. The ANT mapping exercise is the process through which the analysis unfolds. The mapping process attempts to come to an understanding of how the different associations between humans and non-humans lead to an emergence of a network of relations. Notably, and somewhat controversially, ANT holds that material (non-human) objects possess an "agency" that is independent of humans. That is, despite not having consciousness, non-human objects may "act", in the sense that they can resist human efforts to control them. In this context, Latour refers to such objects as "actants" (i.e. actors-without-consciousness). Actants operate or function in society in such a way as to demand a response from human beings. For example, a speed bump demands the response that the attentive driver slows down. Further, an actant may call forth, or set into motion, a whole series of human activities and other material objects. As an illustration one may consider how a virus is a central and pivotal actant that precipitates an outbreak situation involving the mobilization of many different actors and actants that are all related to each other in a human–material network. This network would include, for instance, the contacts of the infected individuals, the public health system, possibly the airline and transportation system depending on how the virus is carried by humans and animals, the media system which transmits information about the outbreak, and so on. Critics of ANT object to its overly co-constructionist emphasis that tends to excessively focus on maintaining the symmetry between the natural and social in analysis. In doing so, ANT does not recognize that action-without-consciousness is fundamentally different from the type of purposeful, meaningful and reflexive actions pursued by humans (Hacking 1999). The problem with this approach, according to the critics, therefore, is that it downplays the responsibilities that humans have as the key actors in the relationship – that is, it fails to give proper significance to humans as the main contributor to the environmental problem under consideration (Young, 2015: 212).

Despite the disadvantages and limitations of the different perspectives mentioned above, they each also have their respective advantages. Thus, in concluding his review of these perspectives, Nathan Young notes:

Political ecology exposes the link between social and environmental inequalities, as well as the deeply political nature of landscapes, natural resources, and economic decision-making. Panarchy theory exposes the impacts that humans have on natural systems large and small, and points to cumulating vulnerabilities that mutually threaten ecology and society. Finally, co-construction gives us a way to "bring nature in" to society – to see natural phenomena and non-human things as partners rather than strangers. Each makes an original (if incomplete) contribution to our understanding of nature–society relations.

(2015: 213)

From our objective of developing critical and alternative approaches to environmental management, these differing views of conceptualizing the nature–society relationship are beneficial. This is because if awareness of this multiplicity and the need for such is recognized and fostered, then conventional environmental management may become more receptive to considering alternative approaches. Further, such a realization would lead to the conclusion that no single answer or strategy can exist as a panacea to the ecological crisis. Rather, the solutions under consideration must be sensitive to the social and biophysical context in which it is being developed and later implemented, otherwise they have no chance of success from the get-go – a point that we will return to in Chapters 10 and 11 when we suggest the need for a philosophical reorientation in environmental management.

Concluding Remarks

Historically, critical social science in general, and critical sociology in particular, has arisen to challenge dominant understandings of society. For various reasons, during the early development of Western social sciences, issues related to the nature and the environment tended to be overlooked as attention focused on that which was considered purely social. The result was an enduring analytical separation between the "natural" and the "social". The serious inadequacies of such an approach came to a head as increased awareness of the worsening ecological crisis in the seventies onwards led to a realization that the environment could no longer be neglected from social analysis. From this time onwards, sociologists interested in environmental issues started to focus their critical lens on the dominant views of the ecological crisis, and not just on the dominant understandings of society. This led some environmental social scientists to reacquaint themselves with the critical writings of the Frankfurt School, who had to some extent begun a critical examination of the unquestioned ideology of dominating nature (that is, considering nature in purely instrumental terms), as a precondition for Western capitalism. Others adopted a critical stance based on a critique of the environmental crisis in terms of the negative consequences the exploitation of nature has had for certain marginalized groups in society – a critique that in the contemporary period has been taken up by the environmental justice movement. Recent developments in environmental social science and sociology have emphasized the need to link the biophysical and social in order to more effectively confront the issues arising from the ecological crisis. In the following chapter we will consider how such attempts to link the biophysical and social can be made in order to understand and address a particularly vexing challenge for environmental managers – global climate change.

Notes

1. This is, of course, not unique to environmental management but is applicable and true with respect to all types of practices and strategies involved in human affairs from the rituals of religious practice based on theology, to the industrial and manufacturing processes based on scientific theory, to child-rearing practices based on psychological theories, to business and marketing practices based on economic theory, to the activities of non-profit organizations based on a vision statement, and so on through all domains of social and organizational life.
2. The concept of historical specificity draws from Hegelian and Marxist traditions. For Marx, as a materialist, the material conditions of a given epoch in history will determine, or at least significantly influence, the consciousness of the people – that is, how people in that epoch think.
3. Although biophysical factors nevertheless did enter implicitly into Durkheim's sociological accounts at various points; see, for example, Catton Jr. (2002) for a full explication.
4. Arthur Mol (2006) notes the situation of environmental sociology in the European context was different than that of the U.S. in several important key respects. First, European environmental sociology did not have a history of debate with the mother-discipline of sociology, whereas in North America the debate stemming from the critique of Catton and Dunlap that mainstream sociology was anthropocentric was a defining element of the subdiscipline's identity. Second, while U.S. environmental sociology were preoccupied about incorporating the environment into sociology, their European counterparts were concerned with getting sociology into studies on the environment. Third, European environmental sociology exhibited a stronger institutionalization of environmental NGOs and green parties in arenas of power.
5. It should be acknowledged that sociology was late to recognize the need to consider both nature and society in the analysis of environmental problems and issues. Other researchers were not so blind, as seen, for example, in the advent of interdisciplinary approaches presumably pursued in the environmental studies programs that began to proliferate in academia in the seventies.
6. In fact, the areas Macnaghten and Urry (1995) suggest are well suited to their choice of approach – namely, the social constructionist approach. This approach analyzes the dynamic of how different claims made about an environmental issue or problem made by different players interact and result in a non-issue becoming an issue, or not (Hannigan, 1995).

References

Barry, J. (1999) *Environment and Social Theory*. London: Routledge.

Bell, M.M. (1998) *An Invitation to Environmental Sociology*. Thousand Oaks, CA: Sage.

Bookchin, M. (1990) *Remaking Society: Pathways to a Green Future*. New York: South End Press.

Bookchin, M. (1996) *Toward an Ecological Society*. Montreal: Black Rose Books.

Buttel, F. (2000) "Classical Theory and Contemporary Environmental Sociology: Some Reflections on the Antecedents and Prospects for Reflexive Modernization Theories in the Study of Environment and Society". In G. Spaargaren, A.P.J. Mol and F. Buttel (Eds.). *Environment and Global Modernity*. Thousand Oaks, CA: Sage, pp.17–39.

Buttel, F.H. (2002) "Environmental Sociology and the Classical Sociological Tradition: Some Observations on Current Controversies". In R.E. Dunlap, F. Buttel, P. Dickens and A. Gijswijt (Eds.) *Sociological Theory and the Environment: Classical Foundations, Contemporary Insights*. Lanham, MD: Rowman & Littlefield, pp.35–50.

Cable, S. and Benson, M. (1993) "Acting Locally: Environmental Injustice and the Emergence of Grass-roots Environmental Organizations". *Social Problems*, 40 (4): 464–477.

Catton, W.R., Jr. and Dunlap, R.E. (1978a) "Environmental Sociology: A New Paradigm". *The American Sociologist*, 13: 41–49.

Catton, W.R., Jr. and Dunlap, R.E. (1978b) "Theories, Paradigms and the Primacy of the HEP–NEP Distinction". *The American Sociologist*, 13: 256–259.

Catton W.R., Jr. and William, R. (2002) "Has the Durkheim Legacy Misled Sociology?". In R.E. Dunlap, F. Buttel, P. Dickens and A. Gijswijt (Eds.) *Sociological Theory and the Environment: Classical Foundations, Contemporary Insights*. Lanham, MD: Rowman & Littlefield, pp. 90–115.

Cudworth, E. (2003) *Environment and Society*. New York: Routledge.

Davies, S. and Zarifa, D. (2009) "New Institutional Theory and the Weberian Tradition". In C. Levine-Rasky (Ed.) *Canadian Perspectives on the Sociology of Education*. Toronto: Oxford University Press, pp. 3–16.

Dunlap, E.R. (1995) "Environmental Sociology". *Encyclopedia of the Environment*. Boston, MA: Houghton Mifflin, pp. 9–11.

Dunlap, R. (2002) "Paradigms, Theories, and Environmental Sociology". In R.E. Dunlap, F.H. Buttel, P. Dickens and A. Gijswijt (Eds.), *Sociological Theory and the Environment*. Lanham, MD: Rowman & Littlefield, pp. 329–350.

Dunlap, R.E. (2008) "Promoting a Paradigm Change Reflections on Early Contributions to Environmental Sociology". *Organization & Environment*, 21(4): 478–487.

Foster, J.B. (1999) "Marx's Theory of Metabolic Rift: Classical Foundations for Environmental Sociology". *American Journal of Sociology*, 105(2): 366–405.

Foster, J.B. and Holleman, H. (2012) "Weber and the Environment: Classical Foundations for a Post-exemptionalist Sociology". *American Journal of Sociology*, 117(6): 1625–1673.

Freudenburg, W. (2008) "Thirty Years of Scholarship and Science on Environment–Society Relationships". *Organization and Environment*, 21(4): 449–459.

Freudenburg, W.R., Frickel S. and Framling, G. (1995) "Beyond the Nature/Society Divide: Learning to Think about a Mountain". *Sociological Forum*, 10(3): 361–392.

Gould, K.A. and Lewis, T.L. (2009) *Twenty Lessons in Environmental Sociology*. New York: Oxford University Press.

Gunderson, L.H. and Holling, C.S. (2002) *Panarchy: Understanding Transformations in Human and Natural Systems*. Washington, DC: Island Press.

Hacking, I. (1999) *The Social Construction of What?* Cambridge, MA: Harvard University Press.

Hannigan, J. (1995) *Environmental Sociology: A Social Constructionist Perspective*. New York: Routledge.

Horkheimer, M. (1982) *Critical Theory*, New York: Seabury Press.

Horkheimer, M. and Adorno, T. (1973) *Dialectic of Enlightenment*. London: Allen Lane.

Huntington, E. (1915) *Civilization and Climate*. New Haven, CT: Yale University Press.

Huntington, E. (1924) *The Character of Races as Influenced by the Physical Environment, Natural Selection and Historical Development*. New York: Scribner.

Jhally, S. (producer) (1997) *Advertising and the End of the World* (video documentary). United States: Media Education Foundation.

Latour, B. (2004) *The Politics of Nature: How to Bring the Sciences into Democracy*. Cambridge, MA: Harvard University Press.

Macnaghten, P. and Urry, J. (1995) "Towards a Sociology of Nature". *Sociology*, 29: 203–220.

Martell, Luke (1994) *Ecology and Society: An Introduction*. Amherst, MA: The University of Massachusetts Press.

Mol, A. (2006) "From Environmental Sociologies to Environmental Sociology? A Comparison of US and European Environmental Sociology". *Organization & Environment*, 19(1): 5–27.

Murdoch, J. (2001) "Ecologising Sociology: Actor-Network Theory, Co-Construction and the Problem of Human Exemptionalism". *Sociology*, 35(1): 111–133.

Murphy, R. (1994) *Rationality and Nature: A Sociological Inquiry into a Changing Relationship*. Boulder, CO: Westview Press.

Pepper, D. (1996) *Modern Environmentalism: An Introduction*. New York: Routledge.

Porter, R. (1994) "The Enlightenment". In A.-L. Northon (Ed.) *The Hutchinson Dictionary of Ideas*. Oxford: Helicon, pp. 174–181.

Young, N. (2015) *Environmental Sociology for the Twenty-First Century*. Don Mills: Oxford University Press.

7
THE CRITICAL ANALYSIS OF CLIMATE CHANGE AS A CASE IN STUDY

In a real sense, global climate change is the exemplary environmental problem of the ecological crisis. It is emblematic of the ecological crisis and is perhaps a defining issue for our times. Indeed, the significance of global climate change for the current era has been substantiated by geologists who have designated the present epoch as the Era of the Anthropocene to highlight the fact that human activities have had a significant impact on the current state of our planet's geology and ecosystems (Crutzen, 2002). Climate change is therefore a particularly apt topic to illustrate how critical science may be employed to shed light on why certain conventional environmental management approaches are adopted to combat climate change, and why they tend to be largely ineffective. As we shall see, certain favored environmental management responses to climate change, such as the creation of a market for carbon pollution permits or the imposition of carbon taxes, tend to take precedence over the consideration of non-market approaches, many of which are based on suggestions for restructuring the institutional base of the economy and society. Although perhaps politically the most expedient in terms of the neoliberal times in which we live, environmental management responses to climate change based on market models may not be the most effective or even logical approach to addressing the climate change problematic. In this chapter, we begin with a very brief overview of what is meant by global climate change. We then begin our discussion of what critical social science and sociology may offer to the understanding of climate change as a socio-ecological phenomenon by examining the unique social and psychological aspects of the climate change phenomenon, and the implications these may have for the responses to climate change we have witnessed thus far. Next, we consider the social process through which the climate change problem becomes a public issue. As discussed in the subsequent section, systems thinking features prominently in thinking about climate change not only as a natural phenomenon, but somewhat surprisingly as a social phenomenon as well. One consequence of this is that the logic of economics and the markets dominates how analysts and policy-makers conceive of the social and behavioral aspects implicated in climate change mitigation and adaptation. Such a development we argue works against the adoption of more critical climate change responses – a theme we will take up towards the end of this chapter.

General Overview of Climate Change

Similar to the ecological crisis in general, global climate change cannot be understood in terms of a single cause or a single set of "effects". In particular, the effects of climate change are very wide-ranging and spatially dispersed. They include numerous types of effects such as increases in Arctic temperatures, reduction in the size of icebergs, the melting of glaciers, reduced permafrost, changes in rainfall, reduced biodiversity, new wind patterns, the increased frequency of extended droughts and heat waves, and other types of extreme weather events. As Dessler and Parson (2006: 1, cited by Young, 2015) note, it is a "new type of environmental problem the likes of which we have never seen before". The disturbance of our planet by climate change is of such magnitude it will affect almost all the natural ecosystems upon which we directly or indirectly rely. And the predictions concerning the consequences of the impacts are dire – flooding of highly populated coastal areas and issue of displaced peoples (i.e. "climate refugees" (Farbotko and Lazru (2012)), changes in the distribution of infectious disease, loss of agricultural productivity due to droughts, social tensions related to climate refugees and the transmigration of people in the context of an intensified struggle for diminishing natural resources, to name just a few.

Climate change is produced by the release of carbon-based compounds (often referred to as greenhouse gases consisting primarily of carbon dioxide but including other gases as well) into the atmosphere due to the combustion of fossil fuels (e.g. oil, coal, natural gas). The accumulation of carbon in the atmosphere is of great concern because the carbon will serve as an insulating layer that will trap excess heat instead of allowing the Earth to dissipate it, thus leading to the situation of global warming (which in turn will lead to changes in the global climate). Scientists have documented a dramatic rise in carbon levels from the time of the Industrial Revolution in which fossil fuels started to be used extensively as a source of energy for various technologies (NASA, 2016). The accumulation of carbon in the atmosphere is a particularly vexing problem today because the burning of fossil fuels is prevalent across many sectors, including, transportation, electricity generation, heating and manufacturing. Climate change is therefore a problem rooted in many facets of our existence and implicates a wide range of factors from the economy to politics and personal habits (Redclift, 2011). It is a problem whose long-term solution requires collective action on a scale the world has never experienced (Young, 2015). As such, political barriers to addressing climate change are faced almost immediately because this global environmental problem requires attention and action from all nations in a cooperative manner. At the same time the stakes are high because addressing the climate change issue will have significant impacts on the economies and societies of all nation states across the globe, with many such states haboring concerns about the loss of competitive economic advantage and political power. International politics is, of course, based on the relationships between individual nation states and, as a consequence, global climate change negotiations tend not to be successful because each nation state continues to defend its own interests, thereby leading to broad failure to address the problem in any meaningful way (Harrison and Sundstrom, 2010).

The Social and Psychological Dimensions of Climate Change

So profound in its impact and pervasive in consequence, it is not unreasonable to assume that global climate change will be overwhelming to the psyche of individuals. Indeed, some social scientists have observed that problems pertaining to the individual and collective motivation necessary for confronting this particular problem represent in themselves a serious obstacle to making any real progress in addressing global climate change (Giddens, 2009; Derber, 2010). Climate change represents a serious existential threat to the social and material systems that essentially support the high quality of life that tends to be taken for granted in the Western experience (Young, 2015). That is, global climate change is a threat similar to nuclear war and global influenza in that the risk of planetary destruction, or the elimination of the human species, may be the ultimate physical realization of that threat (Derber, 2010). Similar to the psychological and political reaction to other existential threats, the issue of global climate change leads to denial and the ignoring of certain kinds of truth claims for the sake of maintaining ontological security – that is, for maintaining the taken-for-granted sense of continuity and order that enables individuals to carry on in their daily lives in an accepted state of unquestioned security. The bracketing out of these sorts of threats to ontological security most readily occurs with respect to climate change because, as Giddens (2009) notes, the threats associated with climate change seem to be abstract and elusive in nature, however potentially devastating they may actually be. Furthermore, since the dangers posed by global climate change are not readily immediate, visible or tangible in the course of the daily lives of most individuals (there are, of course, exceptions such as the Inuit who inhabit polar areas that have drastically changed in a short period of time due to melting ice sheets), the tendency is normally to delay taking action. Known as "future discounting", this psychological predilection is similar and somewhat related to one of the prominent features of the incubation period of disaster identified by Barry Turner (1976) to be discussed in Chapter 9. Specifically, we are referring here to the psychological phenomenon of "minimizing emergent danger" where people tend to underestimate the risks involved, thereby leading them to disregard the warning signs of an impending disaster (see Chapter 9). The serious implication arising from this tendency is that by the time people are stirred to take action, it may be too late as far as climate change is involved. The need for urgent action is especially pressing if one takes into account the role that exceeding a tipping point may play in accelerating the global climate change process. That is, once a critical threshold value or tipping point in temperature is exceeded, climate change would no longer be expected to unfold at a gradual rate, but at an exponential rate.

Despite the high disaster potential associated with global climate change, our social and political institutions seem to be either unaware or choose to not take into account the tendency to minimize the emergent danger. In this connection, Derber observes that "in our short-term culture, long-term truths that we cognitively accept as valid become abstract and disconnected from our urge to act. Our economic and political systems create short-term, ego-centered myopia" (2010: 2). As such, the psychology and sociology of climate change are important areas of knowledge that environmental managers should be aware of in developing responses to global climate change that are in tune with the people and institutions of society. Yet, as alluded to previously, as stated explicitly by Urry in regard to sociology, although the mainstream of this discipline purports to examine the nature of modern society, sociology has failed to analyze the carbon resource-basis of society; sociology has been, in that respect, "carbon-blind" (2011: 163). In particular, what has thus far been neglected in much of the social scientific analysis of the ecological crisis is the question of how modern societies have become so thoroughly dependent upon fossil fuels and how the politics of carbon have become central to contemporary global politics. Without knowledge concerning the social, psychological and political context of the ecological crisis, environmental management strategies will continue to be too narrowly define, short-sighted and out-of-sync with social reality. Consequently, these strategies may very well remain within the narrow parameters of the realpolitik of the ecological crisis in general, and the problem of global climate change in particular, but at the same time they will be out of touch with the large-scale structural changes required to actually address the ecological crisis and climate change in any effective way that is properly informed by sound theoretical and ethical imperatives.

The Social Framing of Climate Change

The social constructionist perspective is an approach within sociology that analyzes the process through which a non-issue becomes an issue (or not). It does so by considering the claims-making process in which various claims-makers put forth and advocate particular positions concerning the issue in question. For example, in the case of environmental issues and problems, John Hannigan (1995) develops and applies the social constructionist perspective to analyze how different social actors (i.e. claims-makers) such as industry representatives, journalists and the mass media, environmental movement groups, politicians, state agencies (including those employing government scientists), and academic scientists are involved in the "construction" of issues such as acid rain, biodiversity loss and biotechnology use. Although there may be many factors and processes involved in the social construction of an environmental issue, one key factor involves the question of how the environmental issue is discursively framed. At the most basic level, "discourse" refers to forms of communication, whether they are in spoken, written, or oral forms. In the sociological sense, "framing" refers to how a discourse is presented in such a way that members of the public become inclined to interpret the meaning of things in certain and particular ways. Framing therefore influences or persuades people to think about things in one particular way as opposed to an alternative way. For example, depending on the discursive framing of the notion of "energy", energy could be thought of in numerously different ways: as a commodity, a social necessity or a natural resource with ecological implications. Each definition will legitimate the position of a different claims-maker and therefore imply that a particular course of action be taken to address the issue. If, for instance, energy is understood to be a commodity, it will follow that business people should be considered as the legitimate actors involved in making decisions about energy. If the social necessity definition is accepted, then the public or the government would be regarded as the legitimate decision-makers. Finally, if energy is regarded as a natural resource, it would be the scientific and ecological experts who would be deemed the proper decision-making authority. Discursive framing, as will now be discussed, plays a central role in how the climate change issue is dealt with by the polity and society.

Climate Change Denial Framing

As repeatedly emphasized throughout this book, of key importance to the development of critical environmental management is knowledge concerning the context in which strategies are to be developed and implemented. Without such knowledge, efforts will remain problematically narrow and ultimately ineffectual. Perhaps one of the most important context-based factors that must be explicitly recognized and dealt with is the understanding that global climate change is ultimately based on human decisions to intervene in nature in particular ways (i.e. in particular, the decision to base the economy and society on the combustion of fossil fuels as the chief source of energy). As was alluded to in our earlier discussion of environmental governance, decision-making is always political and in the case of climate change what should be recognized from the onset is that very powerful interests are involved, especially actors from the carbon-based global energy industries. These social actors have significantly influenced how the climate change issue is framed, and they have expended a great deal of effort and resources to ensure that their power and influence would not be wrestled from them (Urry, 2011). The societal reliance on fossil fuels did not arise "naturally" as is often assumed, but was the distinct historical result of a cluster of high-carbon, path-dependent systems that were set in place then locked in through various powerful and influential economic and social institutions in the oil and transportation sectors and their political allies. We cannot go into the details of this long and complex historical process here, but suffice to say that the process continues to the present day in a somewhat developed and cunningly sophisticated way – as fully elaborated upon, for example, by the work of Tim Mitchell (2011). As will now be discussed, the overall objective of these powerful and influential actors is to sway public opinion in certain directions with respect to climate change and the maintenance of a high-carbon society on which climate change is predicated.

In a series of studies, Riley E. Dunlap and his colleagues have carefully documented how an interlocking network of political and industrial elites – which are referred to as the anti-reflexivity movement – have worked together to undermine climate science and policy (Dunlap, 2009, 2013; Dunlap and Jacques, 2013; Dunlap and McCright, 2010, 2011a, b; Elsasser and Dunlap, 2013; Jacques et al., 2008; McCright and Dunlap, 2003, 2010). What their research reveals is that the American conservative movement, comprising a network of conservative foundations, think tanks, media outlets and public intellectuals, was heavily funded by a number of extremely wealthy conservative families and their foundations and corporations to pursue lobbying measures designed to maintain a high-carbon lifestyle and way of life. This network of actors first gained influence and power during the early years of the neoliberal period with the ascendancy of the Ronald Reagan administration in the early 1980s. McCright and Dunlap (2010) found that the efforts of this particular set of actors were directed at delegitimizing the environmental movement and environmental impact science in the eyes of the public. The strategies the anti-reflexivity movement adopted were different from the past in that "learning from its mistakes in overtly attacking environmental regulations in the early 1980s, this counter-movement has subsequently exercised a more subtle form of power characterized by non-decision-making" (McCright and Dunlap, 2010: 100). Non-decision-making techniques refer to the ways in which a problem remains a non-issue, thereby preventing any significant progress in policy-making with respect to that problem. These non-decision-making techniques are based on the exercise of more subtle forms of power. As such, this exercise of power does not arise in actual situations of direct conflict and debate; rather, non-decision-making power is exercised by confining the scope of decision-making to only those issues that do not seriously challenge the actor's subjective interests. In the case of the anti-reflexivity movement, the non-decision-making techniques included: (1) obfuscating, misrepresenting, manipulating and suppressing the results of scientific research; (2) intimidating or threatening to sanction individual scientists; (3) invoking existing rules or created new procedures in the political system; and (4) invoking an existing bias in the media. All of these techniques were directed at making climate change a non-issue by challenging the legitimacy of climate science and by preventing progress on climate policy-making by introducing doubts that would influence the interpretive framing of the issue.

These non-decision-making tactics were also carried out by various high-profile front organizations where again the focus was primarily on attacking the science behind climate change rather than attacking the notion of environmental protection per se; recourse to the latter was recognized as being ineffective under today's widespread public awareness of the ecological crisis (Dunlap and McCright,

2011a, b). The adoption of these types of approaches has ultimately led to the introduction of a discursive frame based on "skepticism" in the policy debate – a frame also referred to as the "climate change denial" or the "contrarian" position. Specifically, denialists went through great efforts to draw public attention to the ostensible uncertainties of the science involved in predicting temperature changes over the future decades, but in actuality this was a misleading and deceptive ploy that diverted public attention from a true understanding of the problem while at the same time diverting attention away from it.

The interdisciplinary science of climate change has been formalized and institutionalized in a way that is quite distinct from other sciences. This process could be traced to the establishment of the Intergovernmental Panel on Climate Change (IPCC) in 1988 under the auspices of the United Nation Environment Programme and the World Meteorological Organization when leading climate scientist James Hansen announced that anthropogenic global warming was well under way. This body consists of more than 2,500 scientists who examine the links between greenhouse gas emissions and climate change, and are mandated to provide the world with a clear scientific view on the current state of knowledge in climate change and its potential environmental and socioeconomic impacts (IPCC, 2016). The IPCC vigorously reviews and assesses the current literature and scientific findings on climate change to ensure a complete and objective understanding of the phenomena and is considered to be the most authoritative scientific body ever assembled on a single topic. As such, the anti-reflexivity movement expends a considerable amount of effort in trying to discredit the IPCC. They do so by promoting the work of a handful of contrarian scientists who regularly speak out against the consensus position of the IPCC and claim that evidentiary basis of global warming is weak, if not wrong (McCright and Dunlap, 2010: 111). The anti-reflexivity movement claims that the work of the IPCC is "junk science" and occasionally accuses the international body of intentionally altering its reports to "manufacture" its climate change position (ibid.). More often than not, their claims are based on the alleged uncertainty associated with climate change science.

Nathan Young (2015: 53) notes that climate change scientists rarely, if ever, make the claim that they are absolutely 100 percent certain about their conclusions concerning complex natural phenomenon. The conclusions of climate change experts are always couched in the cautionary and careful qualifications demanded as part of the protocol of all the scientific disciplines (Hannigan, 1995: 80). The need for such careful couching of scientific arguments is especially true with respect to climate change science which combines knowledge from many disciplines such as oceanography, geology, atmospheric science, thermodynamics, and so on. Understandably, it should in fact be logically expected that there will always be a certain degree of uncertainty in the claims of climate scientists. However, the presence of scientific uncertainly does not in itself invalidate their conclusions concerning global climate as the scientists themselves have always maintained that they have a high confidence in their findings with respect to this phenomenon (Young, 2015). Yet, the skeptic framing will focus almost exclusively on these uncertainties and claim that the scientific findings are therefore invalid or inconclusive. This, however, is an incorrect inference based on the scientific evidence presented. Unlike the position taken by the chemical industry in an earlier era, in which Rachel Carson was directly attacked, the skeptics position themselves as the voice of reason in that they are arguing that taking action against climate change is premature due to what they see is a lack of conclusive evidence. That is, they claim that taking action when there is no proven evidence of harm will be expensive and misguided (ibid.).

The Gradualist and Catastrophist Framing of Climate Change

Other climate change frames exist and do, in fact, compete for public and political attention. For instance, based on earlier linear models of climate change explicated in the four major reports produced by the IPCC between 1990 and 2007, a perspective was put forth that climate change-induced impacts would unfold in a relatively slow manner, which would give societies adequate time to adjust and adapt. Such a framing is referred to as "gradualism" (Urry, 2011). More recently, a third frame has evolved based on newer considerations that lead to a less optimistic account for the future and a need to act more urgently now. This perspective critiques the IPCC for not considering positive feedback loops in their analysis, especially those pertaining to the melting of ice sheets and thawing of permafrost. If these more systems-based mechanisms are considered, the climate change effects will not occur in a gradual fashion but in a much more dramatic, rapid and non-linear fashion once certain thresholds are exceeded. This framing of the climate change phenomenon is known as "catastrophism".

According to the catastrophism framing, the impacts of global climate change are expected to unfold more quickly and because of the way positive feedback loops and tipping points work, the changes will be abrupt and sudden. This is because positive feedback loops will amplify the warming effects in ways that were not previously identified by the scientific community until recently. An example of such a mechanism involves the melting of Arctic sea ice (Derber, 2010). Normally, the snow covering the sea ice would act as an insulating blanket and reflect back much of the solar energy that impinged upon it. This would help ensure that the sea ice would stay cold and not melt. However, exposed ocean water is darker and will absorb sunlight. With global warming, more of the ice will melt, leading to more exposed water. More exposed water will lead to greater heating, which will then result in even more melting of ice, which will lead to even more exposed water. Consequently, the melting of the polar ice caps (included in these caps is compressed ice of up to 2 miles in height) will occur much more quickly than predicted by the earlier linear models. The implication of this prediction is that populated coastal regions, and those areas under the sea level, will have much less time to prepare for the imminent flooding that global warming will render. Notably, three great ice sheets are in danger due to the amplifying effects of feedback loops; one covers vast expanses of Greenland and two others cover similarly vast expanses of the Antarctic (Urry, 2011: 32). The amplifying effects would be made worse by other phenomena related to climate change. For instance, if the permafrost in Siberia were to thaw, this would lead to the release of methane on a significant scale (as there exists a huge deposit of the more powerful greenhouse gas of methane buried within the permafrost), which would in turn lead to an even more intensified global warming. By 1990, thirteen significant positive feedback loops were identified, providing further support for the catastrophist position that the Earth's climate would change faster and more dramatically than previously thought.

Systems Thinking and the Climate Change Issue

One important point to raise concerns the role that systems thinking has in dealing with the issue of climate change. We have already seen that systems thinking, in terms of tipping points and feedback loops has been employed by scientists to understand and characterize global climate change in biophysical terms. We will engage in a more sustained discussion of complexity and systems thinking in the next chapters. However, for now, based on cursory understanding, it is interesting to note that the social science of economics also employs the logic of systems thinking, but in a very different and specific way. And the way that economists apply their particular systems thinking logic has many implications for the way that society may possibly respond to climate change, especially with reference to the possible types of policy options that are given due consideration. The feedback loops we have discussed above in regard to the natural systems implicated in global climate change involve *positive* feedback loops; economists, on the other hand, tend to base their models on the assumption of working *negative* feedback loops. Positive feedback loops ultimately lead to disasters because processes quickly spiral out of control – that is, they rapidly move away from some stable equilibrium state. With negative feedback loops, the equilibrium system is maintained and disaster or out-of-control scenarios are averted. For instance, the negative feedback loop involved in regulating the heat and temperature of a room is based on a relatively simple system consisting of a thermostat and furnace. If the temperature in the room falls below the set temperature on the thermostat, then the furnace will turn on until the room temperature eventually rises to reach the temperature set on the thermostat by the user, at which point the furnace will turn off. In this way, the temperature in the room remains at the stable equilibrium point. John Urry (2011) notes that much of economics presumes that feedbacks will only be negative and therefore equilibrium-restoring (this is often why there is frequently mention of the action of a "corrective" in the market place that ostensibly returns the market system to a state of equilibrium). Models based on equilibrium dominate economics and in doing so they ignore the huge array of positive feedbacks that exist in reality and will certainly result in taking the market system away from the assumed equilibrium state that the economic models assume.

Urry (2011) further notes that within climate change policy circles, the economists are typically understood to be the specialists who can speak to the "human dimension" of climate change, especially as it involves adaptation and mitigation. At least in part, this emphasis can be traced back to the influential Stern Review of 2006 (the 700-page IPCC report entitled *The Economics of Climate Change*) in which economics was given a central and dominant role in developing climate change responses for society. Indeed, as Urry (2011) notes, much of the Stern Review deploys the language, methods and modelling skills of economics. Consequently, the social science of climate change was not given the chance to become well established or even allowed to undergo significant development, as the lead was taken and dominated by the narrow economic models of human behavior. Due to their preferential status in climate change circles, economists were able to quickly secure the resources and funding to support their particular research work to the detriment of other social scientists. As a consequence, today it is the economic model of human behavior that has the most significant influence on the worldwide development of environmental policy in general, and global climate change policy in particular. Such a bias, it should be noted, works in concert with the neoliberal conditions that prevail today. According to this economically informed perspective on human behavior, dubbed "economic imperialism" by Urry (2011: 8), the analysis of human life and patterns can and should be reduced to "economic calculation" and the working of "markets". In particular, "economics performs human behaviour as individualized and hence as agents of market mechanisms" (Urry, 2011: 10). This individualizing tendency is problematic because it reduces complex patterns of collective social life and interaction to an agglomeration of rational individuals. This is especially problematic in recognizing that global climate change is an issue that requires collective rather than individual responses based on preferences, social customs, traditions, and so on that cannot be simply understood in economically rational, maximizing individual self-interest terms. For example, many serious problems arise in addressing climate change through market mechanisms because they do not have a nuanced, subtle and sophisticated understanding of the social world in which many other types of rationality (other than economic) come to play an important role (for example, cultural rationality, a notion we will return to in Chapter 10). In particular, for our purposes, the market-based logic and economic approach are not sufficiently critical and upstream in orientation to be useful. Such approaches, in particular, are often incongruent with the more radical approaches espoused, for instance, by certain streams of the environmental movement and critical social scientists.

Much of contemporary environmentalism engaged with the issue of climate change seeks to contest the excesses that Urry refers to as "carbon capitalism" (2011: 92) – a form of capitalism whose foundation rested upon fossil fuels. Carbon capitalism was well supported by powerful industrial interests such as petrochemical, transportation, manufacturing and energy and oil companies, and their political lobby and think tanks, all of whom argued for the maintenance of a high-carbon society and the luxurious lifestyles that were predicated on that. Indeed, it cannot be taken for granted that, as Leggett (2005) notes, oil companies are undoubtedly the most powerful interest group in the world, with most oil companies being bigger and more powerful than many governments. Their influence cannot be underestimated. In response, climate change environmentalism developed and posed alternatives that essentially challenged the twentieth-century carbon capitalism, especially in promoting various low-carbon possibilities for society. Their proposed alternatives and action were, however, met with an intense and well-orchestrated opposition by the carbon capitalists who adopted various public opinion-influencing tactics such as actively supporting the "climate change skeptic" frame discussed above; through strategies of "greenwashing" where companies publicly claim that they are engaged in sound environmental practices and by promoting a "green image" when in fact this is simply a deception; "astroturfing" whereby public relations firms were hired by corporations to promote the image that their corporation has extensive grass-roots support; and lobbying efforts to weaken environmental legislation. As the discursive conflict between carbon capitalists and climate change environmentalists continues, critical environmental managers must be cognizant of the tactics both sides employ in order to be clear on their tasks at hand with respect to charting the way towards alternative and critical environmental management strategies. This is where critical social science can assist in the endeavor.

Important guiding insights for critical environmental management can be gleaned from our review above concerning the social scientific understanding of how climate change frames have been constructed and contested. One important insight stems from recognizing that climate change, and the ecological crisis in general, are the result of societal (or perhaps more correct "socio-ecological") processes. And, as a partially societally constructed phenomenon, there can be no natural point of equilibrium to which we can return. Yet, the skeptic and gradualist framing of climate change is predicated on the notion of returning to a state of equilibrium with no attention given to the role that positive feedback loops may play in taking us away from equilibrium. It is in this light that Urry notes that:

> The 'normal' state then is not one of balance. Policies never straightforwardly restore equilibrium, as opposed to the typical claims of policy-makers. Indeed, actions often generate the opposite or almost the opposite from what is intended. So many decisions intended to generate one outcome, because of the operation of a complex system, generate multiple unintended effects different from those that are planned.
>
> (2011: 41)

For instance, Barnett and O'Neill (2010: 212) give the example of how climate change was suspected in leading to lower water levels in Melbourne, Australia. To deal with this problem, desalination plants were constructed, but running these facilities requires a great deal of energy, which in turn results in the worsening of the climate change problem. Thus, although energy-intensive adaptation actions may have addressed the current needs, they created a positive feedback by increasing greenhouse gas emission, thereby increasing the likelihood that further adaptation to climate change will be required in the future. This example also illustrates another common problem faced by environmental and disaster managers wishing to address global climate change – namely, the tendency for managers to focus on a well-structured problem first rather than addressing more an urgent ill-structured problem – a variant of the "decoy problem" identified by Barry Turner (1976) in his disaster incubation exposition to be explored in the next chapter.

Concluding Remarks

From the perspective of environmental management, perhaps the most valuable contribution that an environmentally conscious social science may make is to direct explicit attention to developing and informing strategies that are context-sensitive – that is, to both the social and environmental context. The particular advantage of this type of context-sensitivity is that it opens up the analysis of an environmental problem to socially viable, and therefore more comprehensive and realistic assessments of the situation. In this way, a notably critical edge is added to the assessment to counter the narrow and somewhat conservative approaches to conventional environmental management. This is seen most vividly in the case of global climate change in that the scope of analysis will be considerably broadened to consider such factors as the social and psychological dimensions of climate change; how the framing of the climate change issue may influence response strategies (such as the types of mitigation and adaptation responses taken); as well as how larger political currents such as neoliberalism bias the selection towards market-based responses to the ecological crisis over all other alternatives. These types of factors are not normally considered to fall under the purview of technocratically defined approaches to environmental management, but because of this very reason, a critical dimension to environmental management continues to be absent. A critical understanding of the ecological crisis, however, is necessary if environmental management is to evolve at the accelerated pace required to properly address the consequences of the crisis. This is an especially pressing need if one considers that in the future it may be inevitable that the worlds of environmental management and disaster management, that for the moment are separate, will undoubtedly converge. As the phenomenon of global climate change reveals, the ecological crisis will be of mutual concern for both fields. As global environmental change accelerates, resilience and adaptation at both the community and societal level will become increasingly more important and environmental and disaster managers will need to jointly organize their efforts to respond effectively – a cross-fertilization that may help cultivate alternative approaches. In the two chapters that follow, we discuss how this may be so.

References

Barnett, J. and O'Neil, S. (2010) "Maladaptation". *Global Environmental Change*, 20: 211–213.
Crutzen, P.J. (2002) "Geology of Mankind: The Anthropocene". *Nature*, 415: 23.

Derber, C. (2010) *Greed to Gree: Solving Climate Change and Remaking the Economy*. London: Paradigm.
Dessler, A. and Parson, E. (2006) *The Science and Politics of Global Climate Change: A Guide to the Debate*. New York: Cambridge University Press.
Dunlap, R.E. (2009) "The Conservative Assault on Climate Science: A Successful Case of Deconstructing Scientific Knowledge to Oppose Policy Change". In J. Nagel, T. Dietz and J. Broadbent (Eds.), *Sociological Perspectives on Climate Change*, Washington, DC: National Science Foundationpp, 67–73. .
Dunlap, R.E. (2013) "Climate Change Skepticism and Denial: An Introduction". *American Behavioral Scientist*, 57: 691–698.
Dunlap, R.E. and Jacques, P.J. (2013) "Climate Change Denial Books and Conservative Think Tanks: Exploring the Connection". *American Behavioral Scientist*, 57: 699–731.
Dunlap, R.E. and McCright, A.M. (2010) "Climate Change Denial: Sources, Actors and Strategies". In C. Lever-Tracy (Ed.), *Routledge Handbook of Climate Change and Society*. Abingdon: Routledge, pp. 240–259.
Dunlap, R.E. and McCright, A.M. (2011) "Organized Climate-Change Denial". In J.S. Dryzek, R.B. Norgaard and D. Schlosberg (Eds.), *Oxford Handbook of Climate Change and Society*. New York: Oxford University Press, pp. 144–160.
Elsasser, S.W. and Dunlap, R.E. (2013) "Leading Voices in the Denier Choir: Conservative Columnists' Dismissal of Global Warming and Denigration of Climate Science". *American Behavioral Scientist*, 57: 754–776.
Farbotko, C. and Lazru, H. (2012) "The First Climate Refugees? Contesting Global Narratives of Climate Change in Tuvalu". University of Wollongong Research Online. Available at: http://ro.uow.edu.au/cgi/viewcontent.cgi?article=8119&context=scipapers (last accessed April 23, 2016).
Giddens, A. (2009) *The Politics of Climate Change*. Cambridge: Polity Press.
Hannigan, J. (1995) *Environmental Sociology: A Social Constructionist Perspective*. New York: Routledge.
Harrison, K. and Sundstrom, L.M. (Eds.) (2010) *Global Commons, Domestic Decisions: The Comparative Politics of Climate Change*. Cambridge, MA: MIT Press.
Intergovernmental Panel on Climate Change (IPCC) (2016) "IPCC Intergovernmental Panel on Climate Change". Available at: www.ipc.ch/organization/organization/shtml (last accessed July 25, 2016).
Jacques, P., Dunlap, R.E. and Freeman, M. (2008) "The Organization of Denial: Conservative Think Tanks and Environmental Scepticism". *Environmental Politics*, 17: 349–385.
Leggett, J. (2005) *Half Gone: Oil, Gas, Hot Air and Global Energy Crisis*. London: Portobello Books.
McCright, A.M. and R.E. Dunlap. (2003) "Defeating Kyoto: The Conservative Movement's Impact on U.S. Climate Change Policy". *Social Problems*, 50: 348–373.
McCright, A.M. and Dunlap, R.E. (2010) "The American Conservative Movement's Success in Undermining Climate Science and Policy". *Theory, Culture & Society*, 27 (2–3): 100–133.
McCright, A.M. and Dunlap, R.E. (2011a) "The Politicization of Climate Change: Political Polarization in the American Public's Views of Global Warming". *Sociological Quarterly*, 52: 155–194.
McCright, A.M. and Dunlap, R.E. (2011b) "Cool Dudes: The Denial of Climate Change among Conservative White Males". *Global Environmental Change*, 21: 1163–1172.
Mitchell, T. (2011) *Carbon Democracy: Political Power in the Age of Oil*. London: Verso.
National Aeronautics and Space Administration (NASA) (2016) "Climate change: How do we know?" Available at: http://climate.nasa.gov/evidence/ (last accessed April 23, 2016).

Redclift, M. (2011) "The Response of the Hermeneutic Social Sciences to a 'Post Carbon world'". *International Review of Social Research*, 1(3): 155–166.
Turner, B.A. (1976) "The Organizational and Interorganizational Development of Disasters". *Administrative Science Quarterly*, 21: 378–397.
Urry, J. (2011) *Climate Change and Society*. Cambridge: Polity Press.
Young, N. (2015) *Environmental Sociology for the Twenty-First Century*. Don Mills: Oxford University Press.

8
DISASTER STUDIES AND THE ECOLOGICAL CRISIS

This chapter begins by explaining why the analysis of disasters is likely to become an increasingly relevant topic for environmental management as the ecological crisis continues to unfold. Following that, we will give a brief overview of the field of disaster studies. As we shall see, disaster research has grappled with similar themes and issues as environmental sociology, especially the need to reconcile the natural with the social analysis. Despite its historical emphasis on practical issues related to disaster management, the field of disaster studies has recently made efforts to build its theoretical foundation. Notable outcomes of such efforts include an increasing focus on disaster vulnerability – how particular groups in society are more susceptible to disasters and their effects – and an understanding of how a disaster is best conceptualized not as an event, but as a process that is informed by the complex interplay of material and social factors.

Disasters and the Ecological Crisis

In his book entitled *Climate Change and Society*, the sociologist John Urry (2011: 166) remarks that global climate change will most likely lead to a future in which, as a society, we will be put in a position in which we will have no choice but to prepare for various catastrophes and extreme weather events. That is, events that will inevitably be precipitated by the massive changes to the Earth's biosphere induced by human activities such as large-scale fossil fuel consumption, deforestation, and so on. With the expected onslaught of extreme environmental events, Urry predicts that sociology's main future contributions will likely be in the field of disaster studies. Similarly, Rudel et al. (2011) surmise that with the expected intensification of climate change, the political economy of the environment perspective will likely shift its focus directly towards the political economy of disasters.

In light of the above, Urry (2011) argues that issues pertaining to vulnerability and resilience to disasters will necessarily receive increased attention from the social sciences in the coming century. Indications pertaining to the need for the type of reorientation in the future already appear to be coming forth. Various sources have reached the similar conclusion that over the last few decades natural disasters have occurred with greater frequency and increased severity of impacts. For instance, the United Nations International Strategy for Disaster Reduction (UISDR) (2012) has found that between 1992 and 2012, disasters affected over 4.4 billion people, causing 1.3 million deaths and economic losses of over $2 trillion. Similarly, findings were produced by the International Federation of Red Cross and Red Crescent Societies (IFRC) (2002: 185–7) which note that there was an increase of over 93 percent in the decade from 1992 to 2001, as the number of reported disasters rose from 368 to 712. Furthermore, during the same period the number of people affected rose from 78,292,000 to 170,478,000. Typically, the various agencies that keep track of the number of natural disasters found that four to five times more disasters occur today in comparison to 1960 (Smith, 2001: 32; Hilhorst and Bankoff, 2004). Although the number of recorded disasters may be an artifact of improved reporting and media channels, as well as perhaps the advent of greater incentives for affected locales to officially declare a "state of emergency" in order to access national and international aid (Young, 2015: 179), it is nevertheless clear that the overall impact of natural disasters has increased (as measured in terms of human and financial losses). The recognition of such circumstances has led some disaster researchers such as Alexander (1997) to argue that we currently live in an "age of disasters" that is unlike any other period in human history if we are to consider issues of context rather than simply the frequency of natural disasters. That is, although it may be, for instance, that the number of earthquakes in the current epoch is similar to the past, what is different is the effects are amplified because of greater exposure to earthquake hazards as the population and the number of buildings and property developments has increased. These developments highlight the importance of disaster research and, as we shall see, such research can offer some important insights into the very nature of the ecological crisis. In fact, in considering the nature of the unfolding environmental circumstances and conditions, it is very likely that in the near future there will be a convergence of environmental management with disaster management as different dimensions of the ecological crisis manifest themselves in the form of "natural" disasters. Before engaging in that discussion, however, it will be useful to first undertake a very brief overview of the current state of disaster research and the types of issues and problems this academic field focuses upon. This will help us to better situate and contextualize our subsequent discussions.

The Development of Disaster Research: A Brief General Overview

Academic research on disasters to some extent holds much in common with social scientific research on the environment. At the same time, though, some important divergences do also exist, particularly with respect to theoretical development. Arguably, it could be said that disaster research has always had much more of an applied and interdisciplinary focus in comparison to environmental sociology, and this difference could in turn be traced to the distinct origins of the two respective fields. The academic study of disasters was predicated on practical, real-world questions. Such an emphasis is understandable given that much emphasis in the aftermath of disaster is naturally directed towards immediate response, recovery and rebuilding so that the disruptive physical, social and economic aspects of the disasters are quickly addressed and minimized with an eye towards the resumption of the normal everyday activities of life as the guiding principle and overall objective of such response/recovery/rebuilding efforts. Today, response, recovery and rebuilding have come to be understood as components of an overall disaster management cycle, where recovery and rebuilding are to now include and incorporate mitigation efforts to reduce the effects of future disasters, thus feeding in to the next phase of the cycle – namely, preparation and prevention of future disasters. According to this cyclical perspective, a delineated set of disaster management activities is associated with each phase of the cycle, with the understanding that there will necessarily be some overlap in the activities between phases.

One can quickly surmise that each phase of the disaster management cycle will require different types of expertise. For instance, efforts in the response phase will require the involvement of emergency-response officials as well as those lay persons already physically present at the scene of the emergency and who wish to assist in the response, as well as government bureaucratic officials and medical and allied health professionals; while the mitigation phase will require the expertise of land use planners and other municipal officials and structural engineers involved with the built environment (e.g. those dealing with building codes and their enforcement) as well as those involved in education and community outreach. Similarly, preparedness and response will also draw upon varied expertise, such as those from the military who are trained in logistics and are in a position to effectively mobilize human and material resources necessary for emergency exercises and search and rescue operations. The necessity of intersectoral involvement and cooperation in disaster management has also meant that disaster research has had to be more open to interdisciplinarity at a professional and practical level, in a much more urgent and direct way than was the case with environmental studies (and to some extent environmental management). This is because the human actor is an integral and intrinsic element of the disaster management cycle, centrally involved in carrying out the activities of the different phases of the cycle as well as being the targeted subject of such directed activities (i.e. the ones being directed). The recognition of the centrality of people to issues of disaster management in general, and to the disaster management cycle in particular, is also why, generally speaking, the social and behavioral sciences are much better received in disaster research relative to conventional environmental management research, as the latter, even today is framed in more scientific and technically operational terms. As such, conventional environmental management is often thought to fall into the exclusive domain of the natural rather than the social sciences. In contrast, as disaster research has developed as a formalized academic field of inquiry, the field has given special attention to the social, organizational and behavioral context of disasters – at least in its more recent incarnations (to be discussed).

Similar to what was found in our overview of environmental sociology, the field of disaster studies has also had to grapple with ontological and epistemological issues related to the questions of how the natural and social worlds are interconnected. At first, under the continuing influence of the Enlightenment tradition on the background assumptions adopted, the field of disaster research had come to be informed by a more positivistic or scientifically defined view of disasters. In this sense, disaster research was similar to the case of environmental management vis-à-vis environmental problems. That is, disasters were conceived of as purely natural phenomena that could be analyzed according to the well-established principles of the biophysical sciences. According to this science-based approach, it was thought that science and technology could be used to help control the natural forces themselves – for example, through flood control, or if this were not possible, science and technology could be used to reduce losses by improving the capacity for forecasting and understanding where and when extreme events would be more likely to occur (Burton, 2016: xv). The latter reasoning, for example, continues to be influential today and can be discerned by considering the underlying logic that informs various managerial approaches to disaster management such as the Hazards Identification and Risk Assessment (HIRA) protocol used by emergency managers in Ontario (for details see Box 8.1).

When completed, the resulting grid essentially summarizes and visually depicts the relative disaster potential of each type of hazard. On this basis, a plan of action can be developed by using the grid to help prioritize, through comparison, the different types of disaster potentials that the community may face – that is, those which have a high probability of occurrence and high impact, all the way down to those with a low probability and low impact potential. In turn, this will aid disaster managers in their decisions for contingency planning and allotment of resources in that endeavor. As one can see, the HIRA protocol is very systematic in its approach and evidence-based, and clearly inspired by a scientific approach to prediction.

The predominant emphasis on conceptualizing disasters as natural phenomena clearly contributed to the adoption of a technocratic approach to disasters. In fact, during the post-World War I era, this was the approach popularized in the American context by the U.S. Army Corp of Engineers (Smith, 2001). During this period, the Corp started to become directly and actively engaged with issues related to flooding and by the mid-1920s they started to conduct comprehensive investigations into ways of dealing with the massive devastation from flooding experienced throughout the U.S. during that period. Such work also stimulated the interest of academic geographers, which in turn led to the founding of a subfield within their discipline – "hazards research" – the predecessor to what would later

BOX 8.1 THE HAZARDS IDENTIFICATION AND RISK ASSESSMENT (HIRA) PROTOCOL

The formalized Hazards Identification procedure is based on first identifying all the hazards that exist within a defined locale. These may include, for example:

Agricultural and food emergency
Building/structural collapse
Civil disorder
Critical infrastructure failure
Cyber attack
Dam failure
Drought/low water
Earthquake
Energy emergency (supply)
Erosion
Explosion/fire
Extreme temperatures
Flood
Fog
Forest/wildland fire
Freezing rain
Geomagnetic storm
Hail
Hazardous material
Human health emergency
Human-made space object crash
Hurricane
Land subsidence
Landslide
Lightning
Mine emergency
Natural space object crash
Nuclear facility emergency
Oil/natural gas emergency
Radiological emergency
Sabotage
Snowstorm/blizzard
Special event
Terrorism/CBRNE
Tornado

82 Disaster Studies and the Ecological Crisis

Transportation emergency
War and international emergency
Water quality emergency

Once identified, for each of these hazards the emergency manager will determine and assign the probability of occurrence of that hazard becoming a disaster. This can be done through the following type of scoring metric based on research of the historical record:

Scoring – Probability of Occurrence

1. No history of incidents in the last fifteen (15) years.
2. Five (5) to fifteen (15) years since last incident.
3. One (1) incident in the last five (5) years.
4. Multiple or recurring incidents in the last five (5) years.

Next, the potential consequences and scale of the impacts of the disaster can be estimated by another type of scoring metric.

Scoring: Consequence/Impact on Public and Property

1. Negligible impact.
2. Limited (injuries, minor or localized damage).
3. Substantial (widespread injuries, widespread and/or severe damage, temporary disruption of basic services).
4. High (fatalities, widespread and severe damage disrupting delivery of essential services, long-term disruption of basic services).

Once the probability and potential impacts are estimated, each hazard can be situated on a risk-assessment matrix or grid, as follows:

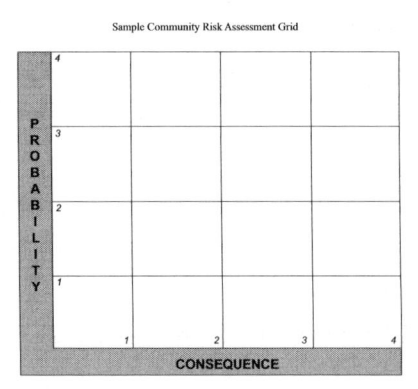

Sample Community Risk Assessment Grid

Source: Adapted from Slideshow Presentation of Emergency Management Ontario, York University, February 15, 2011. Available at: www.emergencymanagementontario.ca/english/emcommunity/ProvincialPrograms/hira/hira.html

become disaster research. Notably, geographers started to involve themselves with the practical issues of assessing the human impacts of construction projects associated with altering the course of rivers, the erection of dams, and so on.[1] Indeed, by the 1930s, geographers were instrumental in developing new environmental planning techniques that focused on the identification and analysis of strategies to minimize flood damage, ultimately resulting in the development and enactment of the 1936 Flood Control Act. During the subsequent decades, especially through the pioneering work of the geographer Gilbert F. White (1973), geographic research on hazards expanded and was no longer limited solely to issues related to flooding. Rather, the repertoire expanded to focus on other types of natural hazards such as drought, earthquakes, landslides, hurricanes, snow storms, and so on, especially as greater funding support began to flow in from the National Science Foundation (NSF). Although geographers at the time did emphasize the physical aspects of the many hazards, there was a growing recognition that hazards and disasters arose from the interplay of material and non-material systems. It was in this connection that Gilbert F. White noted that:

> Hazard always arises from the interplay of social and biological and physical systems; disasters are generated as much or more by human actions as by physical events; the present forms of government intervention in both traditional and industrial societies often exacerbate the social disruptions from extreme events; if we go on with the present public policy emphasis in many regions upon technical and narrow adjustments, society will become still less resilient and still more susceptible to catastrophes like the Sahelian drought.
> (1978: 230)

Following upon White's conceptual framework, hazards research began to focus more explicitly on human and societal adjustments to natural hazards. These adjustments included considerations such as avoiding hazards entirely – for example, through land-use planning and development restrictions; mitigating the impacts of extreme events through measures such as building codes; spreading risks through the provision of insurance; preparing for extreme events, focusing on different units of analyses, such as households and entire communities; and response and recovery from such events (White, 1973; Burton et al., 1978).

The practical emphasis in disaster research, as illustrated by the type of work that was pursued in hazards geography, is mirrored in another founding area within disaster research – namely, disaster sociology. The institutionalization of formal disaster sociology can be traced to the emergence of the Disaster Research Center at Ohio State University in 1963 (later moving to Delaware in 1985). Notably, the Center conducted hundreds of sociological field studies that focused on how people, organizations and society react and respond to disasters (Nigg and Mileti, 2002). In the context of the Cold War, such research took a decidedly practical focus as much research funding and sponsorship was provided by the U.S. military establishment and various government agencies interested in how civilians would respond to various military incursions, particularly air raids and nuclear missile attacks (Fritz, 1961; Gilbert, 1998; McEnaney, 2000). In this context, disasters were viewed as natural experiments that emulated wartime situations in that both situations were thought to ostensibly give rise to similar psychological reactions. This was because in both cases, people would be responding to some sort of external aggression. In accordance with such reasoning, external agents such as floods, hurricanes, or earthquakes were akin to bombs and missiles. As such, it was presumed that victims of natural disasters would act in ways similar to how people would react during bombing raids as well as how they would react in response to nuclear war. Thus, it was thought that the study of peacetime disasters could lead to knowledge that would be relevant to the types of events and conditions that could result during a wartime emergency (Kreps, 1984). In particular, the military was interested in how civilians would respond to natural and industrial disasters so that managerial instruments of social control could be developed. Thus, as Tierney (2007: 504) notes, funding priority was given to sociological research that initially focused on the study of collective behavior during and immediately following disaster impact such as: Would the public panic in the face of a nuclear attack? Would victimized populations be so demoralized that they would be unable to participate actively in wartime recovery efforts? Would civil unrest break out among populations suffering the depredations of nuclear war? The influence of the Cold War-inspired civil defense emphasis on sociological disaster research was perhaps further reinforced with the civil disturbances of the late 1960s, where governmental and military concern with maintaining the social order gained renewed urgency and significance. Similar to the case of geography, sociological disaster research was supported by the National Science Foundation – in fact, sociologists have managed the hazards and disaster research program in the NSF Engineering Directorate since the program's inception in the 1970s (ibid.).

In particular, as part of its practical and applied emphasis, much of the sociological research on disasters carried out during the ensuing decades focused on debunking common-sense assumptions and popularly held myths about how people act during disaster situations. As such, much of the classical empirical work in disaster sociology challenged commonly held, but untested and uncontested ideas pertaining to widespread public panic and irrationality after disasters, including post-disaster lawlessness, as well as assumptions about disaster shock, and negative mental health outcomes. Generally speaking, this work found that positive behaviors and outcomes characterized disaster settings, including the enhancement of community morale, declines in crime and other antisocial behavior, reduction in status differences, suspension of pre-disaster conflicts in the interests of community safety, the development of therapeutic communities, and organizational adaptation and innovation (Fritz 1961; Barton 1969; Dynes 1970; Quarantelli and Dynes 1972).

Recently, criticism of disaster sociology has arisen. Much of the critique has been directed at the atheoretical focus of the field which, it is argued, has led to analytical stagnation. Kathleen Tierney (2007) notes several reasons that could account for this development. A first reason involves the repercussions of having only a relatively small number of social scientists involved in disaster research. According to the National Research Council (2006), the number of core disaster researchers from all social sciences combined was estimated to be around two hundred. However, according to Tierney (2007), despite the presence of a number of well-known and respected disaster sociologists, the field itself has lacked visibility within the mainstream of the discipline because of a narrow focus that has persisted over the years. Tierney attributes this persistence to the strong paradigmatic nature of the disaster sociology field in which a strong consensus is built up among the core researchers with respect to conceptual frameworks, research methods and appropriate topics for study. This is especially problematic in light of the inertial quality that arises in situations where so many scholars have been trained by so few mentors, and over time by the students of those mentors, thereby leading to an inbred quality to the field. Consequently, advances in the field have been hampered by resistance to new approaches, especially with regard to the prospect of enrichment via theoretical diversity.

The problem-focused origins of sociological research in disasters has also hindered possibilities for conceptual innovation in the field to take hold. For Tierney (2007), this is especially evident when considering that disaster sociology has not kept pace with theoretical developments in sociology at the most general level. That is, North American sociological research on disasters has remained largely isolated from major theoretical developments that have occurred within the broader discipline of mainstream sociology. This is because the concern with solving problems, especially those problems defined in the terms specified and deemed important by government institutions and practitioners, has completely overshadowed any interest in advancing theoretical work in disaster research – a development which reflects how the field of environmental management has also evolved. For this reason, although disaster research in sociology has produced studies that have yielded a large number of sound empirical generalizations, they have by and large remained unlinked to existing general theory. Thus, Tierney notes that "it is more accurate to say that funding programs, especially multidisciplinary ones, have not encouraged the growth of theory and discipline-based knowledge and that funding priorities have been shaped by problem definitions developed largely by non-social scientists" (2007: 516).

Lastly, a further offshoot of the strongly applied nature of disaster sociology is that the core disaster sociologists have become almost exclusively preoccupied by issues of knowledge-transfer, practitioner and policy-oriented concerns and activities, as opposed to pure research. This tendency may have become further reinforced and entrenched in recent years in the aftermath of the terrorist attacks of September 11, 2001. The establishment of the U.S. Department of Homeland Security shortly after the terrorist attacks may have contributed to the adoption and institutionalization of a hyper-intensified interest and concern with security, securitization and emergency preparedness. As part of this development, disaster sociologists have been called to sit on various government boards and become involved in the drafting of disaster management and security legislation (Herring, 2005).

In addressing the limitations of sociological research on disasters, Tierney (2007) argues that disaster researchers must halt, or at least make efforts to lessen the tendency to organize their inquiries according to the dictates of the institutions charged with managing disasters, and instead concentrate on problems that are meaningful to the discipline. As such, she recommends that disaster sociologists should integrate their research with core sociological concerns, such as social inequality, societal diversity and social change. Crucial to such a reorientation is to adopt an emphasis in which disasters can be traced either directly or indirectly to the way in which society is organized, especially in relationships of the institutions of a given society with nature, thus consolidating the linkages between disaster and environmental sociology. In fact, Tierney argues that as more and more of these linkages become evident through research on disasters and the environment, the less justification there will be for the two specialty areas to remain distinct. As will now be discussed, indications of movement in this direction may in fact be currently discerned.

Contemporary Issues in Disaster Research

Within the field of disaster studies, one major development or conceptual breakthrough in recent years has been the emergence of the vulnerability paradigm or the adoption of a focus on the identification and analysis of what makes particular groups or individuals within a society more susceptible to the negative effects of a disaster relative to others. As Oliver-Smith (2004:1) notes, the significance of the vulnerability perspective stems from the fact that it emphasizes the interpretation of social forces and environmental conditions that informs a larger effort to rethink the relationships between society, economy and nature.

Sociologist John Urry (2011) notes that in the coming century, as the world is inevitably forced to move beyond the carbon century that precipitated the ecological crisis, issues of disaster resilience and vulnerability will most certainly be crucial topics for future societies and social science. In particular, as global environmental change accelerates with the ecological crisis, resilience and adaptation at both the community and societal level will become even more resonating and salient issues. What should be noted at this point is that it is unlikely that the consequences of the ecological crisis will be felt evenly throughout the future population. Some people and societies are far more vulnerable to natural disasters than others, and these divisions usually reflect established social inequalities (as was also alluded to in Chapter 7 with reference to "climate refugees"). Thus, as the vulnerability paradigm warns, entrenched social, economic and political inequalities will expose particular groups to greater risks than others, although it should be kept in mind that at the same time, a greater proportion, or more and more people in sheer numbers will be exposed to higher risk than today.

The Natural versus Social Dimensions of Disaster

As discussed above, a central problematique for environmental sociology was the question of how to reconcile the natural with the social, especially in light of the fact that throughout much of the disciplinary history of sociology, the two domains were kept analytically separate for the various types of reasons we have mentioned in Chapter 6. As we have seen, attempts to analytically bridge the two domains were met with resistance by mainstream sociology. In a similar manner, but with perhaps a different focus and outcome, disaster research has also grappled with the ontological and epistemological issues pertaining to the relationship between the natural and social. In the particular context of disaster research, this has meant addressing the analytical question of how natural and technological (i.e. human-made) disasters are similar and/or different in terms of onset and consequences. Interestingly, convergence of the natural and social/technological as analytical categories may have come a little easier in disaster studies (compared to mainstream sociology) in light of its own particular trajectory as a field of inquiry. That is, because of the explicitly practical focus of disaster studies in the past, there has always been interest and attention directed to the issue of overlap between natural and technological disasters. Recall, for instance, that the military was greatly interested and sponsored much research on how people responded to natural disasters in order to gain insights into how people would react in cases of human-made disasters such as those pertaining to military excursions, while the U.S. Army Corp of Engineers in alliance with hazards geographers traditionally considered how the effects of a "natural" disaster such as flooding could be exacerbated by social conditions such as living arrangements and land-use decisions.

Despite the historical tendencies in disaster studies to focus on the similarities between natural and technological disasters, some disaster researchers have found differences which they have emphasized in subsequent debate and analyses (Quarantelli, 1998). This is particularly true in relation to individual and collective responses to the new types of environmental threats characteristic of the "risk society" such as chemical and nuclear contamination (Beck, 1992). Such threats are said to be qualitatively and quantitatively different from the risks of an earlier, pre-modern era for a number of reasons (Ali, 1998: 4). First, modern environmental risks may not be detectable to our physical senses, thus forcing us to rely on technological means of detection (Beck, 1992). Second, these types of risks are remote from most people's day-to-day experiences, thus leading to a dependence on the knowledge claims of experts (and the counter-claims of counter-experts) to engender understanding. This means that environmental risks controversies are amenable to social construction in the manner discussed in Chapter 7 in relation to global climate change (see also Hannigan (1995) for a detailed account of the social construction of environmental risks). Third, the long chains of complex causal interactions inevitably involved in the transmission of and exposure to modern environmental risks means that a great deal of scientific uncertainty is inherent to such risk situations. A further implication of this is that conclusive attribution of culpability through available evidence is always difficult to establish, thereby establishing the social preconditions for community fragmentation and litigation as different parties vie to obtain or deny responsibility and compensation. Lastly, modern environmental risks such as chemical and nuclear pollution, the thinning ozone layer and global climate change, are all ultimately due to our own decisions to intervene in the environment in ways that are harmful. In light of the influence and effects of these characteristics of modern environmental risks, some disaster scholars have concluded that it is best to analytically distinguish between natural and technological disasters.

Proponents calling for this analytical separation contend that consideration must be given to the particularities of the disaster agent – that is, to the nature of the "cause" of the disaster (Ali, 2008). An important consideration in this context is the degree to which human beings have control over the disaster agent and its consequences. In line with this reasoning, Kai Erickson (1991) argues that technological and natural disasters are qualitatively distinct because the former are the product of human hands while "natural" disasters "visit" us from afar, then exit the scene. As such, human-caused disasters (such as technological ones) imply a *loss* of control over systems we have ourselves created, while natural disasters imply simply a *lack* of control over systems which we had no role in creating. The implication is that human-made disasters are in theory preventable. The further implication of the preventability of human-made disasters is illustrated in considering the much greater prominence given to arguments over culpability in the case of technological disasters compared to natural disasters (Edelstein, 2004; Ali 2003; Freudenburg, 1997; Fowlkes and Miller, 1987). As such, in the aftermath of technological disaster a "corrosive community" is said to form in which a great deal of community fragmentation occurs as different groups point the finger at each other in a context of public anger and distrust (Freudenburg, 1997) – usually directed towards those actors accused of harboring corporate greed or those accused of government corruption (as well as government ineptitude and/or bureaucratic bungling). This is said to contrast to the many situations arising in the aftermath of a natural disaster where a "therapeutic community" forms on the basis of collectively faced setbacks that require cooperation and the consolidation of community members to respond effectively. The formation of a therapeutic community is only made possible because the divisiveness arising from blaming an individual party is not present in the case of the aftermath of natural disaster (where the event is understood as an "act of God" rather than the act of an individual where the former cannot be sued or made to financially recompense the loss). In other words, in the case of natural disasters, the response is characterized by acceptance or resignation because there can be no individual human party that can be held as solely responsible for the disaster. However, as will be discussed later, recent analyses of several high-profile disasters such as Hurricane Katrina in the context of New Orleans has led to a questioning of such a conclusion.

It is argued that another set of differences that differentiate natural from technological disasters may be identified by considering the mental health and psychological effects of each type of disaster. Kai Erickson has observed that in a human-made disaster, such as in a chemical contamination event, the toxic risks are internalized, which produces an inherently different psychological response than an external injury. This is because the physical effects may be more ambiguous and uncertain due to unbounded quality of internalized toxic risks. In the words of Erickson: "Chemical disasters involve toxic poisons, that is, they contaminate rather than merely damage, they pollute, befoul, taint, rather than just create wreckage, they penetrate human tissue indirectly rather than assaults of a more straightforward kind" (1991: 15). "Toxic risks also have an unbounded quality, wreaking not direct but chronic, long-lasting damage on people who in a sense do not become victims until well after the noxious offense" (ibid.: 20).

The unbounded quality of technological disasters means that victims are forced to deal with the potential for harm – that is, toxic effects that have not yet manifested, but may develop in some unforeseeable point in the future because of the exposure, creating a sense of lasting dread. Consequently, a lingering sense of anxiety is experienced that may persist long past the time of the disaster onset. Although these lingering effects may also be found with respect to natural disasters (as illustrated, for example, in the experience of the effects of post-traumatic stress disorder), the situation is much more pronounced in the aftermath of technological disasters in relative comparison to natural disasters (ibid.). The effects of natural disasters are more often overtly physical – for example, bodily injury due to a falling tree limb or building debris that breaks the arm of the unfortunate victim. With this type of injury, the harm is more evident and works itself from the outside in. The reverse is true with respect to human-made chemical or nuclear contamination disasters where the effects are much more insidious and personally traumatic as the effects work themselves from inside the body outwards, as would be the case of the development of cancer due to exposure to toxic materials or nuclear radiation. That is, toxic risk represents an internal violation of the integrity of the body that stimulates a different psychological response than in the case of an external injury.

As we have discussed, although a case has been made for making an analytical distinction between technological and natural disasters, more recent research has led to reverse arguments. Mirroring the hybrid (i.e. the duality of the natural and social) emphasis of recent environmental sociology with respect to its approach to environmental problems and phenomena, disaster sociology has likewise gradually edged towards an orientation that tends to blur the distinction between the natural and the social in the conceptualization of disasters. Indeed, as will now be discussed, the adoption of such an orientation has proven influential in emerging perspectives and new points of focus in disaster studies, especially well illustrated by the notion of "disaster vulnerability".

Vulnerability to Disasters

Sociologist Eric Klinenberg's (1999) ground-breaking and influential work on the 1995 Chicago heatwave dramatically illustrates the effects of differential vulnerability to disaster. In his study Klinenberg focused on how residents in different neighborhoods of Chicago experienced the effects of extreme heat quite differently. This contradicted the taken-for-granted and commonly held notion that residents, regardless of the neighborhood in which they resided, would be exposed to the same intensity of heat in the same way. The differential vulnerability was starkly documented by the significantly different mortality rates found in different neighborhoods. Klinenberg found that various structural conditions could help account for the differential mortality rates. It was clear, for example, that the mortality rate was much higher for poor, African-American, "literally socially isolated" senior citizens living in single-resident occupancy units in particular areas of the city. So isolated were these individuals, that many of the deceased in these areas were only discovered several days after their death by neighbors who had detected the scent of decay. Furthermore, these isolated and vulnerable individuals had limited mobility to seek shelter from the heat by traveling to air-conditioned facilities, and even if they had the ability to move about outside, they would likely have been reluctant to do so due to fear of assault (which would also explain why they did not leave their windows and doors open for ventilation in their single residency units as per the advice of municipal officials). Of course, due to the cost of electricity, such individuals could not afford to run air conditioners even if they had them in their own apartment units. At the same time, much of the inner-city housing stock where the higher rates of mortality were found, consisted of units in a state of deterioration and disrepair, which in turn increased the level of heat exposure the occupants experienced. In the end, Klinenberg's somber analysis revealed how the structural and spatial inequalities of the city – in part related to neoliberal cuts to social and health programs for the city's poor by the municipal government – reflected the mortality pattern of the heatwave and brought to the fore the issue of social vulnerability in the context of a "natural" disaster. Thus, although the heatwave itself may have been a natural phenomenon that appears to have its origins in the workings of the Earth's physical systems (though some would argue that the heatwave was an extreme weather event was a consequence of anthropogenic (i.e. human-caused) climate change), the effects of the disaster on the community were very much influenced by human decisions and sociopolitical factors, thus blurring the distinction between the social and natural. A similar conclusion can be drawn with reference to Hurricane Katrina.

In August 2005, Hurricane Katrina struck the Louisiana, Mississippi and surrounding states, leading to the tragic loss of over 1,700 lives (Youngman, 2009: 176). One of the areas most impacted was the City of New Orleans, Louisiana, which experienced a loss of about 1,100 lives. Much of the devastation and loss of lives in this city (which is located below sea level) was due to the flooding that accompanied the hurricane as the city's levy system was overcome by the hurricane's storm surges. The effects of the flooding were exacerbated because of a combination of poor engineering practices, unwise land-use decisions and the local government's insistence on prioritizing economic growth over public safety (ibid.). Most deaths were of those who were poor, African American and/or elderly.

Thus, similar to the case of the Chicago heatwave, Hurricane Katrina also directs our attention to how natural and social factors combine to make particular groups particularly vulnerable to disasters.

Based on an extensive review of the numerous studies of Hurricane Katrina and New Orleans conducted by social scientists, Picou et al. conclude that "there is a need for a paradigm shift in disaster research or a reorientation and redirection of important research themes throughout the broader discipline of sociology" (2010: 1). They support this contention on several grounds (Picou et al., 2010: 9–10). First, some disasters that were historically perceived as natural have increasingly come to be viewed as anthropogenic. This understanding, holding aside the scientific veracity of the claim, will have increasing political, legal and social relevance in the future (Marshall and Picou, 2008). Second, even though a "natural" disaster itself may be perceived as an "act of God", the aftermath may involve impacts that result in contamination and other effects that can be attributed to human actors, thus leading to the type of corrosive community discussed in a previous section. For example, in the case of Katrina, the issue of contaminants arose in terms of the hurricane's disturbance to oil refineries in the New Orleans area, resulting in the release of hazardous materials, or through purposeful recovery actions such as pumping polluted water into various water bodies (e.g. Lake Pontchartrain which represents the northern boundary of the city). In this context, attribution of responsibility for the negative effectives were ascribed to the government for: (1) not enforcing regulations; (2) not being prepared for disasters; and (3) not responding in the manner required. Third, the sheer magnitude of the impacts of Katrina – maximum damage to the built environment, widespread mortality, the experience of serious physical and mental health impacts on survivors and a massive relocation of individuals from the impact area – implies that the hurricane event could be considered as a "worst-case" disaster (Clarke, 2006). A worst-case disaster is a disaster in which there is a synergistic combining of the damage potential from all types of past disaster events. In the case of Katrina, this involved the interplay of natural forces, technological failure, ecological contamination, the response failure of human institutions, and the massive displacement of people, all of which interacted in ways that amplified and exacerbated the severity of the impacts. In light of the above, Picou et al. (2010: 10) conclude that there needs to be shift in the conceptualization of disasters in a manner that considers the changing nature of hazards in the modern world. Furthermore, they note that "worst-case catastrophes invite a broader consideration of the organization of social vulnerability, resiliency, manufactured uncertainty and socioenvironmental policy" (ibid.).

Concluding Remarks

As the ecological crisis continues to unfold, it is very likely that the field of environmental management will have to deal with mitigating the effects of disasters in some way. Arguably, this may be due to an expected increase in the number of "natural" disasters and extreme weather events we experience due to the effects of global climate change.However, even if this is not borne out, it is clear that the social context for disaster has changed. This is seen, for instance, in terms of increased population, greater numbers of people living in disaster-prone areas such as on sea coasts, increased interconnectivity of networked infrastructure, less investment in disaster preparedness due to neoliberalism, and so on. As a result, the impacts of both "natural" and "technological" disasters will be much more magnified because more people and property are exposed to disasters than in the past. Thus, the ecological crisis coincides with the "age of disasters" (Alexander, 1997) and responding to disasters will mean responding to the ecological crisis (and vice versa). The future merging of the two fields of disaster and environmental management may prove very useful in terms of developing alternative approaches to address the ecological crisis. In the next chapter we will explore how social scientific concepts from environmental and disaster studies may be brought together to help develop one such alternative – namely, a socio-ecological approach.

Note

1. Scholars tend to distinguish between "hazards" and "disasters" in that the former is defined as a natural and technological source of danger that can potentially threaten life or property or both, while a disaster is the physical manifestation of the hazard as an actual event.

References

Alexander, D. (1997) "The Study of Natural Disasters, 1977–97: Some Reflections on a Changing Field of Knowledge". *Disasters*, 21(4): 284–304.
Ali, S.H. (1998) "The Search for a Landfill Site in the Risk Society". *The Canadian Review of Sociology and Anthropology*, 36 (1): 1–19.
Ali, S.H. (2003) "Dealing with Toxicity in the Risk Society: The Case of the Hamilton, Ontario Plastics Recycling Fire". *The Canadian Review of Sociology and Anthropology*, 39(1): 29–48.
Ali, S.H. (2008) "Analyzing Environmental Disasters". In S.D. Gupta (Ed.) *Understanding the Global Environment*. New Delhi: Pearson Press, pp. 245–264.
Barton, A. (1969) *Communities in Disaster: A Sociological Analysis of Collective Stress Situations*. New York: Doubleday.
Beck, U. (1992) *Risk Society: Towards a New Modernity*. London: Sage.
Burton, I. (2016) "Foreword". In D. Etkin, *Disaster Theory: An Interdisciplinary Approach to Concepts and Causes*.Waltham, MA: Butterworth-Heinemann, pp. xv–xvi.
Burton, I., Kates, R.W. and White, G.F. (1978) *The Environment as Hazard*. New York: Oxford University Press.
Clarke, L. (2006) *Worst Cases: Terror and Catastrophe in the Popular Imagination*. Chicago: University of Chicago Press.
Dynes, R.R. (1970) *Organized Behavior in Disaster*. Lexington, MA: Lexington Books.
Edelstein, M.R. (2004) *Contaminated Communities: Coping with Residential Toxic Exposure* (2nd ed.). Boulder, CO: Westview Press.
Erikson, K. (1991) "A New Species of Trouble". In S. Couch and J.S. Kroll-Smith (Eds.) *Communities at Risk: Collective Responses to Technological Hazards*. Oxford: Peter Lang, pp. 11–29.

Fowlkes, M.R. and Miller, P.Y. (1987) "Chemicals and Community at Love Canal". In B. Johnson and V. Covello (Eds.) *The Social and Cultural Construction of Risk: Technology, Risk, and Society*. Boston, MA: D. Reidel.

Freudenburg, W. (1997) "Contamination, Corrosion and the Social Order: An Overview". *Current Sociology*, 45(3): 19–39.

Fritz, C. (1961) "Disasters". In R. Merton and R. Nisbet (Eds.) *Contemporary Social Problems*. New York: Harcourt Brace, pp. 651–694.

Gilbert, C. (1998) "Studying Disaster: Changes in the Main Conceptual Tools". In E.L. Quarantelli (Ed.) *What is a Disaster? Perspectives on the Question*. New York: Routledge, pp. 11–18.

Hannigan, J. (1995) *Environmental Sociology: A Social Constructionist Perspective*. New York: Routledge.

Herring, Lee (2005) "Sociologist Testifies at House Hearing on Disasters". *Footnotes*, 33 (December 9): 1. American Sociological Association.

Hilhorst, D. and Bankoff, G. (2004) "Introduction: Mapping Vulnerability". In G. Bankoff, G. Frerks and D. Hilhorst (Eds.) *Mapping Vulnerability: Disasters, Development and People*. London: Earthscan, pp. 1–9.

International Federation of Red Cross and Red Crescent Societies (IFRC) (2002) *World Disasters Report 2002*. IFRC: Geneva.

Klinenberg, E. (1999) "Denaturalizing Disaster: A Social Autopsy of the 1995 Chicago Heat Wave". *Theory and Society*, 28(2): 239–295.

Kreps, G.A. (1984) "Sociological Inquiry and Disaster Research". *Annual Review of Sociology*, 10: 309–330.

McEnaney, L. (2000) *Civil Defense Begins at Home: Militarization Meets Everyday Life in the Fifties*. Princeton, NJ: Princeton University Press.

Marshall, B.K. and Picou, J.S. (2008) "Post-Normal Science, the Precautionary Approach, and Worst Cases: The Challenge of 21st Century Disasters". *Sociological Inquiry*, 78(2): 230–247.

National Research Council (2006) *Facing Hazards and Disasters: Understanding Human Dimensions*. Washington, DC: National Academy Press.

Nigg, J.M. and Mileti, D. (2002) "Natural Hazards and Disasters". In R.E. Dunlap and W. Michelson (Eds.) *Handbook of Environmental Sociology*. Westport, CT: Greenwood Press, pp. 272–294.

Oliver-Smith, A. (2004) "Theorizing Vulnerability in a Globalized World: A Political Ecological Perspective". In G. Bankoff, G. Frerks and D. Hilhorst (Eds.) *Mapping Vulnerability: Disasters, Development and People*. London: Earthscan, pp. 10–24.

Picou, J.S., Brunsma, D.L. and Overfelt, D. (2010) "Introduction – Katrina as Paradigm Shift: Reflections on Disaster Research in the Twenty-First Century". In D.L. Brunsma, D. Overfelt and J.S. Picou (Eds.) *The Sociology of Katrina: Perspectives on a Modern Catastrophe*. Toronto: Rowman & Littlefield, pp. 1–24.

Quarantelli, E.L. (1998) *What is a Disaster? Perspectives on the Question*. New York: Routledge.

Quarantelli, E.L. and Dynes, R.R. (1972) "When Disaster Strikes (It Isn't Much Like What You've Heard and Read About)". *Psychology Today*, 5: 66–70.

Rudel, T.K., Roberts, J.T. and Carmin, J. (2011) "Political Economy of the Environment", *Annual Review of Sociology*, 37: 221–238.

Smith, K. (2001) *Environmental Hazards: Assessing Risk and Reducing Disaster* (3rd ed.). New York: Routledge.

Tierney, K.J. (2007) "From the Margins to the Mainstream? Disaster Research at the Crossroads". *Annual Review of Sociology*, 33: 503–525.

Urry, J. (2011) *Climate Change and Society*. Cambridge: Polity Press.

White, G.F. (1973) "Natural Hazards Research". In R.J. Chorley (Ed.) *Directions in Geography*. London: Methuen, pp. 193–216.

White, G.F. (1978) "Natural Hazards and the Third World – A Reply". *Human Ecology*, 6(2): 229–231.

Young, N. (2015) *Environmental Sociology for the Twenty-First Century*. Don Mills: Oxford University Press.

Youngman, N. (2009) "Understanding Disaster Vulnerability: Floods and Hurricanes". In K.A. Gould and T.L. Lewis (Eds.) *Twenty Lessons in Environmental Sociology*. New York: Oxford University Press, pp. 176–190.

9
A SOCIO-ECOLOGICAL APPROACH TO THE ECOLOGICAL CRISIS

The intrinsically multifaceted character of the ecological crisis implies the need for environmental management strategies that are attentive to this multidimensionality. With this in mind, in this chapter we attempt to develop an orienting approach that does justice to the inherent complexity involved in dealing with environmental problems. We develop this approach based on the insights we have gained from social scientific and sociological treatments of environmental problems and disasters reviewed previously. As such, a central aspect of the approach we develop here is an insistence on considering both the social and biophysical factors involved in the production of the environmental problem or disaster. This socio-ecological approach, as we shall call it, takes as a starting point and emphasizes throughout its analysis, the notion of process. As we have alluded to in the last chapter, this processual understanding is a key element of certain strands of disaster research – notably, perspectives interested in questions and issues related to vulnerability, and, as we shall discuss in this chapter, research that explores disaster incubation – how the factors that contribute to a disaster go unnoticed until a hazard actualizes into a disaster.

We begin this chapter by further developing the notion of vulnerability and related concepts that would help inform a socio-ecological approach. As we shall see, segments of the environmental movement have to a certain extent already engaged with vulnerability in terms of raising issues of environmental justice, such as dealing with the unequal distribution of risks or the negative impacts of an environmental problem. Environmental justice may also be relevant and of value to a socio-ecological approach in environmental management, particularly in regard to developing the critical dimensions of this approach. The next sections will delve in more detail into the process-based orientation to disasters and the disaster incubation perspective. Lastly, we will illustrate how a socio-ecological approach can be used in environmental management by applying it to the case of infectious disease outbreaks as an example of a new and emerging type of disaster that is likely to occur with increasing frequency in the future.

Vulnerability, Resilience, Adaptation, Mitigation

Over the past few years, the interrelated concepts of vulnerability, resilience, adaptation and mitigation have come to represent a core set of principles that have guided the study and practice of contemporary disaster management (Etkin, 2016: 105). Undoubtedly, the environmental and disaster management approaches based on these concepts, as well as the issues related to them, will continue to gain prominence as the ecological crisis unfolds (Urry, 2011). At present, numerous definitions and understandings of these concepts exist. For the purposes of our discussion here, however, we will focus only on those key features of these concepts that will help and guide the development of a critical disaster and environmental management perspective.

In the broadest sense, vulnerability refers to susceptibility to the damaging effects of a hazard or disaster. This definition was the starting point for the understanding of vulnerability by the United Nations International Strategy for Disaster Reduction (UNISDR). The UNISDR went on to qualify this understanding in asserting that:

> There are many aspects of vulnerability, arising from various physical, social, economic and environmental factors. Examples may include poor design and construction of buildings, inadequate protection of assets, lack of public information and awareness, limited recognition of risks and preparedness measures, and disregard for wise environmental management. Vulnerability varies significantly within a community and over time.
>
> (Cited by Etkin, 2016: 113)

Vulnerability, therefore, can be understood to be a multidimensional and wide-ranging concept but at the most general level, vulnerability is about susceptibility to risk. Through the adoption and influence of this concept, key questions started to be raised by disaster researchers in regard to how and in what ways this disaster vulnerability develops and becomes manifest. Taking into account the expansive characteristics of vulnerability, the geographer Susan Cutter (1996) has called for the establishment of an interdisciplinary field of Vulnerability Analysis to identify and analyze those circumstances that put people and places at risk, including those related to: (1) the physical dimension: buildings, infrastructure, critical facilities; (2) the social dimension: vulnerable groups, livelihoods, local institutions, poverty; and (3) the economic dimension: related to direct and indirect financial losses. As we can see, Cutter's multipronged approach to disaster vulnerability incorporates both the physical and social in the analysis, which may encourage the adoption of or at least garner greater receptivity to, the hybrid conceptualization of a disaster we have discussed in the previous chapter. For the purposes at hand, though, with an eye towards consciously developing a critical perspective, we are interested in how vulnerability is socially produced and the implications that insights drawn from this type of emphasis will have for the study, practice and philosophical reorientation of disaster and environmental management.

In adopting the perspective of disaster vulnerability, a key focus is on how and why certain groups within a community are more susceptible than others to the effects of natural and technological disasters. And since it is almost always the case that such vulnerable groups are from marginalized populations, the critical question becomes how is it that the marginalized are more susceptible to hazards and disasters (and their effects)? In particular, how does vulnerability reflect established inequalities in society? The importance of such questions in the context of the unfolding ecological crisis cannot be underestimated because issues of environmental inequality and the unequal distribution of environmental risks will undoubtedly intensify in the future (Beck, 1992; Homer-Dixon, 2000).

As a concept, resilience is similar to the notion of vulnerability in that it is also multidimensional and wide-ranging. Etkin (2016: 122–134) notes that different fields define resilience in different ways in accordance with the respective contexts each field is associated with. The concept of resilience can therefore be applied to a wide range of settings, including the physical, environmental, individual and societal. Originally, the concept arose from the domain of physics with the discovery of Hooke's Law in 1678. The law mathematically describes how an increasing application of force to a spring (or a material) will lead to a linearly proportional increase in the amount the spring deforms (i.e. stretches or compresses). This relationship holds true until a threshold is surpassed, after which point the spring loses its elastic property and will not be able to return to its original state (i.e. it is unable to regain its original form, thus resulting in what is referred to as "plastic deformation"). The threshold limit at which plastic deformation occurs represents a breaking point whereupon the material is not able to "snap back into shape". The range in which the spring is able to snap back is known as the "elastic" region, whereas the point after the threshold is referred to as the "plastic region". The general idea behind the notion of engineering resilience – the elastic property of materials – has since been applied to other fields. As such, in the more general sense, resilience refers to the ability of social and natural systems to respond to changes without breaking down (Young, 2015: 188). Today, we can speak of ecological, psychological and community resilience (Etkin, 2016). For instance, ecological resilience finds application in describing how ecosystems change in ways that lead to new states of stability and equilibrium – an approach most fully developed in the panarchy theory of C.S. Holling (1973). In this ecological context, resilience is not just about returning to the original state but adapting to changes that may be permanent (Adger, 2000). The underlying assumption of this understanding of resilience is that the system has capacity to absorb some disturbance or perturbation while undergoing some change that will enable the system to retain essentially the same function (Wilson, 2012: 15 cited by Young, 2015: 190).

Similar to the ecological resilience, psychological resilience emphasizes the importance of flexibility and adaptability. That is, psychological resilience refers to the ability of the individual to "rebound back" to a functioning state after experiencing trauma, but not necessarily to the functioning state that was originally found previous to the trauma experience. As Etkin (2016: 128) points out, psychological resilience may involve certain unique aspects such as identity, faithand spirituality not present in engineering or ecological perspectives on resilience. In line with the other types of resilience, community resilience refers to how a community can "bounce back" to a state of functioning after a disaster. Notably, the UNISDR refers to this type of resilience in their definition:

> The ability of a system, community or society exposed to hazards to resist, absorb, accommodate to and recover from the effects of a hazard in a timely and efficient manner, including through the preservation and restoration of its essential basic structure and functions . . . The resilience of a community in respect to potential hazard events is determined by the degree to which the community has the necessary resources and is capable of organizing itself prior to and during times of need.
>
> (Cited by Etkin, 2016: 123)

Understandably, the notion of community resilience has great relevance for disaster and ecological management. In fact, community resilience is central to some of the strategies that are currently being formulated in these management areas. For instance, resilience thinking is consistent with, and implicit in, the all-hazards approaches to disaster management, such as the Hazards Identification and Risk Assessment Approach (HIRA) discussed in the previous chapter. In this connection, Etkin (2016) notes that thinking in terms of community resilience is useful for disaster management because it enables a way to look at and think about how community systems respond to crisis.

Implicitly interwoven throughout our discussion of vulnerability and resilience are references to the notions of mitigation and adaptation (and the related idea of adaptive capacity). Recall that these notions have already been introduced in our discussion of the disaster management cycle as efforts to adapt and develop initiatives to reduce the impacts of future disasters have now been explicitly incorporated as strategic objectives of this cycle. In the context of disaster and environmental management, Nicole Youngman (2009: 182) notes that mitigation efforts – that is, the measures that can be taken to lessen or prevent impacts – may be of three kinds. The first is structural mitigation that emphasizes large engineering "megaprojects" such as floodwalls and bank stabilization to lessen the impacts of flooding and erosion. The second is infrastructural mitigation which refers to the strengthening of built systems such as drinking water, sewerage and drainage systems, roads and bridges, phones and Internet lines and towers, and power and gas lines, so that they become more resilient to high winds, flooding or seismic activity. Third, non-structural mitigation initiatives deploy strategies such as implementing stricter zoning laws that prohibit or restrict construction of buildings in vulnerable areas such as in floodplains or coastal areas. The focus here is on keeping people and property out of harm's way.

By pre-emptively lessening the potential future impacts, mitigation strategies in effect help also to build the adaptive capacity of a community – that is, the ability of a community to absorb shocks and adapt to long-term changes (Young, 2015; Agrawal, 2010; Cutter et al., 2008). Yet, as Youngman (2009) observes, for various reasons, political leaders, especially at the local level, are reluctant to talk about adaptation in response to an environmental problem – that is, changing the way things are done in order to confront and live with the changing reality and circumstances brought on by the environmental problem in question. First, this reluctance to discuss vulnerability and environmental change is based on the feeling that this type of discourse will scare away business and investment in the community. Second, there is a pervasive belief that we will simply be able to address the problems related to vulnerability and environmental change by putting our faith in future generations. This means that difficult decisions involving the reformation of environmentally destructive practices or the adoption of comprehensive planning can be postponed to the future. Such a mindset is similarly found in the socio-psychological phenomenon of "future discounting" in which there is a tendency to forego future benefits in favor of gaining immediate benefits – a significant barrier to addressing many types of environmental problems. Third, environmentalists may themselves be hesitant to support adaptation measures because to do so implies an abandonment of efforts to mitigate or eliminate environmental impacts altogether.

The merging of the concepts of vulnerability, resilience, mitigation and adaptation into one framework may make sense from the perspective of environmental and disaster management. This is because such a synthesis may lead to a more holistic approach to disaster reduction compared to the use of each approach by itself. Certainly, at first sight barriers to synthesis exist because of trying to reconcile conceptual differences, but these may be more apparent than real. For example, Etkin (2016) notes that resilience tends to emphasize the positive features involved in disaster management such as strengths and capacities within communities, whereas vulnerability emphasizes weaknesses. However, as Etkin (2016) also notes, both the notions of resilience and vulnerability essentially address responses to adversity – and recognition of such may open up the possibility for developing a more encompassing approach. Another possible barrier pertains to the tendency of the resilience perspectives to engage with concepts from the engineering and ecological disciplines, which means that resilience perspectives are underlain by a positivist approach that may perhaps be more in line with conventional (and uncritical) managerial approaches to environmental and disaster management. In contrast, vulnerability theory tends to be more informed by social constructionism, which is a more interpretist perspective (Etkin, 2016: 123). Again, however, positivist and social constructionist perspectives need not be mutually exclusive as we will try to illustrate by our case study analyses presented at the end of this chapter.

For our purposes, the crucial advantage of the vulnerability-related perspectives is that they provide the opportunity to open up the analysis in terms of being receptive to critical sociological and social science perspectives. Notably, the incorporation of the concepts of vulnerability, resilience, mitigation and adaptation into ecological and disaster management strategies will help broaden the horizons of these management approaches and allow for the consideration of alternative approaches. The adoption of these concepts will also address a failing of current disaster studies identified by Kathleen Tierney (2007) – namely, the need to link disaster research with core sociological concerns such as social inequality, diversity, and social change. As Tierney notes, a shift in orientation in this direction may have already been set into motion, as indicated by critiques of traditional ways of conceptualizing disasters, the greater acceptance of constructivist formulations; the willingness to acknowledge that disasters are accompanied by both social solidarity and social conflict; and a recognition of the significance of the interaction of disasters and risk with gender, class and other axes of inequality. In this context, the incorporation of vulnerability and related concepts will also represent an important step in this direction.

The potential for an expanded focus that is brought to bear on disaster analysis by vulnerability-related concepts is also useful in that they have the potential to serve as starting points for a more radical critique of the prevailing technocratic paradigm. This is because the vulnerability perspective places the emphasis on that which renders communities unsafe – a condition which in turn depends primarily upon a society's social order and the relative position of advantage or disadvantage that a particular group occupies within the given society (Hewitt, 1997: 141). To target and change these structurally informed social aspects of disasters and the ecological crisis will require the adoption of, or at least increased receptivity to, a critical approach. In other words, the vulnerability perspective has the potential to move us in this direction because, as Oliver-Smith observes, "the concept of vulnerability, with its emphasis on social forces and environmental conditions, is part of a larger effort to rethink the relationships between society, economy and nature" (2004: 19).

Notably, the expanded focus of the vulnerability perspective is not limited to broadening the analytic scope for only the social dimension of disaster studies, but the ecological dimension as well (or more accurately the hybridized socio-ecological dimension). That is, it should always be recognized that it is not the exclusive entrenchment in social, economic and political inequalities alone that exposes certain groups to higher levels of risk, but also because of increased exposure resulting from changing environmental conditions (for example, increased flooding in low-lying areas due to climate change). That is, disaster vulnerability should really be thought of as a function of social and environmental conditions and it cannot be divorced from the combined influence stemming from both these sets of conditions. Thus, Wisner et al. (2004) argue that although it may be that events such as hurricanes, floods and earthquakes are triggers for disaster, the disasters themselves originate from socio-ecological processes that may, in fact, be far removed from the actual events themselves. Such socio-ecological processes may include, for instance, deforestation, environmental degradation, factors that encourage settlement in hazardous areas, poverty and other forms of social inequality, low capacity for self-help among subgroups within populations, and failures in physical and social protective systems. By pointing us towards an expanded view with respect to the origins of disasters, the adoption of the vulnerability perspective reminds us of our environmental limits (so crucial to understanding the ecological crisis), while at the same time helping us understand how vulnerability is created and imposed by human social arrangements and decisions that ultimately pertain to how we intervene in the natural environment (e.g. how natural resources are distributed, the impact of neoliberal capitalism, colonialism, etc.). Thus, Anthony Oliver-Smith (2004: 16) notes, the study of disasters informed by a vulnerability perspective can contribute to clarifying the relationship between the environment and society – an important precondition to developing sound environmental and disaster management strategies.

Vulnerability and Environmental Justice

As the vulnerability perspective gains greater prominence in the future, it may be likely that the work of future environmental and disaster managers will become more open to incorporating the types of critiques raised by the environmental justice movement. Although perhaps not yet fully recognized and institutionalized, the vulnerability perspective is philosophically in line with the environmental justice movement. Environmental justice groups deal with issues related to the unequal distribution of environmental risks, where those in subordinate positions are exposed to a greater frequency of environmental risks than those who are in dominant positions in society. Since its inception over a quarter of a century ago, the environmental justice movement has since evolved and matured, and in doing so it has expanded its mandate. Today, concerted efforts are made by environmental justice groups to link occupational, economic, environmental and social justice issues. With this broadened array of concerns, the contemporary environmental justice movement is involved in a multitude of activities such as eliminating the unequal enforcement of environmental, civil rights and public health laws; the differential degree of exposure to harmful chemicals in the home, school, neighborhood and workplace, as well as discriminatory zoning and land-use practices (Haluza-Delay et al., 2009). The environmental justice movement today has already for some time cultivated a critical ethos in which attention is focused on the social and environmental conditions that facilitate or hinder the possibility of progressive social change. As discussed in Chapters 2 and 3, with the increasing institutionalization and influence of environmental governance in both the thought and practice of official environmental decision-makers, a space has opened up for the involvement of social movement organizations, such as environmental justice groups. It is within this context that the opportunity arises for the environmental justice movement to infuse their critically based approaches into environmental and disaster management more generally. In particular, the opportunity window may open for both the environmental justice movement and the broader environmental movement to critique the existing theory and practice in environmental and disaster management in a more significant way than in the past. This in turn may allow for the possibility of considering more seriously alternative approaches to conventional environmental and disaster management that are based on the critical insights and findings from contemporary environmental and disaster social science.

From an Event-Based to Process-Based Orientation to Disasters

Disasters are often conceptualized in event-based terms – that is, as having a beginning (the period of onset), a middle (the emergency period), and ultimately an end (when social life returns more or less to normal and when recovery takes place). This type of conceptualization of a disaster implicitly guides the underlying orientation found in conventional disaster management strategies such as those based on the disaster management cycle or an all-hazards approach (e.g. the Hazards Identification and Risk Assessment protocol reviewed in the previous chapter). An accumulating amount of research has found that an event-based approach to disasters is too limiting for an accurate account and understanding of how a disaster arises, which in turn will logically have implications for developing effective disaster management responses (see, for example, Ali, 2003, 2008; Ali and Novogradic, 2008; Beamish, 2001, 2002; Klinenberg, 1999; Oliver-Smith, 2004; Turner, 1976). What is perhaps the greatest shortcoming of an event-based approach is that it overlooks the possibility that disasters may be an inherent and emergent product of the social structure and processes themselves – just as we have argued that the ecological crisis may be an outcome of the capitalist system itself, or, more generally, a function of the way the relationship between economy and society is institutionally and ideologically organized. That is, what is not recognized or at the very least not given the proper credence, is the understanding that disasters are episodic and symptomatic manifestations of the broader political–economic and cultural forces that shape societies (Tierney, 2007). It is only by acknowledging and engaging with this important realization that we can move forward in developing alternative environmental and disaster management strategies that are innovative and critical, yet at the same time are in touch with reality on both the material and social levels. Without this broader context-based understanding of disaster, disasters will be simply depoliticized by being attributed to purely natural forces. In other words, the view that a disaster is simply a departure from a state of normalcy to which a society returns on recovery denies the wider historical and social dimensions of hazard while concurrently (though perhaps inadvertently) encouraging the consideration and adoption of exclusively technocratic solutions (Bankoff, 2004: 29) – as is similarly the case with environmental management strategies vis-à-vis the ecological crisis. And, as we have seen, such an orientation is quite often uncritical and out of touch with the reality imposed on the biophysical setting due to social, political economic and cultural forces. Furthermore, as Hewitt (1995: 118–121) notes, this type of technocratic approach has permitted hazards and disasters to be treated as specialized problems that call for the advanced knowledge of scientists, engineers and bureaucrats, the result of which is the appropriation of the knowledge pertaining to disaster management (and we would add environmental management) by experts – a development that would run counter to the more democratizing tendencies inherent to environmental governance in which external critique by outside bodies, such as environmental groups, would be better received. We will return to this important point later in Chapter 10 when we discuss the potential for what is known as post-normal science.

A discernable movement away from this classic event-based approach to disaster has become increasingly evident over the recent years. Part of the impetus for this change in focus is likely related to the increased emphasis on vulnerability (and the associated concepts of resilience, adaptation and mitigation) discussed above. With the recognition that the vulnerability of individuals and a community to disasters and the ecological crisis is actually just an endpoint to something more, the analytical focus has switched to the antecedent process that has led to this endpoint as disaster. As such, in addressing the question of how people have become vulnerable to disasters and environmental hazards, investigative focus has naturally turned towards a consideration of the historical trajectory on which basis people are put in harm's way – an issue that environmental justice actors have implicitly raised (Ali, 2009). Once the historical trajectory becomes part of the analysis, the analysis naturally moves away from an endpoint focus to a process orientation. The historical context in which a disaster emerges has now come to be an important consideration in disaster analysis (Ali, 2003; Beamish, 2002; Molotch et al., 2000).

The process-orientation to disaster clearly has significant implications for conceptualizing disasters and it may hold the promise for leading to new and fruitful ways of gaining insights not only for researchers, but for disaster and environmental managers as well. As discussed, conventionally, a disaster has been conceived as an unexpected and non-routine social event that arises from one-off natural forces. However, with the adoption of a process-orientation, disasters come to be viewed and approached differently. That is, far from being non-routine, disasters come to be understood as somewhat common occurrences that are expected to emerge from the particular societies in which they are embedded. In turn, these societies can be characterized by the particular historical factors that have informed their development, including the myriad of social influences stemming from industrialization, urbanization, globalization, the legacy of colonialism, political economic forces, and the mechanisms of control exercised over both the environment and civil society (Ali, 2008, 2009). Notably, all these influences arise from, and are exerted through, social *processes*. Thus, in this light, it is through the adoption of a process-orientation that the analysis of disasters "opens up" in the sense that it encourages a consideration of a larger array of social and material factors that may exert their influences at different scales – local, regional, national and global – and through their complex interplay.[1] A process-orientation to disaster will discourage the adoption of a conventionally narrow and technocratically defined approach to disasters while at the same time making room for more critical approaches that bring to the fore the role of broader social and political processes involved in the production of a disaster.

One significant benefit of the process-orientation to disaster is that it draws attention to the important question of how a hazard (i.e. potential disaster waiting to happen) becomes transformed into an actual disaster. One way to investigate such transformative processes is through the adoption of the "disaster incubation" perspective.

Disaster Incubation

Disaster incubation refers to the period before the actual onset of a disaster. In his seminal work, Barry Turner (1976, 1978) refers to this stage of a disaster as the period in which a series of discrepant events accumulate unnoticed until a precipitating event or trigger leads to the actual disaster onset. What is most noteworthy concerning the chain of discrepant events that contribute to the "incubation" of a disaster is that they are allowed to accumulate *unnoticed*. For Turner, therefore, the key question is why do they go unnoticed? To answer this question the incubation period must be closely examined so as to identify those conditions that make it possible for unnoticed, misperceived, and misunderstood events to accumulate. According to Turner, the factors that contribute to a disaster may go unnoticed because either the events are not known to anyone or they are known but not fully understood by all concerned. As such, a key aspect of the disaster incubation period is that it is during this time that a "failure of foresight" is fostered – understood by Turner in terms of "the collapse of precautions that had hitherto been regarded culturally as adequate" (1976: 380). Guided by this insight, Turner then proceeds to identify those conditions that foster this failure of foresight. He does so by focusing on the identification of those *organizational features* that have fostered the failure. Through a meticulous analysis of numerous disaster case studies, he identifies the following organizational features that are frequently found in the disaster incubation period: rigidities in institutional beliefs, distracting decoy phenomena, neglect of outside complaints, multiple information-handling difficulties, exacerbation of the hazards by strangers, failure to comply with regulations, and a tendency to minimize emergent danger (Turner, 1976).

What is so useful about the disaster incubation approach is that it implicitly recognizes and analytically engages with the processual nature of a disaster by focusing attention on what is often the least dramatic, and therefore most neglected, part of the disaster process. The limitation of the approach developed by Turner, however, may be its exclusive focus on the organizational aspects of disaster incubation. The incubation of a disaster may also be influenced by larger social forces, such as those related to globalization and the political economy, often invoked by critical social scientists. At the same time, disaster incubation may very well be influenced by the face-to-face or human-to-human interactions taking place as well.

In other words, disaster incubation may result from social factors and processes that are not only associated with the exclusively meso-scale implicit in Turner's organizational emphasis, but also from the macro and micro scales. Similarly, all disasters must necessarily implicate biophysical factors and processes (ultimately involving matter, energy and the natural and built environment), and in this light, an exclusive focus on the social may be remiss unless it also considers the material factors that contribute to the disaster incubation as well. Thus, in other works we have incorporated other spatial scales and the biophysical dimension into the disaster incubation analysis in what may be referred to as a socio-ecological approach to disaster incubation (Ali, 2004, 2008; Mulvihill and Ali, 2007).[2] We would expect that the expansion of disaster incubation analysis along these lines may not receive favor with those ascribing to conventional environmental and disaster management strategies. However, this is precisely the point. The socio-ecological approach to disaster incubation focuses attention on to factors that will originate from outside the specific organization in which environmental and disasters managers normally work. As such, the socio-ecological approach opens the door to the messy world of "politics" – the nemesis of technocrats. This is, however, necessary if a critical reorientation in disaster and environmental management is to take hold and be supported.

As an alternative orientation to those normally found within conventional disaster and environmental management, the socio-ecological approach to disaster incubation offers distinct advantages that resonate well with the types of issues raised in previous chapters. First, by explicitly focusing on both the social and ecological, the socio-ecological approach is, in fact, epistemologically consonant with the hybrid (nature–social) analytical emphasis currently found within contemporary environmental and disaster sociology (see Chapters 6 through 8). Thus, the socio-ecological is itself an avenue of opportunity for encouraging the incorporation of research and insights from environmental and disaster sociology into the work of environmental and disaster managers. Second, the socio-ecological approach is intrinsically process-oriented. Thus, it discourages disaster and environmental managers from narrowing their consideration to one point in time while encouraging them to look backwards and forwards in time, thereby putting the disaster or ecological crisis into proper perspective. Such an outlook is tied to a third benefit – namely, the advantages of contextualizing the disaster/ecological crisis. The adoption of a socio-ecological approach would enable less parochial perspectives to have a place in the development of new and innovative environmental and disaster management strategies. That is, by directing attention to upstream causal contributions to the disasters and the ecological crisis, other pertinent social and environmental factors not normally considered by officials would be given consideration, particularly those types of factors that encourage critical thinking in the sense that we are discussing in this book. For instance, this would include a consideration of how the decisions and actions of government, political and economic elites (and their financial supporters) who occupy global industries and financial institutions played a role in the incubation of disaster or the ecological crisis more generally.

Lastly, the socio-ecological approach will sensitize those in disaster and environmental management to the need to consider and incorporate issues of vulnerability, resilience, adaptation and mitigation into the strategies they develop. Such considerations would again naturally follow through the adoption of a process orientation that takes into account the social dimension more seriously and critically – for example, social groups that are more vulnerable to the effects of disaster and the ecological crisis. To help illustrate some of these benefits of the socio-ecological approach to disaster incubation, let us turn our attention to a case study.

The Socio-Ecological Analysis of Disease Outbreaks as Disasters

During the last part of the last century, there was tremendous optimism that in light of the various successfully implemented infectious disease eradication campaigns it would soon be time to "close the book" on infectious diseases and with that, attention could be focused on chronic diseases such as cardiovascular disease, cancer and diabetes. This has proven to be a false prognostication. Over the last three decades, an unprecedented number of new and (re)emerging diseases have risen around the world (McMichael, 2001). Examples of these abound and include such pathogenic threats as (to name just a few): the Severe Acute Respiratory Syndrome (SARS) coronavirus, HIV/AIDS, West Nile, Huntavirus, Ebola, the Lyme disease virus, the avian flu virus, the Zika virus, *clostridium difficile*, and the hoof-and-mouth pathogen (Drexler, 2003; Levy and Fischetti, 2003; Garrett, 1994; Institute of Medicine, 1992). Why has this come about? According to McMichael (2001) such changes in infectious disease emergence occur at key points in history when the relationship between humans and nature changes significantly. Thus, he outlines how the proliferation of various specific types of disease outbreaks historically accompanied socio-ecological changes related to the advent of agriculture and the domestication of livestock in early human history, the intensified trade, travel and military movement as part of various conquering empires (Roman, Mongol, etc.), and the process of colonization pursued by European countries. Today, through globalized processes involving the intensified and extensive movement of people, foodstuffs, and goods at ever expansive distances and shorter periods of time, we may be witnessing a fourth great transition that has resulted in the plethora of new and (re)emerging diseases we now face. Notably, in current times, the number of disease outbreaks is expected to rise as increased human intervention in nature through development pressures will lead to even greater types of environmental changes that are conducive to the onset of epidemics. To understand how this is so, we briefly turn towards a consideration of disease ecology.

A fundamental principle of disease ecology is that an infectious disease outbreak can only occur if three sets of circumstances and conditions are aligned. Referred to as the Epidemiological Triad (see Figure 9.1), this perspective holds that at the most basic level, there needs to exist a disease-causing agent (e.g. virus, bacteria or other pathogen), a host that can be infected by that agent, and the presence of a conducive environment in which both the agent and host can survive. Moreover, the environmental media and conditions must be suitable for the disease-causing agent to be able to expeditiously travel to infect the host.

One illustration of how the epidemiological triangle can be used to account for disease outbreaks is the case of the Nipah virus outbreaks in Malaysia in 1999 (McMichael, 2001). Ecosytems were disturbed by development pressures involving the removal of large tracts of tropical forests to accommodate an airport extension. With the removal of trees, bats carrying the Nipah virus (but which were themselves immune to the disease caused by the virus) were deprived of the forest fruits upon which they relied for food. Deprived of their food source, the bats raided food troughs on pig farms, thereby infecting the pigs, which were not immune. Humans who came into contact with these infected pigs also became infected, leading to an outbreak situation.

McMichael (2001) also gives an historical example. The period in which iron tools were first produced in West Africa coincided with the introduction of slash-and-burn agriculture. Such activities then created a new breeding ground for the mosquitoes that carried the parasite that causes malaria, thus leading to the spread of this disease in this particular period.

As a third illustration, take the case of tuberculosis. Tuberculosis outbreaks have been known to occur in particular sites such as urban homeless shelters and jails (Ali, 2010). This is because all the facilitating conditions for a disease outbreak vis-à-vis the epidemiological triad are often found in these types of settings. Focusing on the former setting, the tuberculosis bacterium (i.e. the agent) needs an available host, and of course the hosts are the residents in the shelters. Lastly,

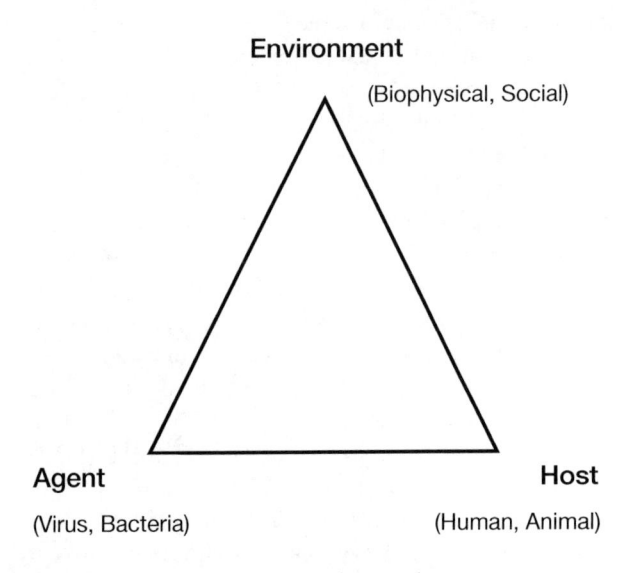

FIGURE 9.1 The Epidemiological Triangle

the environmental conditions for the spread of tuberculosis include the existence of poor ventilation and overcrowding. In many large metropolitan centres, due to neoliberal funding cuts to social welfare, housing and poverty programs, the state of homeless shelters has deteriorated, with many beds housed clustered together in close confines (ibid.) – and with the lack of upkeep and investment in these shelters, many do indeed have poor ventilation. The environmental conditions for a tuberculosis outbreak are therefore met. To break any of the linkages in the triad would require investment and attention, which would in turn necessitate political clout, policy change and funds. In this context, for instance, if more suitable and appropriate accommodation space were provided, including, for example, beds that were much more spaced out, investment within the shelter system infrastructure to ensure proper ventilation, and decreasing the sheer number of homeless people through the provision of better housing and other social programs designed to eliminate homelessness, such improvements would lead to less crowded and healthier environments in the shelter system. Attention to such improvements in the end would ensure that a tuberculosis disease outbreak would not occur in this particular setting.

The approaches and insights from environmental and disaster sociology that we have discussed in previous chapters and above are particularly apt in the study of disease outbreaks. First, consistent with the logic of the Epidemiological Triad, the relationships implicated in a disease outbreak are inherently socio-ecological – that is, the relationships described by the triad have both social and biophysical components. Thus, for instance, a conducive biophysical environment for the spread of tuberculosis can be "socially manufactured" through the politics and policies governing homeless shelters, such as the number of occupants permitted to stay at a given site. Thus, to make sense of a disease outbreak, the notion of the environment must be broadened to include not only the biophysical, but the social and political environment as well. Second, a disease outbreak is an emergent phenomenon that arises from the convergence of various flows – pathogen, animal, human and environmental (e.g. wind, soil, water). As such, an outbreak conceptualized as a disaster clearly has a processual dimension associated with it. Third, the social and biophysical factors and processes that contribute to the disaster incubation may go unnoticed in the pre-disaster phase due to organizational and broader political economic factors at play. For instance, government cost-saving neoliberal cuts to public health and inspection programs may result in an increased likelihood that shelters will be poorly maintained as infrastructure elements of the facility that need attention will be overlooked and neglected, and thus allowed to deteriorate (for example, the maintenance of good ventilation), thereby increasing the disaster potential for a disease outbreak to occur.

In terms of vulnerability, it is instructive to consider Paul Farmer's (1997) observation that infectious diseases tend to "hide" among the poor because the poor are often socially and medically segregated from those whose deaths might be considered more significant. As such, the homeless, who have little option except to stay at shelters and other such facilities, are the ones most vulnerable to diseases such as tuberculosis. Further, in the case of tuberculosis, because of the nature of this particular disease, those whose immune system are compromised are the most susceptible to its deadly effects. It should be noted that an immune system may become compromised due to the influence of such environmental factors as poor nutrition and constant stress – the very conditions faced on a daily basis by the homeless. Since homelessness remains a low-priority public concern for many North American municipalities, not only does the plight of the homeless remain neglected but so too does the recognition of the potential for tuberculosis outbreaks. This neglect in turn works against the very possibility for strategies of resilience, adaptation and mitigation to be introduced and adopted. For instance, resilience is difficult to pursue under conditions of "institutional cycling" where the homeless are shuttled between jails, shelters, single-occupancy hotels, hospitals, rehabilitation centers and recovery homes (DeVerteuil, 2003). Institutional cycling is a key aspect of homelessness and represents an important confounding influence in effectively tracing the spread of tuberculosis (Ali, 2010), thus preventing even the possibility for resilience, adaptation and mitigation at a structural level.

One more formalized attempt to develop an explicitly socio-ecological approach to disease outbreaks is given by Ali (2004; see also Muvihill and Ali, 2007; Bowden, 2011) who introduces a socio-ecological matrix to guide efforts in analyzing the incubation of a disaster.

The socio-ecological matrix approach enables the identification and analysis of a much greater range of disaster incubation factors and processes than would normally be the case. Notably, it does so by considering a wider range of scales ranging from the micro to meso to macro on both the social and ecological dimensions. As factors/processes are identified, they are situated in the appropriate cells of the matrix. Once complete, the matrix can serve as a template for discussion on how to develop targeted disaster prevention and/or management strategies by helping to identify those issues and matters that need more careful attention – for example, the protection of vulnerable subpopulations or environmental features. Notably, this approach tries to incorporate one of the major insights of disaster sociology – namely, that the roots of a disaster may be quite deep, extending far beyond the local spatial and temporal circumstances of a particular place. Thus, taken into consideration are such factors/processes related to global environmental changes on the "macro" ecological level (cell 3) – for example, global climate change – and the forces of the global political economy at the "macro" social level (cell 6) – for example,

	Downstream ←———————→ Upstream		
	Micro Level	Meso Level	Macro Level
Ecological Dimension	1	2	3
Social Dimension	4	5	6

FIGURE 9.2 The Socio-Ecological Matrix

neoliberal policy trends at the international level. At the "meso" ecological level, the matrix facilitates the consideration of regional environmental factors (such as the specific geographic features of a given bioregion or locality) or the organizational features of the specific bureaucratic agencies implicated in the disaster. The "micro" factor or process acting at the local social level refers to those human factors/processes occurring at the disaster onset scene, such as the actions of operators of a technology. Finally, the example of a localized extreme weather event illustrates a micro factor/process unfolding at the ecological level.

Two other notes should be considered in adopting the socio-ecological matrix approach. First, in the attempt to develop a more complete and comprehensive, yet workable account of the incubation of a disaster, the socio-ecological matrix appears to artificially separate out elements/processes that in reality interact with each other in a dynamic way. As such, it should be kept in mind that the matrix serves as a sort of generic template that serves as a sensitizing tool and a launching point for further detailed examination and discussion that considers explicitly how the different cells of the matrix are related to one another. Second, as we go from a consideration of micro to macro factors, we are also focusing our attention from the downstream disaster incubation factors to the upstream ones. In this context, the upstream factors are those that relate to the ultimate source of the disaster, while downstream factors refer to those that permit or allow the outbreak to occur once the upstream processes are already unfolding. Let us briefly consider a previous study which has applied this approach to the largest waterborne outbreak of *E. coli* O157:H7 in Canada (for a more detailed discussion, see Ali, 2004).

Walkerton is a small farming community of 4,800 people that is located about 180 km north-west of Toronto. During the period of May 23–24, 2000, close to half the residents of this community became ill with bloody diarrhea, vomiting, severe stomach cramps and fever; and tragically, seven people eventually succumbed to their illnesses (Bruce-Grey-Owen Sound Health Unit, 2000). The cause of the illnesses was traced to the presence of *E. coli* O157:H7 in the community's drinking-water supply. The incubation of the outbreak can be traced through the completion of the socio-ecological matrix presented above. For instance, media attention quickly focused the blame for this particular outbreak on the operator of the local water-treatment facility who was found to be negligent in his responsibilities by not identifying a broken chlorinator and then falsifying records of the added chlorine levels to conceal his mistake; this factor was situated in cell 4. He was further found not to be trained properly for the job (a factor that would be situated in cell 5). Popular accounts held this particular individual as wholly responsible for the outbreak. Such an account, however, is simplistic in that it does not consider other factors that contributed to the outbreak. The operator failure was a downstream factor. Questions remained as to why operator failure was allowed to occur – for example, why was the training not properly completed, and why were the high bacterial counts in the water not automatically reported to the appropriate public health agency and the medical officer of health who would be able to immediately issue a boil-water advisory and warn the community against

A Socio-Ecological Approach to the Crisis **111**

drinking the water (cell 5). To consider such factors requires a more upstream focus that considers the organizational basis of the disaster. In this case, the adoption of neoliberal measures, including the privatization of lab testing for bacterial counts, meant that there was a breakdown in communication for the reporting of dangerous levels of bacteria, which influenced what happened at the meso level. The focus could, however, go further upstream, to the global level where considerations of how agribusiness restructuring under international political economic agreements has led to the intensification of livestock operations (also known as factory farming), particularly in response to the demands of the burgeoning fast-food industry and the increased demand for beef at that time (cell 6). In turn, it was due to the excessive amount of manure that was produced by such intensified livestock operations in the region that led to contamination of the drinking-water supply (cell 2), a contamination process that was aided by an unprecedented level of torrential rainfall in the area just prior to the outbreak, which enabled water contaminated with the pathogen to enter into a well that was hydraulically connected to the community water source, thus contaminating the source of water for the community (cell 1). An understanding of the evolution of the bacteria itself, from a harmless variant of *E. coli* to this more virulent strain requires an even further upstream gaze that takes into account how acid rain may have served as an evolutionary inducement for the bacteria to be able to more readily survive harsh conditions and how the global trade in cattle and meat products may have enabled the harmless variant of the *E. coli* bacteria to acquire a gene from the deadly *Shigella* bacterium (present in the Argentinian cattle reservoir) through a viral agent, thus transforming the *E. coli* into a deadly form (cell 3).

The socio-ecological approach to the disaster incubation is not typical of conventional approaches to environmental and disaster management because, in particular, it takes a more critical approach. It thus takes into account factors that are not normally considered, such as how government agencies operate under conditions of neoliberalism, the role of larger upstream factors such as the global fast-food industry, and how that has influenced and is connected to problems experienced at a local level. Analyses of this type have important implications for the manner in which disasters are subsequently "managed" because they direct attention to larger structural issues pertaining to the source of the disaster (or the ecological crisis). In particular, they encourage the idea that attempts to control the environment need to be replaced by approaches that emphasize ways of dealing with unexpected events in a manner that is accompanied by flexibility, adaptability, resilience and capacity.

Concluding Remarks

As a proposed strategy for environment management, using conventional criteria, the socio-ecological approach seems a bit too broad, vague and imprecise – say, in comparison to typical and familiar approaches that are usually adopted, such as environmental impact assessment, adaptive environmental management, integrated resource management, or environmental monitoring and auditing. This is, however, precisely the point. The socio-ecological approach is meant to be an orientating strategy for environmental management that is explicitly intended to broaden the range of factors normally considered. It is meant to help gain a properly informed and situated understanding and insight into the social and ecological contexts in which the environmental (or better, socioenvironmental) problem is embedded. The socio-ecological approach and conventional environmental management approaches need not be considered as mutually exclusive, although the immediate reaction by many practitioners may very well be to treat the two approaches as separate, so as not to venture too far outside established comfort zones and defined roles. Rather, the socio-ecological approach should be used to help broaden the horizons of conventional environmental management and enable a better selection of response strategies. That is, better in the sense that the selected strategy will be more appropriate in terms of suitability to the context. The ultimate goal, therefore, is to ensure a better and more effective response based on the promotion of a more upstream and critical approach. In the next two chapters we propose and discuss other alternative ways of pursuing this objective. We do so by considering other confounding factors that thwart current conventional environmental management efforts – namely, the issue of dealing with the normative aspects of environmental decision-making, and how decisions can be made under conditions of uncertainty and limited knowledge.

Notes

1. A complex interplay that is perhaps akin to the notion of interactive complexity referred to in the Normal Accident theory of Charles Perrow (1984). Interactive complexity is a property of a system that emerges when two or more discrete failures interact in unexpected ways. According to Perrow, a sufficiently complex system will always exhibit failures of this type, which will inevitably lead to disasters. Consequently, this makes us perpetually vulnerable to this type of disaster as long we are dependent on such technological systems – we would argue socio-ecological systems, a distinction that will be more fully developed later in this chapter.
2. Similar consideration with respect to the temporal scale is not warranted because the processual characterization of a disaster implies that the consideration of time is already implicitly incorporated into the analysis.

References

Adger, W.N. (2000) "Social and Ecological Resilience: Are They Related?" *Progress in Human Geography*, 24: 347–364.

Agrawal, A. (2010) "Local Institutions and Adaptation to Climate Change". In *Social Dimensions of Climate Change: Equity and Vulnerability in the Warming World*. Washington, DC: World Bank, pp. 173–198.

Ali, S.H. (2003) "Dealing with Toxicity in the Risk Society: The Case of the Hamilton, Ontario Plastics Recycling Fire". *The Canadian Review of Sociology and Anthropology*, 39(1): 29–48.

Ali, S.H. (2004) "A Socio-Ecological Autopsy of the *E. coli* O157:H7 Outbreak in Walkerton, Ontario, Canada". *Social Science and Medicine*, 58(12): 2601–2612.

Ali, S.H. (2008) "Analyzing Environmental Disasters". In S.D. Gupta (Ed.) *Understanding the Global Environment*. New Delhi: Pearson Press, pp. 245–264.

Ali, S.H. (2009) "Analyzing Environmental Disasters". In S.D. Gupta (Ed.) *Understanding the Global Environment*. New Delhi: Pearson Press, pp. 245–264.

Ali, S.H. (2010) "Tuberculosis, Homelessness and the Politics of Mobility". *Canadian Journal of Urban Research*, 19(2): 80–107.

Ali, S.H. and Novogradec, A. (2008) "Disasters and Emergency Preparedness". In J. Golson and Y. Zhang (Eds.) *Encyclopedia of Global Health*. London: Sage, pp. 532–535.

Bankoff, G. (2004) "The Historical Geography of Disaster: 'Vulnerability' and 'Local Knowledge' in Western Discourse". In G. Bankoff, G. Frerks and D. Hilhorst (Eds.) *Mapping Vulnerability: Disasters, Development and People*. London: Earthscan, pp. 25–36.

Beamish, T. (2001) "Environmental Hazard and Institutional Betrayal". *Organization and Environment*, 14: 5–33.

Beamish, T. (2002) "Waiting for Crisis: Regulatory Inaction and Ineptitude and the Guadalupe Dunes Oil Spill". *Social Problems*, 49(2): 150–177.

Beck, U. (1992) *Risk Society: Towards a New Modernity*. London: Sage.

Bowden, G. (2011) "Disasters as System Accidents: A Socio-Ecological Framework". In R.A. Dowty and B.L. Allen (Eds.) *Dynamics of Disasters: Lessons on Risk, Response and Recovery*. London: Earthscan, pp. 47–60.

Bruce-Grey-Owen Sound Health Unit (2000) The Investigative Report of the Walkerton Outbreak of Waterborne Gastroenteritis, May–June, 2000. Released October 10, 2000. Walkerton, Ontario.

Cutter, S.L., Barnes, L., Berry, M., Burton, C., Evans, E., Tate, E.and Webb, J. (2008) "A Place-Based Model for Understanding Community Resilience to Natural Disasters". *Global Environmental Change*, 18: 598–606.

Cutter, S. (1996) "Vulnerability to Environmental Hazards". *Progress in Human Geography*, 20(4): 529–530.

DeVerteuil, G. (2003) "Homeless Mobility, Institutional Settings, and the New Poverty Management". *Environment and Planning A*, 35: 361–379.

Drexler, M. (2003) *Secret Agents: The Menace of Emerging Infections*. New York: Penguin.

Etkin, D. (2016) *Disaster Theory: An Interdisciplinary Approach to Concepts and Causes*. Waltham, MA: Butterworth-Heinemann.

Farmer, P. (1997) "Social Scientists and the New Tuberculosis". *Social Science and Medicine*, 44(3): 347–358.

Garrett, L. (1994) *The Coming Plague: Newly Emerging Diseases in a World out of Balance*. New York: Penguin.

Haluza-Delay, R., O'Riley, P., Cole, P. and Agyeman, J. (2009) "Introduction. Speaking for Ourselves, Speaking Together: Environmental Justice in Canada". In J. Agyeman, P. Cole, R. Haluza-Delay and P. O'Riley (Eds.) *Speaking for Ourselves: Environmental Justice in Canada*. Vancouver: UBC Press, pp. 1–26.

Hewitt, K. (1995) "Excluded Perspectives in the Social Construction of Disaster". *International Journal of Mass Emergencies and Disasters*, 13: 317–340.

Hewitt, K. (1997) *Regions of Risk: A Geographical Introduction to Disasters*. Longman: Harrow and Essex.

Holling, C.S. (1973) "Resilience and Stability of Ecological Systems". *Annual Review of Ecology and Systematics*, 4: 1–23.

Homer-Dixon, T. (2000) *Environment, Scarcity and Violence*. Princeton, NJ: Princeton University Press.

Institute of Medicine (1992) "Emerging Infections: Microbial Threats to Health in the United States". Washington, DC: National Academy of Science.

Klinenberg, E. (1999) "Denaturalizing Disaster: A Social Autopsy of the 1995 Chicago Heat Wave". *Theory and Society*, 28(2): 239–295.
Levy, E. and Fischetti, M. (2003) *The New Killer Diseases: How the Alarming Evolution of Germs Threatens Us All*. New York: Three Rivers Press.
McMichael, A.J. (2001) "Human Culture, Ecological Change and Infectious Disease: Are We Experiencing History's Fourth Great Transition?" *Ecosystem Health*, 7(2): 107–115.
Molotch, H., Freudenburg, W. and Paulsen, K. (2000) "History Repeats Itself, but How? City Character, Urban Tradition, and the Accomplishment of Place". *American Sociological Review*, 65: 791–823.
Mulvihill, P. and Ali, S.H. (2007) "Disaster Incubation, Cumulative Impacts and the Urban/Ex-Urban/Rural Dynamic". *Environmental Impact Assessment Review*, 27: 343–358.
Oliver-Smith, A. (2004) "Theorizing Vulnerability in a Globalized World: A Political Ecological Perspective". In G. Bankoff, G. Frerks and D. Hilhorst (Eds.) *Mapping Vulnerability: Disasters, Development and People*. London: Earthscan, pp. 10–24.
Perrow, C. (1984) *Normal Accidents: Living With High-Risk Technologies*. New York: Basic Books.
Tierney, K.J. (2007) "From the Margins to the Mainstream? Disaster Research at the Crossroads". *Annual Review of Sociology*, 33: 503–525.
Turner, B.A. (1976) "The Organizational and Interorganizational Development of Disasters". *Administrative Science Quarterly*, 21: 378–397.
Turner, B. (1978) *Man-Made Disasters*. London: Wykeham.
United Nations International Strategy for Disaster Reduction (UNISDR) (2004) "Defining a Few Key Terms". Available at: www.unisdr.org/eng/media-room/facts-sheets/fs-Defining-a-few-key-terms.htm (last accessed April 26, 2016).
Urry, J. (2011) *Climate Change and Society*. Cambridge: Polity Press.
Wilson, G.A. (2012) *Community Resilience and Environmental Transitions*. New York: Routledge.
Wisner, B., Blaikie, P., Cannon, T. and Davis, I. (2004) *At Risk: Natural Hazards, People's Vulnerability, and Disasters*. New York: Routledge.
Young, N. (2015) *Environmental Sociology for the Twenty-First Century*. Don Mills: Oxford University Press.
Youngman, N. (2009) "Understanding Disaster Vulnerability: Floods and Hurricanes". In K.A. Gould and T.L. Lewis (Eds.) *Twenty Lessons in Environmental Sociology*. New York: Oxford University Press, pp. 176–190.

10
TOWARDS A PHILOSOPHICAL REORIENTATION IN ENVIRONMENTAL MANAGEMENT I

Post-Normal Science Thinking

It is a central contention of this book that the guiding principle for environmental management should begin with the awareness and appreciation that all environmental management efforts are ultimately concerned with addressing the ecological crisis writ large. At first sight, the very idea of addressing the ecological crisis seems overwhelming and beyond our individual and collective means, and perhaps rather naive and even absurd. We would concede that it may indeed appear that the task of dealing with the ecological crisis is truly daunting, but we do not agree that it is beyond our means to address it. Rather, we would argue that it is beyond our current and conventionally understood ways of addressing the challenges through existing environmental management approaches. For this reason, we have argued that a new approach is needed based on an altogether different orientation informed by a distinctly broader conception of the ecological crisis and environmental management. In this regard, recall that we have mentioned in the introductory chapter that narrow definitions of environmental management that conceive of this field as a business activity are not helpful with respect to the broader goals of the "management of the environment" or sustainability. Indeed, we have made the case throughout this book that environmental management is a broad, collective, and collaborative endeavour – that it involves nothing less than governance for sustainability with conscious efforts directed at addressing both the root causes and downstream elements of the ecological crisis. With this expansive understanding of environmental management in mind, we propose that a new orientation to environmental management must be built on insights from ecological *and* social sciences – two areas of research that themselves eschew reductionist approaches to the phenomena they respectively study (i.e. ecosystems and societies). We have further argued that this new type of orientation must be imbued with a decidedly critical stance that is receptive to more unorthodox and expansive ways of thinking about the ecological crisis. The adoption of a broader orientation is necessary to overcome the resistance and inertia of conventional modes of thinking about the ecological crisis, as currently found within the field of environmental management – approaches that typically tend to focus on particular and specific ends to managing the environment in the narrowly defined terms of partisan political and policy objectives. As many of the barriers to more innovative ways of thinking about the ecological crisis tend to be social and political in nature, in this monograph we have opted to focus on and emphasize more explicitly the critical social-scientific rather than ecological side of the equation (recognizing, of course, that the two are intertwined as we have argued throughout).

First and foremost, it should be kept in mind that the ecological crisis is a crisis *of* society and *for* society. Thus, Nathan Young (2015) writes that environmental problems are problems *of* society in the sense that they are the result of societal decisions about how to intervene in nature, as well as how we as human beings relate to nature more generally. As such, a critique of the type of social order that contributes to and maintains the ecological crisis must be considered as one important area of concern for the profession of environmental management. In the present day, we are dealing with the social order of modern capitalism, a social organizational form predicated upon, among other things, continued economic growth, a consumer culture and a rapid urbanization accompanied by suburban forms dependent solely upon the automobile for transport. As Bhagwati (2007) observes, capitalism is taken for granted as the dominant global economic system, and further capitalist development is currently seen among both rich and poor countries as the best and only way to improve quality of life and standards of living. As a consequence of the sway of such an ideological stance, most perspectives that are formulated to deal with the ecological crisis end up merely "tinkering at the edges" of the major environmental problems produced by global capitalism. Consequently, these perspectives do not promote any real change with respect to the ecological crisis (which in the meantime worsens) because they do not address the root source of the crisis – namely, capitalism – while at the same time attention becomes diverted towards specific downstream environmental impacts which are merely the outward symptoms or manifestations of the larger underlying problem of the ecological crisis itself. To go beyond this narrow mindset, the conversation must be broadened. For example, as Bhagwati (2007) suggests, this could be pursued by considering questions such as what an economic system with no externalities would look like. This would lead to a different emphasis than considering only market-based solutions to environmental problems such as pollution permits or carbon taxes, and would open the possibility to consider, for instance, the institutional restructuring of the whole of society along ecologically sensitive lines. Capitalism, at this juncture, as Peter Newell (2011: 4) remarks, is very much the "elephant in the room". Yet, due to the pressing nature of the ecological crisis, the integral role that capitalism plays in the ecological crisis can no longer be simply ignored. This realization must be explicitly acknowledged by policy-makers and environmental managers alike since this would be an important first step in the development of more effective strategies that would explicitly engage with the impositions on thought that capitalism as ideology and practice have on thinking about ways to address the ecological crisis. Such impositions on thought have included, for instance, the encouragement of the adoption of narrow ad hoc, managerial, instrumental and reductionist approaches in addressing environmental problems. This is why a critical approach to environmental management is so important – it helps us recognize some of these cognitive and structural limitations faced in addressing the ecological crisis writ large.

If the objective is to find ways to address the ecological crisis, both within and perhaps more controversially beyond, the context of capitalism, then critical perspectives of capitalist society will need to be engaged with in some way, shape or form. Second, once created by society, environmental problems come to threaten our existing patterns of social organization, as we struggle to adapt to the material impacts and consequences of the ecological crisis. In other words, the ecological crisis is a crisis *for* society. This is an especially important point to keep in mind if one recognizes that any form of social organization must ultimately depend on some material base, whether this is thought of in terms of matter and energy and material flows, or "nature" and "natural resources". If the material basis of our lives is disrupted, then so too will the social basis of our lives – a perhaps obvious point to those living in marginalized and deprived areas of the world where day-to-day experiences are replete with reminders and instances of material deprivation. It may not, however, be so obvious to those who take the material basis of life for granted due to the privileged or otherwise fortunate circumstances of living in what is assumed to be an age of exuberance. The "age of exuberance" refers to the characterization of the post-war period onwards in which people unquestioningly and unfailingly presume that we live, and that we can continue to live indefinitely, in a time of accelerated economic growth and endless possibility (Catton and Dunlap, 1980). Today, however, it must be realized that ecological scarcity and the ecological crisis need to be taken into account and incorporated into the very fabric of our social life – that is, as an organizing principle for society. This point is emphasized, for example, in Ulrich Beck's (1992) risk society thesis where he discusses the politicization of environmental risks predicated by the realized collective need for civil society to confront such risks. This recognition, of course, is especially important for professionals officially and formally involved in addressing the ecological crisis (i.e. those involved in environmental management).

How, then, can the field of environmental management first broaden its perspective on the ecological crisis and then start on taking measures to address the ecological crisis? The in-the-field particulars of how this can happen can only be developed and pursued once an overarching philosophical or theoretical blueprint has been laid out, otherwise we will run the risk of continuing to reproduce the ineffective and narrow approaches of the past. Building on the insights of our previous discussions, in this chapter we suggest and discuss some guiding principles that may help move forward the endeavor of establishing a new philosophical/theoretical foundation for environmental management, with the understanding that the specifics can be developed in the future once a firm theoretical scaffolding is established. We begin our discussion with the following caveat. From our discussion above, it may appear that what we are suggesting is somewhat grandiose or overly ambitious, but this is not intended to be the case. Our intent is actually much more modest than that; it is to simply initiate a larger discussion on what would be involved in developing a critically informed alternative approach to existing technocratic approaches to environmental management and to get "the ball rolling" on that topic of conversation.

We begin our discussions by considering some of the existing challenges faced in environmental management. We will focus on two key sets of challenges as these will be particularly crucial in considering how alternative philosophical orientations can be developed. The first is dealing with the issues pertaining to the analysis of complex phenomena, and the second with the issue of uncertainty and the incompleteness of knowledge. The second section will introduce the perspective of "post-normal science" and discuss how this perspective is well suited to deal with the challenges identified. How the adoption of a post-normal science is advantageous will also be discussed in terms of bridging the social and natural, and this will be the topic of the third section. Our final section will consider the normative aspect of environmental decision-making in the context of post-positivism – a perspective emanating from a critique of policy science. Post-positivism, as we shall see, is a natural follow-through to post-normal science in that it emphasizes an enhanced role for lay-citizen involvement and participation in environmental governance.

Confronting the Limitations of Conventional Environmental Management

One way to delve into the opportunities and prospects for alternative environmental management is to first consider the existing limitations of environmental management and then do a scan of the critical social science literature on environment and disasters to see what ideas and concepts from these fields hold the most promise in terms of addressing the identified limitations. At various points in this book we have already briefly mentioned and/or alluded to some issues and matters pertinent to the discussion of the limitations of environmental management, and at this point it will be helpful to review some of these.

In our discussion of the challenges facing environmental management in Chapter 2, we noted that dealing with the issue of complexity is particularly difficult. This is especially true when one recognizes that social systems and natural ecosystems are each inherently complex systems in and of themselves. As emphasized in Chapters 6 through 9, to make progress in the development of alternative approaches to environmental management, we suggest that one important precondition is a change in the overall analytical orientation. Specifically, we refer to a reorientation wherein greater analytical attention, credence and considerations are given to understanding the combined effects or interplay of social and biophysical systems. The adoption of such a socio-ecological reorientation, as we have argued, better captures the actual multifaceted reality of the ecological crisis and helps encourage the development of a broader and critical backdrop necessary for the formulation of alternative environmental management approaches. The ostensible drawback to such a decidedly socio-ecological approach is that we would then be dealing with the combined influences of two systems (i.e. the social system and ecosystem) which are inherently complex in and of themselves – that is, we are dealing with double complexity. The need to deal with complexity may, however, be unavoidable due to the very nature of the types of systems with which we are dealing. In the formal sense, complex systems arise when elements of a given system interact in a non-linear way (Byrne, 1998). Consequently, it becomes impossible to predict the behavior of the system as a whole from knowledge about the constituent elements themselves – ecosystems and social systems are both cases in point. As grappling with intrinsic systems complexity is inevitable, it behooves us to find and/or develop innovative ways to deal with situations characterized by complexity, if we are to position ourselves better with respect to discovering more effective ways to understand and respond to the ecological crisis.

A second set of interrelated challenges that would need to be taken into account in developing an alternative, yet sound, foundation for environmental management would involve the issue of working with uncertainty and incompleteness of knowledge. As discussed in Chapter 2, an inadequacy in baseline data on the many ecosystems of our world severely limits the quality of scientific knowledge and depth of understanding that may be attained. For many ecosystems, true baseline measurements can never be made because the point at which the ecosystem in question was unadulterated has long since vanished. Consequently, the best that can be done under these circumstances is to measure a baseline at some point in time after the impact or contamination has already occurred. The implication is that our understanding of the ecological crisis will always be limited and incomplete because pre-crisis ecosystem baseline data does not exist. Second, uncertainty enters into the discussion of the ecological crisis in terms of our limited ability to forecast and predict future effects when dealing with complex phenomena (or, in the case of the ecological crisis, a doubly complex phenomenon). We will never have the necessary accuracy in data and precision in methods to make error-free predictions of complex phenomena such as climate change and ecosystem collapse, as these will always involve long and complicated causal chains, non-linear effects and feedback loops. As such, as mentioned in Chapter 2, in light of the recognition of our limitations in data and methods, we are led to the sobering conclusion that the full magnitude of the effects of the ecological crisis will remain largely unknown. Acknowledging these existing challenges and limitations to environmental management – that is, dealing with complexity, uncertainty and limits to technical knowledge – we suggest that one possible way forward in establishing an alternative foundation for environmental management would be to incorporate the insights from the "post-normal science" perspective and "black swan" thinking. Notably, both of these perspectives are sensitive to issues of uncertainty, complexity and the limitations of knowledge in different ways. We will deal with "black swan" thinking in the next chapter, but for the present we will focus on "post-normal science". As we shall see, one of the main advantages of the latter approach is that it brings to light the normative context in which environmental management takes place. The normative context is very important to consider with reference to environmental management because it is in this context that the political, economic, social and cultural forces pertaining to the ecological crisis play out.

Post-Normal Science

Post-normal science was originally formulated and proposed by Functowicz and Ravetz (1991) as a problem-solving framework for the field of ecological economics. The approach has since evolved to apply to all situations involving issue-driven science – notably, those situations unfolding at the interface of science and policy. Typically, such situations are characterized by circumstances in which the facts are uncertain, values are in dispute, the political and social stakes of the decisions are high, and decisions are to be made in a somewhat urgent manner (Functowicz and Ravetz, 2003: 1). Post-normal science arises as a response to the limitations of the use of traditional science in environmental decision-making. Traditional science, as found in research science, professional practice or industrial development, is based on controlled experimentation, quantification and the building of abstract theory. Such science, it is argued, is problematic when applied to the domain of environmental decision-making because:

> This situation is a novel one for policy makers. In one sense issues of environment and sustainability are in the domain of science: the phenomena of concern are located in the world of nature. Yet the tasks are totally different from those traditionally conceived for Western science. For that, it was a matter of conquest and control of Nature; now we must manage, accommodate and adjust.
> (Functowicz and Ravetz, 2003: 2)

In some ways, then, post-normal science is reminiscent of the previously expressed need to blend the natural and the social dimensions of the ecological crisis, as raised and discussed in earlier chapters. But with post-normal science another dimension is brought into the mix in a more explicit way. Scientific knowledge and approaches in environmental decision-making must take into account and with systems that are inherently complex. Moreover, under the conditions of uncertainty, complexity and limitations of knowledge, there can be no single privileged point of view for measurement, analysis and evaluation of knowledge (ibid.). As we shall see, traditional science cannot do justice to phenomena that lie at the intersection of life, society and the environment because the reductionist approach of traditional science is not appropriate for the analysis, characterization and understanding of complex systems phenomena – a position that would likely be supported by ecological thinkers who often adopt a systems (as opposed to reductionist) perspective for that very reason. On the basis of this rationale, Functowicz and Ravetz call for a different type of science – namely, "post-normal science".

The term "normal" in the phrase "post-normal science" is used in two senses, each referring to a different but related type of "normality". The first meaning is based on Thomas Kuhn's (1962) work in the history and sociology of science. According to the perspective developed by Kuhn, significant advances in sciences only occur if there first exists some pressing scientific anomaly that cannot be resolved on the basis of applying the existing methods and approaches of what Kuhn calls "normal science". Normal science refers to the regular and routine activities of laboratory science (e.g. theorizing, observing and experimentation) that are carried out in accordance with the guiding principles laid out by the prevailing explanatory framework. As such, with normal science, findings slowly accumulate and add supportive detail to the general theory that has already been accepted through consensus by the scientific community (referred to as a "paradigm" by Kuhn). The paradigm serves as the theoretical scaffolding under which the regular working activities of normal science is guided. The paradigm guides the routine working activities of scientists and frames the problems or puzzles that scientists endeavor to solve through their research. Explanatory weaknesses in the paradigm become evident when contradictory findings continually accumulate over time, until the point is reached that they cannot be ignored. Consequently, the existing paradigm increasingly becomes recognized by some within the given scientific community as being inadequate in terms of serving as the foundation for guiding normal science activities. At that point there is a realization that there is a need to find an alternative paradigm to account for the accumulating weight of non-explained anomalous findings. If a major break-through occurs, and a plausible and tested alternative paradigm is proposed and accepted, a revolution in the scientific community will occur as the new all-encompassing theory will come to supplant the old paradigm because of its better explanatory power. Such a paradigm shift is seen, for instance, when classical Newtonian mechanics became supplanted by quantum mechanics and wave/particle duality in order to explain the dynamics of subatomic particles.

According to Functowicz and Ravetz (1991), the degree to which there exists uncertainty and the level of sociopolitical stakes involved with the decisions pertaining to the science being used leads to distinctly different situations (see Figure 10.1) For example, in the case of research science done in a university laboratory, the theoretical emphasis of such science means that it carries little in the way of political stakes at the moment. The research findings will simply further theoretical knowledge with little implications for the broader society. The uncertainty involved in this type of science will also be low, owing to the controlled conditions demanded by experimental design in the laboratory setting. This situation of low uncertainty coupled with low stakes is referred to in Figure 10.1 as "Applied Science", but we can think of this as "normal science" in the Kuhnian sense. In contrast, when dealing with the science involved in environmental impact

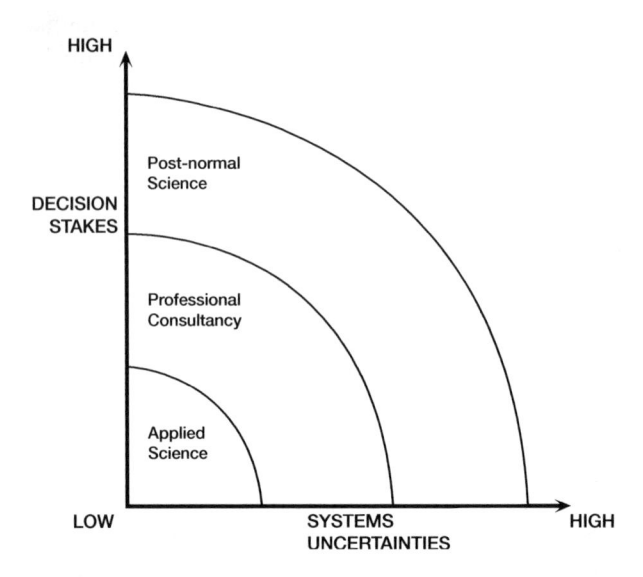

FIGURE 10.1 The Relationship between Decision Stake and Systems Uncertainties

Source: François DM, own work, CC B-SA 3.0, https://commons.wikimedia.org/w/index?curid=16042041

assessment, for instance, the uncertainty is often very high because of the need to deal with large and complex ecosystems and social systems. Since the environmental impact decisions will have consequences for many in the community, the political stakes are also very high. This situation of very high uncertainty coupled with very high stakes refers to the situation of post-normal science. Professional consultancy refers to the intermediate range of moderate uncertainty and stakes, and includes, for instance, the work of medical clinicians.

For Functowicz and Ravetz (2003), the normal science of the laboratory is simply not suitable or up to the task of dealing with environmental problems because the type of science employed in the decision-making will almost always be associated with a great deal of systems uncertainty that is coupled with a high level of associated political and social stakes. For instance, decisions pertaining to the establishment of environmental regulations or actions for environmental remediation are based on much uncertainty due to the very nature of dealing with complex social and ecological systems. Yet, decisions based on risk assessment do go forward because of the urgent need for environmental regulations or remedial action to address the problem to the extent possible under the existing ways of and approaches to managing environmental problems. At the same time, the political and social stakes are high, as evidenced by the frequent controversies that arise in such situations where industry, the state and environmental groups clash over the appropriateness, strictness or laxity of the environmental regulation or action being proposed. As such, there is always a normative context associated with environmental management, despite technocratic claims to scientific "objectivity" and political neutrality.

Another illustration of how normal science may fail in the service of addressing the ecological crisis is the example of global climate change. As mentioned in Chapter 7, the types of natural systems involved in the climate phenomenon are almost unfathomable – global systems of ocean currents, wind patterns, atmospheric systems, hydraulic systems, materials cycles, and so on. The number of variables to be considered and the amount of data to be compiled to characterize such systems are overwhelming. The challenge becomes even more formidable if one needs to consider the interactions between multiple global ecological systems as, for instance, required in forecasting the effects of climate change. The complexity is further multiplied if one considers the interactions of these natural systems with the social systems – again, a must for climate change scientists who are trying to demonstrate how human decisions to intervene in nature have contributed to anthropomorphic climate change and the possible societal responses to such. At the same time, even though uncertainties exist when dealing with such complex systems, as discussed in Chapter 7, this does not undermine or invalidate the scientific conclusions reached about global climate change.

The political and social stakes in the decisions pertaining to climate change are very high, and it is for this reason that we can account for the proliferation of political disputes and controversies involved in reaching international agreements on limiting carbon contributions. The full-scale active mobilization and involvement of the large number of players beyond the nation state politicians, such as industry representatives and environmental movement groups, is also revealing of the magnitude and far-reaching qualities of the social and political stakes involved in decisions related to addressing climate change. In contrast, such controversy does not arise in the case of the research laboratory science setting of normal science, where, as was mentioned above, the controlled conditions of the experiment reduce uncertainty in explanation, and the political and social stakes of the relatively obscure research being conducted are not very high.

The term "normal" in "post-normal" also refers to the continuing influence and unquestioned understanding and confidence in the idea that the routine problem-solving that constitutes the lifeblood of normal science will provide an adequate knowledge base for environmental decision-making in the policy context. That is, it is thought that, in an unquestioned and uncritical way, conventional science can be used and applied in the "normal" way in the context of environmental policy-making and decision-making context. In this light, what post-normal science proposes essentially lies outside the expert-based investigative processes which have been defined by scientists as "normal" (Waltner-Toews and Wall, 1997). More precisely, post-normal science is seen to be outside what conventional science defines as normal because post-normal science takes into account complexity, uncertainty and decision stakes. One prominent way that post-normal science seeks to incorporate these types of factors is through the rejection of the conventionally held idea of "value-free" science. By doing so, post-normal science brings together "facts" and "values" into a unified conception of problem solving – an emphasis that is reinforced by replacing "truth" by "quality" as the core evaluative concept for the science involved in environmental management (ibid.: 4). By adopting the post-normal science perspective, environmental problem solving becomes open to the incorporation of the plurality of legitimate perspectives with a focus on dialogue, and on mutual respect and learning.

Funtowicz and Ravetz (2003) note that different types of normal science have established different means for ensuring quality control for the respective products of their work. For instance, for the assurance of quality, research science uses peer review, professional practice is subject to the standards of their professional association, and industrial development is subject to the market. For the case of the science employed in environmental management, however, they argue that ensuring quality depends on an open dialogue with all those affected by the environmental impacts. Notably, those affected in the context of environmental problems will usually involve a much larger number of people as part of what Funtowicz and Ravetz refer to as the "extended peer community" (2003: 7). This enlarged grouping will consist not only of individuals with some form of institutional accreditation, but rather all stakeholders who wish to participate in the resolution of the environmental problem in question. As Waltner-Toews and Wall (1997) note, environmental problems often necessitate the involvement of a large number of people because such problems extend over large spatial and temporal scales, thereby affecting many more and different types of people. This involvement does not refer to just a change in quantity (i.e. involving a greater number of people), but to a qualitative shift in orientation whereby members of the community are viewed as legitimate participants and peers in the investigative and evaluative processes. Significant movement in that direction has already started to become formally institutionalized. At this time, such initiatives have taken different forms, or are at least referred to by different labels, such as multi-stakeholder consultation (Ali, 1997, 1999), citizen science (Irwin, 1995), post-positivism (Fischer, 2000), the democratization of science (Beck, 1992), and in the realm of environmental health, popular epidemiology (Brown, 1992, 1997). As we shall see, post-normal science, by emphasizing a place for different and often competing values at the table of environmental decision-making, opens up the governance process, thereby enabling the possibility for more critical and innovativ approaches to enter into the discussion.

Post-Normal Science and Bridging the Social and Natural

Post-normal science could be construed as a practical response to the previously discussed need of blending the natural and the social in analysis and approach. Other than the considerable analytical benefits of bridging the natural and social in understanding environmental problems (as emphasized in Chapters 6 through 9), one particularly important benefit in adopting a post-normal science perspective in environmental management is the infusion of a normative element in the problem-solving process. Paul Robbins (2012) notes that ecological science thus far tends to be "apolitical ecology" in that ecology willfully ignores the role of politics in shaping the natural world. The consequence of such a framing is that it encourages the notion that human impact on the environment can only be understood in ecological terms. This apolitical ecology position directly opposes the view of post-normal science and environmental and disaster sociology, which emphasize the need to consider how environmental impacts are the result of human decision-making and larger social structures. In other words, the latter perspectives challenge the notion held by many environmental managers that environmental matters are purely "technical" matters that can be solved by the natural sciences alone. In contrast, post-normal science and critical social science enable and encourage thinking about the social and institutional origins of the ecological crisis – the latter emphasis being a point we have stressed throughout this monograph. Moreover, by allowing for critical perspectives to enter into the discussion, post-normal science better facilitates the rejection of shallow explanations of environmental problems. For instance, as Young (2015) notes with reference to the critical perspective of political ecology, rather than accepting that the ecological crisis is caused by blanket conditions such as "overpopulation", post-normal science allows researchers to probe deeper by considering issues such as who controls the resource, how it is used, and what impact it has on other potential users.

Post-Positivism

As mentioned in Chapter 1, it is helpful to think of environmental management as an integral component existing within an overall framework of environmental governance. In this context, post-normal science serves as a conduit to bring issues of governance into the fold of environmental management. That is, post-normal science represents an orienting strategy for environmental management that would help bring issues of environmental governance to the fore. Also recall from Chapter 1 that the success of environmental governance is measured by the degree to which the governance strategy in question fosters dialogue, debate and collaboration among stakeholders. Governance and the issues associated with it constitute central elements of an approach closely allied with post-normal science – namely, post-positivism. Originally, political scientist Frank Fischer (2000) introduced the notion of post-positivism as a critique of existing approaches in the policy sciences. He begins by questioning the fundamental positivist principle of separating facts and values. In arguing that it is not possible to separate facts and values, Fischer goes on to reject the positivist idea that it is possible for empirical research to proceed independently of the normative context or the normative implications involved therein. Especially problematic for Fischer was his assessment that policy science, by actively encouraging the separation of facts and values, had at the same time actively encouraged the adoption of a decidedly technocratic form of policy analysis (and we would add governance) that emphasized efficiency as the only criterion that need be considered in decision-making. That is, important value debates became eliminated in the decision-making process as the emphasis switched solely to the most efficient means of achieving politically pre-established goals.

Consequently, policy analysis devolved into the process of translating inherently normative political and social issues into technically defined ends to be pursued through administrative means. This was problematic because in the effort to evade the type of goal-value conflicts that frequently arose in dealing with policy, economic and social problems, the complex issues involved were reduced and simplified in ways that were amenable to simple adjustments in management and program design. Such approaches would not directly address the core of the problems being discussed. As such, the solutions posed tended to rely on the technical application of generic and prescriptive administrative approaches developed within the policy sciences of the day (Amy, 1987). Reflecting a subtle antipathy towards democratic processes, terms such as "pressures" and "expedient adjustments" were used to denigrate pluralistic policy-making. This led to the adoption of a view in which Fischer notes, was based on the idea that, "If the politics doesn't fit into the methodological scheme, then politics is the problem" (1998: 131).

As mentioned in Chapter 1, citizens and environmental groups are often skeptical or ambivalent about the narrowly defined schemes of environmental management, giving them relatively less significance and often viewing them as simply one element involved in the complex puzzle of environmental governance. One of the key reasons for this, we contend, is precisely because of the limitations of the technocratic approach discussed above. The technocratic approach that informs much of conventional environmental management is exclusionary, in the sense that "experts" retain exclusive control over the analysis of environmental data and decision-making. This is especially unacceptable to a critically minded constituency, which, on the basis of past experiences, frequently feels that expert professionals are less dedicated to the public good than the goal of increasing their own authority, power and wealth. This is a reasonable and understandable concern given, for instance, the role that the fossil fuel industry with all its wealth and power plays in framing how the climate change issue is viewed and treated (see Chapter 7). As such, as an alternative approach that opens up decision-making, Fischer (2000) proposes a post-positivist orientation to approaching environmental problems.

Of central importance to environmental governance practice based on a post-positivist orientation is an emphasis on participatory inquiry and local knowledge. The adoption of this type of orientation is meant to give citizens and policy-makers an equal voice in the deliberations pertaining to an environmental problem or policy. In this context, an important aspect of the post-positivist orientation is that it enables "cultural rationality" to enter into the environmental management and governance process (Fischer, 2000: 123). Cultural rationality refers to the distinctive type of reasoning that lay individuals use in assessing the nature and risks of the environmental problems they confront. Notably, the reasoning process embodied in cultural rationality is very different from the perspectives adopted by the technocratic experts. The latter tends to use a more narrowly defined technical rationality often informed exclusively by quantitative assessments. One of the major shortcomings of this narrow approach is that it tends to focus only on the technical issues related to environmental decision-making (particularly risk assessment), thus shifting the political ground and debate on risk to simply the search for "acceptable risk" (Fischer, 2000: 126). In other words, technocratic environmental management and governance renders an uncritical approach to environmental matters and narrows the scope of vision instead of opening it up to broader concerns. In contrast, the infusion of cultural rationality into the decision-making process may open things up. Once cultural rationality is given due respect and credence and allowed to enter into deliberations, it should help bring forth a better and more satisfactory environmental governance framework.

In contrast to the formal and impersonal nature of technocratic rationality and its emphasis on depersonalized technical calculations, cultural rationality is informed by personal experience, local knowledge and the unique level of familiarity the individual or community has with the risk or environmental problem in question (Ali, 2003). As such, cultural rationality is based on a much broader approach to environmental problems and incorporates non-technical considerations such as accountability, personal values and trust (Powell and Leiss, 1997: 10). In this context, Fischer notes that cultural rationality is informed by the circumstances "under which the risk is identified and publicized, the standing or place of the individual in his or her community, and the social values of the community as a whole" (2000: 132). Thus, for example, by viewing developments through the lens of cultural rationality, citizens would like to know how environmental decision-making conclusions were reached, whose interests were at stake, who is responsible and what protection would be provided if something goes wrong – it is these types of questions and the answers to them that would inform cultural rationality (Fischer, 2000: 137). The rationality used by citizens in approaching environmental problems is therefore based on social processes unfolding in the particular context that they are involved in. For instance, one can see cultural rationality at work when citizens are distrustful of the evidence presented by industry representatives in the aftermath of a contamination event, or the arguments made by climate change deniers. The citizens' past experiences have often led to a situation where they are skeptical, thus compelling them to act on the basis of such experiential knowledge. This is an understandably rational course of action – indeed, not to do so would in fact be irrational under these social and political circumstances.

Within existing conventional and technocratically informed environmental management approaches, cultural rationality is viewed as an impediment to adopting "objective" strategies to deal with an environmental problem. In this light, many technical experts see the involvement of more people as merely clogging up the process. But as Fischer (2000: 42) notes, these types of objections fail to recognize or give proper credence to the insights of cultural rationality, and especially the importance of cultural rationality to drawing attention to considerations that normal science has failed to appreciate. In other words, the culturally rational assessments of the environmental problem are not "irrational" or based on "ignorance" as the experts are apt to claim. Rather, cultural rationality relates to a different part of the problem that experts have neglected.

The infusion of cultural rationality in environmental decision-making has implications for better environmental governance practices. This is because the incorporation of cultural rationality into environmental decision-making would mean that the ways in which citizens may object to the very way in which the environmental problem is defined and framed by technical experts and government officials would have to be taken into account in the deliberative process (Fischer, 2000: 129). For example, some environmental problems may have as much to do with local politics about land use as they do with biophysical impacts and safety per se. By recognizing and accepting cultural rationality as a legitimate aspect of the process, environmental management and governance expand the scope for involvement. Notably, this would allow space for the involvement of environmental justice groups who are not only interested in pursuing environmental improvement but also enacting sociocultural transformations and societal restructuring to deal with the ecological crisis writ large. As Fisher (2000: 121) notes, as opposed to conventional approaches that focus mainly on the environment in external physical terms, the environmental justice movement conceptualizes environmental degradation in terms of the links between the physical degradation and other social and political problems, particularly in relation to how they manifest themselves in the daily realities and condition of people's daily lives. With this emphasis, we again see a return to an effort to bridge the natural and the social with the possibility for more critical discussions to enter into the decision-making. As such, what is notable about the expanded scope and, in particular, the opportunity for the involvement of environmental justice groups, is that the critique of society may form part of the deliberations, thereby enabling a broader and more critical discussion of the ecological crisis to be taken up within the environmental management context. Such broader discussion may in turn enable discussion of how environmental problems are linked together, vis-à-vis the ecological crisis and living in a high-carbon society – discussions that are notably absent in current environmental management approaches.

Concluding Remarks

A key element of environmental management in the contemporary era involves issues pertaining to the broader domain of environmental governance. The conventional technocratic approach to environmental management would hold that the activities of environmental management are solely technical in nature, in that they are focused on purely natural phenomena that are best studied exclusively in terms of the natural sciences. For this reason, the technocratic approaches argue that environmental management is scientifically objective and politically neutral. In other words, according to the technocratic approach, environmental management has little to do with environmental governance and the separation of experts who make decisions about environmental problems from those affected by the environmental problems should be retained, lest the situation be "contaminated" by politics through lay involvement. Advocates of post-normal science and post-positivism argue the opposite – namely, that since the ecological crisis and the environmental problems that contribute to the overall crisis are so complex and multidimensional, involving the consideration of issues at the intersection of nature and society, and dealing with serious limitations of knowledge, and with so much at stake, the decision-making process, they contend, can no longer be the exclusive preserve of technical experts.

Several social developments over the past few decades have paved the way for the opening up of space for post-normal science and post-positivism. As Ulrich Beck (1992) has noted in his risk society thesis, the limitations and failings of scientific analysis to effectively deal with environmental problems have increasingly become known to the public as competing technical claims regarding a particular environmental problem are aired in the public and covered by the media. Thus, according to Beck, in the past, science was acknowledged as the great demystifier of the Enlightenment tradition in that it replaced religion as the explanatory authority of our day. With greater awareness of the limitations of science to deal with environmental risk issues, science as the great demystifier has itself become demystified in the eyes of the public. As part of this demystification, science and technical experts have lost their privileged or monopoly position in environmental decision-making. This is part of a larger trend in declining deference given to professionals more generally, as seen, for example, by the proliferation of lay experts who are prepared to engage in technical debates in public and political fora (especially through their involvement in environmental non-governmental organizations). It is at this juncture that post-normal science and post-positivism takes hold and enters into environmental management deliberations.

Post-normal science and post-positivism are not simply about the use of science in environmental management and environmental governance. Rather, these approaches represent a "foot-in-the-door" that enables formally institutionalized opportunity structures to develop and foster a broader process and context in which the philosophical orientation of environmental management may be rethought. Specifically, this reorientation would take things in a more critical direction that would enable the critique of the existing social order. Notably, such a critique would include a greater receptivity to the consideration of environmental management strategies that would de-emphasize individual profit-maximization and bolster an emphasis on collective well-being and the environment.

In grappling with the limitations and uncertainties that are inherently part of the environmental management, post-normal science and post-positivism direct attention to the normative dimension of environmental governance. In the next chapter, we will consider the "black swan" approach to conceptualizing environmental problems. As we shall see, such an approach also engages with the limitations and uncertainties that arise in environmental management, but its emphasis is more on the analytical rather than the normative basis of environmental and disaster management.

References

Ali, S.H. (1997) "Trust, Risk, and the Public: The Case of the Guelph Landfill Search". *Canadian Journal of Sociology*, 22(4): 481–504.

Ali, S.H. (1999) "The Search for a Landfill Site in the Risk Society". *The Canadian Review of Sociology and Anthropology*, 36(1): 1–19.

Ali, S.H. (2003) "Dealing With Toxicity in the Risk Society: The Case of the Hamilton, Ontario Plastics Recycling Fire". *The Canadian Review of Sociology and Anthropology*, 39(1): 29–48.

Amy, D. (1987) "Can Policy Analysis be Ethical?" In F. Fisher and J. Forester (Eds.) *Confronting Values in Policy Analysis*. Newbury Park, CA: Sage, pp. 45–67.

Beck, U. (1992) *Risk Society: Towards a New Modernity*. London: Sage.

Bhagwati, J. (2007) *In Defense of Globalization* (2nd ed.). New York: Oxford University Press.

Brown, P. (1992) "Toxic Waste Contamination and Popular Epidemiology: Lay and Professional Ways of Knowing". *Journal of Health and Social Behavior*, 33: 267–281.

Brown, P. (1997) "Popular Epidemiology Revisited". *Current Sociology*, 45(3): 137–156.

Byrne, D. (1998) *Complexity Theory and the Social Sciences: An Introduction*. London: Routledge.

Catton, W. R., Jr. and Dunlap, R.E. (1980) "A New Ecological Paradigm for Post-exuberant Sociology". *American Behavioral Scientist*, 2: 15–47.

Fischer, F. (1998) "Beyond Empiricism: Policy Inquiry in Postpositivist Perspective". *Policy Studies Journal*, 26(1): 129–146.

Fischer, F. (2000) *Citizens, Experts, and the Environment: The Politics of Local Knowledge*. Durham, NC: Duke University Press.

Funtowicz. S. and Ravetz, J.R. (1991) "A New Scientific Methodology for Global Environmental Issues". In R. Costanza (ed.) *The Ecological Economics*. New York: Columbia University Press, pp. 137–152.

Funtowicz S. and Ravetz, J.R. (1993) "Science for the Post-Normal Age". *Futures*, 25: 735–755.

Funtowicz, S. O. and Ravetz, J.R. (2003) "Post-Normal Science". *International Society for Ecological Economics: Internet Encyclopaedia of Ecological Economics*. Available at: http://isecoeco.org/pdf/pstnormsc.pdf (last accessed April 27, 2016).

Irwin, A. (1995) *Citizen Science: A Study of People, Expertise and Sustainable Development*. New York: Routledge.

Kuhn, T. (1962) *The Structure of Scientific Revolutions*. Chicago: University of Chicago Press.

Newell, P. (2011) "The Elephant in the Room: Capitalism and Global Environmental Change". *Global Environmental Change*, 21: 4–6.

Powell, D. and Leiss, W. (1997) *Mad Cows and Mother's Milk: The Perils of Poor Risk Communication*. Kingston: McGill-Queen's University Press.

Robbins, P. (2012) *Political Ecology* (2nd ed.). Malden, MA: Wiley-Blackwell.

Waltner-Toews, D. and Wall, E. (1997) "Emergent Perplexity: In Search of Post-Normal Questions for Community and Agroecosystem Health". *Social Science and Medicine*, 45: 1741–1749.

Young, N. (2015) *Environmental Sociology for the Twenty-First Century*. Don Mills: Oxford University Press.

11
TOWARDS A PHILOSOPHICAL REORIENTATION IN ENVIRONMENTAL MANAGEMENT II

Black Swan Thinking

Recall that in our previous chapters we have discussed how the conventional environmental orientation is largely ineffective in addressing the ecological crisis for several reasons. Here we will focus on two of these reasons: the inherent complexity of environmental problems and the related problem of uncertainty and incomplete knowledge. Environmental phenomena involve the functioning of complex systems. For this reason, the influences of complex system mechanisms and attributes such as positive feedback cycles, networks, chaos and non-linear effects must be taken into account in developing sound environmental management strategies. These influences, however, make the complete characterization of environmental systems challenging, if at all possible in the first place. That is, we face a situation of irreducible uncertainty due to the very nature of environmental phenomena. Recall also that the necessity of having to contend with incomplete data pertaining to environmental phenomena is due in part to the magnitude and complexity of environmental problems, which requires innumerable variables to be identified and incorporated into analysis, and because ecological baseline data are not available after the fact – that is, during the post-impact period when it is too late to attain baseline data. Furthermore, as alluded to in our previous discussions, the level of complexity and the degrees of uncertainty multiply when we adopt a more holistic approach that takes into account the socio-ecological basis of the ecological crisis. This is because both social and natural variables (not to mention the interactions between these two sets of variables) would then need to be factored into the account. How, then, can we move towards the development of a philosophical reorientation of environmental management that takes into account these types of formidable limitations?

In this chapter, we consider approaches that are beginning to explicitly engage with the challenges arising from issues pertaining to uncertainty, complexity, surprise, and limitations of knowledge. The first of these is the "anticipatory surprise" approach, which is a more managerial perspective that, as we shall see, has much in common with the existing disaster management approaches reviewed in Chapter 8. This approach is, however, notably quite different from existing disaster management approaches in that anticipatory surprise management brings to the fore issues related to uncertainty and unexpectedness. The theme of uncertainty and incompleteness of knowledge is taken up at a more philosophical level in the "black swan" theory of Naseem Taleb (2010). We will conclude by making the argument that both these types of approaches may serve as a conceptual and philosophical foundation to reorient conventional environmental management in ways that are perhaps better suited to dealing with the current state of the ecological crisis.

The "Anticipatory Surprise Management" Perspective

In our rapidly globalizing, increasingly networked, highly mobile and fluid world, qualitatively new and different types of challenges arise in many different domains of social life (Ali, 2012; Ali and Keil, 2008). Notably, the present context in which we exist can be described as being informed by social and environmental forces related to hyperchange, hypercomplexity and an "unknowable world", which in turn demand new ways of thinking and a new mind-set to understand and situate our current state of affairs (Stacey, 1992). Writing in reference to the field of public administration and disaster management, Ali Farazmand (2007) notes that the key question for governance in the contemporary era becomes, how do we cope with "inconceivability and hyper-uncertainty"? That is, how do we deal with challenges that are "inconceivable" (Dror, 2001), "unthinkable" (Handy, 1998) and "unknowable" (Stacey, 1992)? In response, Farazmand (2007) proposes the perspective of "anticipatory surprise management" as a way to make improvements within the field of emergency governance and disaster management that take into account such features of the contemporary world. As we have discussed in Chapter 8, disaster management and environmental management have much in common in terms of approach and subject matter (especially in the context of the ecological crisis), and we would thus argue the philosophy behind anticipatory surprise management will also be useful for environmental management in terms of dealing with the particular challenges outlined above.

In a world characterized by hyperchange, hypercomplexity and an "unknowable world", especially where non-linear developments and tipping points result in small fluctuations that lead to dramatic and abrupt eruptions of system instability, Farazmand (2007: 156) argues that traditional disaster and emergency management techniques are no longer useful. As a corrective, therefore, new approaches, such as anticipatory surprise management, would be based on preparing for an unknowable world. This could be pursued through the utilization of state-of-the-art knowledge of non-linear systems coupled with training specifically designed to develop crisis expertise with inconceivability (or "worst case") scenarios. Farazmand (2007: 157) notes that foreign policy expert Charles Hermann some time ago noted that "surprise" may be the "most commanding dimension of uncertainty" (1969: 2).

In turn, uncertainty, as we have alluded to above, is a key characteristic of complex non-linear systems wherein there inevitably exists the presence of a large number of inconceivables and unexpecteds that surprise everyone (Farazmand, 2007: 157). For Farazmand, the impact of the surprise element could be lessened if there was some built-in capacity for dealing with chaos and surprise in advance. This anticipatory surprise management capacity would have to be integrated into governance and public administration structures, otherwise, "the lack of such capacity building – planning, preparation, response flexibilities, and so on – will surely lead to a total paralysis in the face of surprise" (ibid.). To help address these limitations, Farazmand (2007: 157) suggests a number of principles that surprise management could be based upon. Among these are:

1. the rejection of anything that is routine and expected, and by extension linear and predictable causal behaviors;
2. the adoption of a management approach that is not rigid, but rather, is fluid, with a degree of flexibility and adaptability;
3. the incorporation of cutting-edge knowledge, skills and attitudes beyond the comprehension of most people in routine settings of governance and administration.

Although Farazmand's work on anticipatory surprise management seems to have been developed independently of the work of Naseem Taleb (2010) on the theory of black swans, there is some conceptual continuity between the two works. Notably, though, anticipatory surprise management entails a meso approach to dealing with the administration and management of disasters as compared to Taleb's much broader philosophical sweep that is not limited simply to disasters. It is towards the latter that we now turn.

The Black Swan Perspective

As an analyst involved in derivatives trading, Naseem Taleb was interested in the question of how risk was managed in the financial sector and how improbable events affect the market. The scope of the analysis has since expanded into a general theory concerning the nature of improbable events, particularly those with high impacts – events he refers to as "black swan events". In his book *The Black Swan: The Impact of the Highly Improbable*, Taleb (2010) introduces the notion of the black swan event by discussing a particular historical circumstance. Specifically, he notes that prior to the discovery of black swans in eighteenth-century Australia, Europeans mistakenly assumed that all swans were white and that a black swan simply did not exist. The black swan was outside the normal experience and expectation of Europeans in that era. Thus, in this context, Taleb (2010: xxii) refers to the "black swan" as a metaphor for a rare event that falls beyond the realm of normal expectation, and for this reason the black swan event can be considered as a type of outlier. Black swan events cannot be predicted with any precision.

Taleb summarizes the three qualities of the black swan event as rarity, extreme impact, and retrospective (though not prospective) predictability. He gives the examples of the terrorist attacks of September 11, 2001, power grid failure, the dramatic rise of the Internet, and rapid climate change, as illustrations of the black swan phenomena. Elaborating on the notion of the black swan, Curry (2011) notes that the theory of black swan events can be used to help explain and deal with certain types of situations that are characterized by the following features. First, it is useful in analyzing situations where a psychological bias blinds people to uncertainty, thus rendering them unaware of the massive role that rare events play in historical affairs. Second, the theory of black swans is applicable to rare event situations that are hard to predict and beyond normal expectations in history, science, finance and technology, but that nevertheless have a high impact on our existence. And third, the theory is particularly well suited to situations where there is an inherent inability in calculating the probability of black swan events with any precision based on current scientific methods.

In discussing the first point concerning psychological bias, Taleb states that a noteworthy aspect of the black swan event is that there is nothing in the past that can convincingly point to even the possibility of the future black swan event. That is, using the swans in Europe example, the cumulative evidence based on seeing only white swans in their day-to-day experience served to reinforce the conclusion for Europeans that the only type of swans that existed were white. That is, on the basis of experience there was no evidence from the past that would lead people to even consider the possibility that a black swan could exist. In fact, it would lead people to the opposite conclusion. The tendency to interpret cumulative evidence in only one exclusive way – that is, of only supporting the predetermined conclusion – has been identified by cognitive scientists as a certain type of psychological phenomenon. Specifically, this natural tendency to look only for corroboration results in a vulnerability to corroboration error known as "confirmation bias" (ibid.: 58). Notably, one implication of confirmation bias is that it may result in a blindness to impending black swan events. That is, the tendency to focus on collaborative evidence leads to a focus on certain preselected aspects of the observed phenomenon, but we use only that "evidence" to generalize from that to the unseen:

> Once your mind is inhabited with a certain view of the world, you will tend to only consider instances proving you to be right. We look for instances that confirm our story and vision of the world, and these instances tend to be easier to find.
>
> (Taleb, 2010: 55)

> Paradoxically, the more information you have, the more justified you will feel in your views.
>
> (Taleb, 2010: 59)

As a result, we run the danger of succumbing to confirmation bias by testing a rule by only looking at instances where the rule works. Taleb points out, however, that another approach to testing a rule is through an indirect approach – that is, by focusing on where the rule does not work – in other words, by looking for disconfirming instances. For Taleb, this latter approach is far more powerful in establishing the truth, but we tend not to be aware of this property:

> We can get closer to the truth by negative instances, not by verification! It is misleading to build a general rule from the observed facts. Contrary to conventional wisdom, our body of knowledge does not increase from a series of confirmatory observations . . . But there are some things I can remain skeptical about, and others I can safely consider certain. This makes the consequences of observations one-sided. It is not much more difficult than that. This asymmetry is immensely practical. It tells us that we do not have to be complete skeptics, just semiskeptics.
> (Taleb, 2010: 56)

Another consequence of what Taleb considers as an excessive focus on what we do know is that we "tend to learn the precise, not the general" (ibid.: xxv). This contributes to the development of another logical flaw when thinking about black swan events.

To gain an understanding and explanation of events in our complex world, Taleb argues that we often automatically attempt to find a pattern or fit a story to a series of connected or disconnected facts – we have a predilection for compact stories over raw truths. Consequently, the stories that we derive may not actually represent the reality we are observing. In other words, we are vulnerable to over-interpretation that severely distorts our mental representation of the world – a predicament that becomes particularly acute when dealing with rare events (ibid.: 63). This is referred to by Taleb as the "narrative fallacy":

> The narrative fallacy addresses our limited ability to look at sequences of facts without weaving an explanation into them, or, equivalently, forcing a logical link, an *arrow of relationship*, upon them. Explanations bind facts together. They make them all the more easily remembered; they help them *make more sense*. Where this propensity can go wrong is when it increases our *impression* of understanding.
> (Taleb, 2010: 64)

The narrative fallacy follows, therefore, from the fact that despite the status of a black swan event as an outlier, human nature compels us to concoct an explanation for its occurrence *after* the fact, which in turn renders the phenomenon explainable and predictable for us (Taleb, 2010: xxii). This leads to retrospective distortion and is the reason why "history seems clearer and more organized in history books than in empirical reality" (ibid.: 8) and why "we fool ourselves with stories and anecdotes" (ibid.: 2). Further, as a consequence of the narrative fallacy, we tend to think we know what is going on in a world that is actually much more complicated (or random) than we realize. Due to the ongoing and significant influence of confirmation bias and the narrative fallacy, Taleb argues that as a society we behave as if black swan events do not exist – that is, human nature is not programmed to deal with such events. This can, however, be corrected through conscious effort, and to do so will have a profound influence on how we conceptualize the ecological crisis and our environmental strategies designed to deal with it.

Dealing with Uncertainty and Unknowns

The black swan event is an asymmetric perceptual outcome because one can never know the unknown since, by definition, it is unknown. As such, a central tenet of Taleb's book is that since black swan events are unpredictable, we need to adjust to their existence, rather than naively trying to predict them (Taleb, 2010: xxv). In other words, calculating the probabilities of black swan events is not possible, but coming to an idea of the impacts of such events are considerably easier to ascertain (2010: 210). As Taleb notes, we can still have a clear idea of the consequences of black swan events despite not knowing how likely they are to occur. For instance, we may not know with any certainty the probability of an earthquake, but we can certainly gain some idea of how a city might be affected by one. For Taleb (2010: 211), then, "[the] idea that in order to make a decision you need to focus on the consequences (which you can know) rather than the probability (which you can't know) is the *central idea of uncertainty*". Notably, for the purposes at hand, we can use this insight to think about how approaches to environmental management decision-making and strategy could be reoriented to take into account uncertainty. Attempts at such a reorientation are, in fact, beginning to be found in other domains of social life. For instance, writing in relation to the world of business, Lehmann (2007) explores how black swan theory can help companies strategically position themselves to deal more effectively with the effects of improbable events.

In considering the utility of black swan theory in the field of technical risk assessment and engineering, Aven (2015) begins his discussion by adopting a more general definition of a black swan event. He conceptualizes a black swan event in terms that are a function of, and relative to, one's existing knowledge and beliefs. On this basis he distinguishes between three different types of situations that may arise with reference to black swan events. These are situations involving: (1) unknown unknowns, (2) unknown knowns (we do not have the knowledge but others do) and, (3) events that are judged to have a negligible probability of occurrence and thus leading to the belief that they will not occur. As an example of a situation of unknown unknowns Aven (2015) refers to the thalidomide drug tragedy. In this situation, pregnant women in the mid-1950s were given thalidomide to alleviate morning sickness, but the children born of those taking this drug were tragically found to have abnormal developments of their limbs. The scientific community was simply not aware of this possibility. The second situation, that involving unknown knowns, arises when events are not captured by the relevant risk assessments, either because experts did not know them, or because they did not give them a sufficiently thorough consideration. Under these circumstances, if the event then occurs, it was not foreseen. The event could have been identified, however, had a more thorough risk analysis been conducted. An illustration of the situation of unknown knowns pertains to the terrorist attacks of September 11, 2001. The third category of black swan events refers to situations where these events occur despite the fact that the probability of occurrence is judged to be negligible. The events are indeed known, but considered so unlikely that they are ignored, thus leading to a situation where cautionary measures are not implemented. This is illustrated in the case where tsunami risk was initially identified as a hazard possibility and added to the list of potential hazards by Japanese authorities. The risk of a tsunami, however, was later removed because the probability of that event was judged as being negligible. Consequently, the 2011 tsunami that affected the Fukushima nuclear plant came as a surprise. Dealing with uncertainty, as alluded to in previous chapters, definitely plays a role in environmental management. In this light, how can the black swan theory help reorient environmental management philosophy to better deal with uncertainty and unknowns?

As alluded to in our discussion of post-normal science, the uncertainties and limits to knowledge with which we must now grapple are to a certain extent the result of the increasing complexity of socio-ecological systems we are immersed in today. One of the implications of this is that the potential for a black swan event to occur has increased as the "the sources of Black Swans today have multiplied beyond measurability" (Taleb, 2010: 61). Indeed, the increase in the potential for black swan events may also help account for the recorded increase in disasters and their impacts over the last few decades, with further increases predicted as the ecological crisis worsens (as noted in Chapter 8).

The complexity upon which the increased potential for black swan events is predicated needs to be taken into account in developing alternative environmental management strategies. That is, if the environment, or more accurately, the relationship between nature and society, has become more complex, then environmental management strategies must reflect this new material and social reality. How, then, has our reality become more complex, and what is it about complexity that increases the potential for black swan events? To a certain extent we have addressed some of the factors that may contribute to this in previous chapters – for example, in our discussions about globalization – but particularly in regard to the role of amplifying feedback loops and non-linearities. The latter is emphasized by Taleb (2010: 88) who notes that in the "real" world, linear relationships are truly the exception. Explanations based on linear models are simplistic accounts in which relationships between variables are seen to be clear, crisp and constant, and therefore easy to understand. This is the reason that Taleb alleges that linear models and thinking are emphasized in the classroom and in textbooks. He contends, however, that the world is actually much more non-linear than we ourselves, and scientists, would like to think.

One reason that linear relationships do not accurately capture the current state of social and natural phenomena is because we live in what Taleb (2010: xxvi) refers to as an increasingly "recursive environment" in which:

> Recursive here means that the world in which we live has an increasing number of feedback loops, causing events to be the cause of more events (say, people buy a book *because* other people bought it), thus generating snowballs and arbitrary and unpredictable planet-wide winner-takes-all effects. We live in an environment where information flows too rapidly, accelerating such epidemics. Likewise, events can happen *because* they are not supposed to happen.
>
> (ibid.)

The recursive potential of the social and natural systems has undoubtedly increased with the facilitating processes of globalization and digitalization that have led to an increasingly networked world (Castells, 2010). This is because modern networked connections facilitate the rapid conveyance of various flows on which the globalized world relies, including flows of people, goods, information, foodstuffs, and even viruses and pathogens, which in turn may accelerate and amplify recursive effects.

The Theory of Black Swan Events and Disaster Management

Quoting Yogi Berra's quip that "The future ain't what it used to be", Taleb (2010: 13) comments that the baseball great seems to be correct. This is because the gains in scientists' (and we would add environmental and disaster managers') abilities to model and predict the world have been dwarfed by increases in the world's complexity, and the influence of amplifying feedback loops and recursive effects. In turn, this implies a greater and greater role for the unpredicted as we live on into the future, adding further that "[t]he larger the role of the Black Swan, the harder it will be for us to predict" (ibid.). Yet we proceed as if this were not the case, not realizing that our environment is more complex than our simplifying assumptions would lead us to believe.

For Taleb, although most people may not realize (or acknowledge) it, black swan events dominate natural and social life. For this reason, there is an urgent need to develop a type of reasoning that is better able to analyze and deal with rare events, randomness and outliers. The current approaches are based on the use of normal distribution (i.e. bell-curve) statistics. With these types of statistics, referred to as Gaussian, the probabilities are known, but this type of statistics is not suitable for dealing with black swan phenomena where the probabilities are not known. Thus, Taleb comments that:

Almost everything in social life is produced by rare but consequential shocks and jumps; all the while almost everything studied about social life focuses on the "normal," particularly with "bell curve" methods of inference that tell you close to nothing. Why? Because the bell curve ignores large deviations, cannot handle them, yet makes us confident that we have tamed uncertainty.

(2010: xxix)

Let us consider an example that illustrates the differences in approach and treatment of probability and statistics between Gaussian and black swan thinking. Say that one is told that two randomly selected authors together sold a total of one million copies of their books. Taleb notes that upon hearing this, most people would almost automatically assume that each author would have sold 500,000 copies each (i.e. equal halves). In actuality, the most likely combination would be 993,000 copies sold for one author and 7,000 for the other. In fact, for any large total, the breakdown will be even more and more asymmetric. In other words, extremes dominate the sale of books. For Taleb, the point is that measures of uncertainty that are based on the normal distribution simply disregard the possibility, and the impact, of sharp jumps or discontinuities. These Gaussian measures are therefore not appropriate for use in many situations in our actual world because the "real world" is dominated by the impacts of extreme events (i.e. black swan events). Thus, Taleb notes that using the statistics of the normal distribution "is like focusing on the grass and missing out on the (gigantic) trees. Although unpredictable large deviations are rare, they cannot be dismissed as outliers because, cumulatively, their impact is so dramatic" (2010: 235). Moreover, the dramatic quality of black swan events cannot be underestimated because it is precisely these events that are responsible for making history not crawl but jump, and are in fact responsible for much of the significant economic, social and political changes evident throughout history (Taleb, 2010: 42). In this connection, an important insight from black swan thinking is that most important events are the least predictable.

In light of the above discussion, one of the key barriers in recognizing the significant role that black swan events play in our lives is that our current methods of approach do not effectively deal with randomness and rare events, thus resulting in an under-appreciation and neglect of black swan phenomena. Taleb suggests some recent mathematical developments in complexity and network science such as statistics based on a power-law distribution as being more appropriate to the analysis of black swan phenomena – or, more correctly, appropriate to a particular subset of black swan events referred to as "grey swans" (discussed below).

We cannot delve further into too much deal with respect to these alternative mathematical approaches because that would simply take us well beyond the scope of our specific exposition of the black swan approach, the goal of which is to help understand the implications of this approach for the philosophical reorientation of environmental management. What can be said at this point, however, is that power-law distribution describes what are referred to as scale-free networks. The presence of scale-free networks is thought to be a generic property of many types of complex systems found in our world. These include the types of networks found in the fields of genetics, neuroscience, power grids, transportation systems, epidemiology and global financial flows through global cities (Urry, 2007). What is a prominent and determining feature of scale-free networks is that although there may be a very large number of small nodes in the network, certain nodes, known as hubs, have a disproportionate influence on the functioning of the network as a whole. Each node has a certain number of connections, or linkages, associated with them. Smaller nodes will only be connected to the network through one or two linkages with other nodes, while larger nodes will have a greater number of connections to the network. It is those nodes with a very large number of linkages that are the hubs. In a scale-free network, there will be a large number of small nodes but only a very few hubs. But, because of the disproportionate importance of the hub for the functioning of the network, disabling just one or two hubs will lead to complete network failure, while disabling a large number of nodes will not, as the network flows can relatively easily circumvent the non-functioning smaller nodes, but cannot so easily circumvent a hub. A good illustration of a scale-free network is the network of airports around the world: an extremely large number of small airports (i.e. nodes with few connections) exist, while the number of huge international airports (i.e. the hubs have a very large number of connections) is relatively few. Yet it is these few hubs that have a dominant influence on the types of air traffic problems that arise in the network of air travel. If the actual number of airports with each particular number of connections is plotted, the resultant graph would depict a power-law distribution and definitely not a normal bell-curve distribution. What should be kept in mind with reference to scale-free networks is that their ability to function properly as a network is very vulnerable to black swan events because the disabling of the entire network can quickly and effectively happen if just one or two of the hubs fail.

For the purposes of our discussion here, it is sufficient to note that conventional Gaussian approaches tend to rely on the statistics of the normal distribution to help predict and characterize the type of phenomena associated with the ecological crisis – for instance, black swan events such as environmental disasters, ecosystem collapse or global warming – are inadequate. It is important to note that it is not just the specific techniques of environmental management that need to be readjusted to take into account black swan events, such as the types of statistics used or the particular models adopted, but rather the assumptions underlying the current environmental management orientation must themselves be rethought – a theme that we have emphasized throughout this book with reference to the broader context in which the general philosophical approach of conventional environmental management is enmeshed.

One important element of black swan thinking that needs to be incorporated in the philosophy of environmental management involves the acknowledgment of how very rare events may have very large effects, and then preparing for those effects. Such reasoning, for instance, can be incorporated in the Hazards

Identification and Risk Assessment (HIRA) protocol discussed in Chapter 8. Recall that the HIRA protocol was based on first identifying all the hazards that can affect a given locale, and then determining/assigning a probability of disaster associated with each identified hazard. The subsequent steps in the process then dealt with the development of appropriate and suitable responses to the potential disasters that could be faced. The usual working logic in developing strategies for response is to focus almost exclusively on those disasters that have the highest probability of occurring based on the determinations of risk (often using the historical record of disaster occurrence in the past). By incorporating insights from the theory of black swan events, the approach to focusing on disasters would be different. Rather than focusing exclusively on high probability events that have high consequences, an equal focus would be on preparing for black swan events – that is, disasters with a low probability that are associated with perhaps moderate to high consequences or impacts for the community. As mentioned, it is particularly important to take note of the fact that the determination and classification of a disaster risk as high, moderate or low is based on a probability assessment that uses the historical record of the past. This is done, for example, through the use of such classificatory designations as "No history of incidents in the last 15 years"; "5 to 15 years since last incident"; "1 incident in the last year"; or "multiple or recurring incidents in the last year". The theory of black of swan events would remind us to be cautious in using such a method. That is, the key to preparing for black swan events rests in understanding the way in which disasters are statistically distributed over time. Specifically, that the frequency and magnitude of the impacts of disasters do not follow a normal distribution, rather, they will follow a power-law distribution, with many limited-consequence disasters with a few large-consequence disasters. Furthermore, in making use of observations from the past to predict the future, Taleb remarks that "Mistaking a naïve observation of the past as something definitive or representative of the future is the one and only cause of our inability to understand the Black Swan" (2010: 42). The potential of the HIRA protocol to deal with environmental black swan events could be enhanced if a different orientation is adopted, one in which much more emphasis is placed in determining the possible consequences and effects of the event rather than predicting the event itself.

"Greying" the Black Swan Event

Perhaps one of the key ways to deal with the phenomenon of black swan events is to first be aware of, then make a conscious effort to deal with, the human tendency to underestimate outliers. It is perhaps due to this inherent tendency that so much emphasis is on the mean (or statistical average) instead of the extremes. By focusing on the observations that hover around the mean, one is focusing on that which is the most typical or to be expected. As alluded to previously, such an approach underlies the traditional Gaussian way of looking at the world with the normal distribution (i.e. the bell curve) as its organizing principle. With this particular type of distribution, the odds of deviation decline faster and faster (i.e. exponentially) as you move away the average situation (i.e. distance away from the mean). The central focus, therefore, is always pegged to the average. As such, a major implication of viewing the world through a Gaussian lens is that it begins by focusing on the ordinary and treats the exceptions (i.e. outliers) as ancillaries (Taleb, 2010: 236).[1] An alternative approach, however, is to take the exception as the starting point and treat the ordinary as subordinate – an approach more in line with the underlying logic of the theory of black swan events. By adopting this alternative approach, the focus switches to those situations that tend to be much beyond the expected (i.e. away from the average where the average value is understood to be the most expected value). With a focus on that which is much less expected, the type of knowledge that will inform the analysis will need to change to reflect this new orientation towards extreme values. In this context, "Black Swan logic makes *what you don't know* far more relevant than what you do know. Consider that many Black Swans can be caused and exacerbated *by their being unexpected*" (Taleb, 2010: xxiii).

What is notable about formalized thinking about black swan events is that it does leave an opening for the existence of some rare and consequential events that may nevertheless be somewhat predictable (Taleb, 2010: 37). In reference to these specific types of events, Taleb notes that:

> They are near-Black Swans. They are somewhat tractable scientifically— knowing about their incidence should lower your surprise; these events are rare but expected. I call this special case of "gray" swans Mandelbrotian randomness. This category encompasses the randomness that produces phenomena commonly known by terms such as *scalable, scale-invariant, power laws, Pareto-zipf laws, Yule's law, Paretian-stable processes, Levy-stable,* and *fractal laws*.
>
> (2010: 37)

In fact, the underlying and implicit working logic of the HIRA protocol is based on an attempt to systematically or scientifically trace disaster incidence from the past. Thus, by careful consideration of the data relating to past disaster incidence, efforts can be made, as Taleb notes, to "turn these Black Swans into Gray Swans, so to speak, reducing their surprise effect" (2010: 213). A gray swan event in this context refers to a black swan event we can somewhat take into account, despite not being able to completely figure out all its properties or being able to characterize the event through precise calculations (Taleb, 2010: 303). The approach of attempting to "gray" a black swan event such as a disaster is only possible because disasters may be considered to follow a power-law or scale-free distribution (what Taleb refers to above as "scale-invariant"), where some disasters may have a limited impact – of which there are many – while other disasters may have extremely large-scale impacts – of which there are fortunately only a few. Adopting a black swan approach to disaster management would therefore mean focusing on the latter.

In light of the above, taking into account the social and material impacts or effects of black swan events must be given greater prominence in environmental management thought. This is an especially pertinent consideration when one considers that the impacts of black swan events today are much more significant in magnitude and pervasive in scale. It may very well be that the nature of environmental disasters, especially weather-related ones such as earthquakes and tornadoes, have not changed much over the centuries (although climate change experts may be starting to have a different view), but what has changed, as Taleb (2010: 61) points out, are the socioeconomic consequences of such occurrences. This is because the extended interlocking relationships and network effects facilitated by globalization (see, for example, Castells, 2010), especially in relation to economics and culture, has enabled the economic and social consequences of black swan events to be much more significant, reverberating and pervasive relative to the state of affairs that was present only a few decades ago. In other words, matters that used to have relatively minor and localized effects in the past may now have major impacts throughout the world because of the networked complexity of the contemporary world.

How, then, can we try to gray the black swan events by minimizing their surprise quality and pervasive effects? One notable way is to consider how natural ecosystems accomplish this very feat.

Bringing Nature Back In

Interestingly, one way to help think about more effective ways to deal with black swan events is by considering the example of how they are dealt with in natural ecosystems. Taleb notes that Mother Nature has a very successful track record in dealing with black swan events, as evident by the fact that natural ecosystems have existed for far longer than human beings – it is the oldest system around:

> Mother Nature is clearly a complex system, with webs of interdependence, nonlinearities, and a robust ecology (otherwise it would have blown up a long time ago). It is an old, very old person with an impeccable memory.
> (2010: 311)

A notable way that the natural world deals with the negative effects of black swan events is that it prevents those effects from spreading through the entire system. That is, the negative effects remain confined and therefore limited in consequence with respect to the impacts they may have for the functioning of the whole system. This strategy, which is prevalent in the natural world, could be emulated in the social world. This would involve an approach where the emphasis would not be on the correction of human mistakes per se, nor would it be the attempt to eliminate randomness from social and economic life through monetary policies, subsidies, and so on, as has been the conventional emphasis since at least the time of the Enlightenment. Rather, the emphasis would be to let the mistakes and miscalculations remain confined. Such an emphasis is similar to the notion of safe-fail, as opposed to fail-safe, used in the fields of systems design and disaster management. For instance, in his discussion of engineering resilience, the disaster researcher David Etkin (2016: 124) describes fail-safe designs as those designed not to fail, in contrast to safe-fail designs where failure occurs with a minimum of harm (as, for example, with a fuse). Doing the opposite – that is, emphasizing the design of fail-safe systems – will ultimately lead to a reduction in the volatility and open randomness of systems, which in turn will increase exposure to the effects of black swan events; it creates an artificial quiet (Taleb, 2010: 322). In addition to the strategy of sequestering the negative effects of black swan events, other strategies may also be revealed by taking a closer look at how Mother Nature deals with such rare but consequential events. The use of redundancies represents another such strategy.

Different types of redundant systems are found within nature. We will focus here on the simplest type for the purposes of illustration – that is, a defensive type of redundancy intended to enable the system to survive under conditions of adversity (Taleb, 2010: 312). Here, we are referring to the availability of spare parts – if one part fails, then another part will take over the function in question. Thus, the human body is equipped with two eyes, two lungs, two kidneys, and so on, where each has more capacity than required under ordinary circumstances. In this context, redundancy equals insurance. The apparent drawback of this is that having redundancies seems to be inefficient in that there is a cost to maintaining the spare parts and to keep them functioning in spite of their idleness. Yet, the costs outweigh the benefits in the long-term in terms of providing insurance in the event of a black swan event. The value of this type of approach has already been recognized in many types of engineering applications where redundancies are built into the technological system – for example, carrying a spare tire in a car or a "zero-force" beam that will take on the surplus load if another beam in the structure fails. These redundancies are integrated into the system despite the additional economic costs associated with doing so because it is largely recognized that it is simply prudent to do so. It is also recognized that using redundancies in this way will actually lead to costs savings in the long term because it will be less expensive to pay the costs of the redundancies in the present rather than paying for the expensive process of rebuilding after a black swan event in the future.

A third strategy to deal with the possibility of black swan events found within natural systems is the tendency not to overspecialize. Overspecialization will limit the positive potential and possibilities of evolution and make species vulnerable to the effects of black swan events. In other words, diversity, including biodiversity, allows ecosystems to be robust by putting them in a better position to adapt by allowing for the opportunity to draw upon alternative resources. Overspecialization, in other words, runs counter to nimbleness and adaptability. This is related to another point that Taleb makes – namely, "Mother Nature does not like anything too big" (2010: 314). The lesson learned from these principles is that human-made constructs should not be allowed to become too large. In the social context, overspecialization may be facilitated by certain developments spurred on by neoliberal economic globalization. Specifically, the phenomenon of large-scale company mergers based on the notion of the benefits of "economics of scale" illustrates what may happen if human-made constructs are allowed to become too large. Taleb (2010: 314–315) argues that company expansions and mergers are usually rationalized according to the idea that companies save money when they become large (i.e. they become more economically "efficient"). This is the accepted logic in the business world despite the fact that the evidence would suggest the opposite. Although large companies may appear to be more "efficient", they are actually much more vulnerable to outside contingencies – that is, to black swan events. Under the illusion of enhanced stability, large companies attempt to optimize their profits and justify their mergers to stakeholders by succumbing to the pressure of Wall Street analysts to "sell the extra kidney" and ditch insurance to raise their "earnings per share" and "improve their bottom line" – hence, eventually contributing to their bankruptcy (Taleb, 2010: 315). A prime example of the vulnerability of overly large entities to black swan events is illustrated by how the failure of one large bank in September 2008, Lehman Brothers, brought down the entire financial edifice. Such fragility of the entire network as a function of a very small number of very large entities also follows logically from our previous discussion of hubs and the power-law distributions. Recall that the failure of one or two hubs will lead to the failure of the entire network because the proper functioning of the network is dependent on these select few hubs.

At the level of human intervention in the natural environment, the principle of not allowing such interventions to become too grandiose was pointed out some time ago by the work of E.F. Schumacher (1973). In his book, *Small is Beautiful: A Study of Economics as if People Mattered*, Schumacher argues that the economic and technological systems constructed by human beings are not compatible with the abilities and actual needs of human beings. Consequently, we are misled by the belief that technology and profit-based economics can solve all the problems faced by humanity. To counter this tendency, Schumacher calls for a shift in lifestyle and worldview on to problems that matter for human happiness rather than only the fulfillment of materialist desires. As part of this this shift, Schumacher contends that there is a need to develop smaller scale technologies that are more in line with the needs of a particular community rather than a mass population. The influence of such thinking is seen in contemporary times in terms of the localism movement or the move to decentralize various production processes upon which we depend (e.g. electricity generation or food production). For instance, the alternative to a very large centralized electricity generation plant would be the construction of smaller renewable energy plants that are based on wind or solar power. Another example would be the pursuit of small-scale local farming instead of large intensified livestock operations. These types of decentralized projects would help spread the risk and effects when a black swan event is faced. That is, by ensuring that the project is limited to a smaller scale, the effects emanating from a black swan disaster would be limited. For example, if one large hydro-electricity plant were to fail, it could affect an entire city, but the failure of one of many small hydro-electricity plants would not lead to depriving the entire city of electricity, but would affect just one or two specific neighorhoods. Similarly, in another context, Patricia Adams (1991) documents how large-scale hydro-electric development projects sponsored by the World Bank have led to huge environmental impacts and the displacement of indigenous peoples when large dams have failed. This has led to extensive flooding and damage across significantly large tracts of land. Such damage could have been limited if these types of development projects were less ambitious and were of a decidedly smaller scale.

A fourth relevant principle that may be discerned by observing the workings of natural ecosystems is expressed by Taleb as "Mother Nature does not like too much connectivity and globalization—(biological, cultural, or economic)" (2010: 316). Essentially, too much connectivity in a system allows the consequences of a black swan event to spread quickly throughout the network, thus leading to the rapid catastrophic failure of the network as a whole. Taleb refers to the vulnerability of highly connected systems to black swan events as "interlocking fragility" (2010: 225). The deceptive aspect of interlocking fragility, especially in the context of globalization, is that because volatility in the system may become reduced, it gives the appearance of system stability. Taleb (2010: 225) again refers to economic globalization for illustration. He notes that the mergers of small financial institutions have resulted in a smaller number of very large banks. This has resulted in a situation were almost all banks are now interconnected such that when one bank falls, they all fall. As such, this has led to a new type of threat which the world had not previously faced – namely, the threat of global financial collapse.

For Taleb, many of the current ideas on the positive effects of globalization and globalized interconnectivity are a little too naive and perhaps dangerous for society. This is because they do not take into account the side effects of globalizing processes. Thus, "[g]lobalization might give the appearance of efficiency, but the operating leverage and the degrees of interaction between parts will cause small cracks in one spot to percolate through the entire system" (2010: 313). For instance, with reference to the possibility of global pandemics, in their volume *Networked Disease: Emerging Infections in the Global City*, Ali and Keil (2008) found that one of the reasons that there has been a documented dramatic increase in disease outbreaks is due to the effects of an increased level of interconnectivity between global cities as well as between remote and urban areas. In regard to the latter, it was noted that in the past, prior to the onset of widespread global air travel, an infectious disease outbreak in a remote village would remain an isolated incident. The disease outbreak would run its course in a particular village and its effects would be limited exclusively to that village. Under the current circumstances of increased interconnectivity, there is an increased likelihood that a person from an urban area may contract the infectious disease and spread that to an urban area, where the greater prevalence of potential human hosts would allow the disease to spread quite expeditiously. Furthermore, the risk of global disease spread increases because the flight times between any two cities in the world have become so reduced these days, that the time to fly between any two locales is less than the incubation period of many infectious disease pathogens. Consequently, travelers do not exhibit symptoms of the disease until they are already established in their destination locales and have already interacted with a great number of people there without any awareness that they are, in fact, ill, thus amplifying the risk potential and effects.

Taleb points out that he is not opposed to the globalized connectivity per se and he recognizes the positive aspects it offers. What he wants to emphasize rather is that society needs to be aware of the side effects and trade-offs associated with this. Such awareness will enable us to be better positioned to deal with the negative repercussions that may develop. For example, such an awareness may help to preemptively prepare for the case of financial collapse or pandemic disease spread.

Concluding Remarks

Developing approaches to deal with black swan events will surely be an indispensable need as the world becomes much more complex. The increasing complexity of the social world will also have implications for the nature of relationship human beings will have with the environment. As that relationship itself becomes more complex and unpredictable, environmental management will need to add other considerations to its tool kit, including the consideration of such factors and phenomena as non-linear effects, rapid change and uncertainty. For this reason, a reorientation of conventional environmental management may be necessary. In this context, we surmise that anticipatory surprise management and black swan thinking will become key components of the new tool kit. In the next chapter, we will discuss some promising leads that have the potential to develop and incorporate these aspects – in particular, research on scenario development and weak signals.

Note

1. Taleb (2010: 236) notes that the Gaussian approach is well suited and appropriate to certain specific types of situations only. These are situations where there would be a rational reason that most extreme values would not fall too far away from the average value. This would be the case if, for instance, there were some physically imposed limitation that would prevent very large values from arising, or if there were strong equilibrium forces that ensured that values would stay close to the mean rather than diverging away from the equilibrium state. It is in reference to the latter that Taleb observes that so much of economics is based on the notion of equilibrium – it allows the analyst to treat economic phenomena as Gaussian.

References

Adams, P. (1991) *Odious Debts: Loose Lending, Corruption and the Third World's Environmental Legacy*. Toronto: Probe International.

Ali, S.H. (2012) "Infectious Diseases as New Risks for Human Health". In S. Kabisch, A. Kunath, P. Schweizer-Ries, A. Steinfuhrer (Eds.) *Advances in People-Environment Studies,*

Volume 3: Vulnerability, Risks, and Complexity: Impacts of Global Change on Human Habitats. Gottingen: Hogrefe, pp.13–25.

Ali, S.H. Ali and Keil, R. (2008) (Eds.) *Networked Disease: Emerging Infections in the Global City*. Oxford: Wiley-Blackwell.

Aven, T. (2015) "Implications of Black Swans to the Foundations and Practice of Risk Assessment and Management". *Reliability Engineering & System Safety*, 134: 83–91.

Castells, M. (2010) *The Information Age: Economy, Society and Culture Volume 1: The Rise of the Network Society* (2nd ed.) Oxford: Wiley Blackwell.

Curry, Judith (2011) "The Climate Black Swan". Available at: https://judithcurry.com/2014

Dror, Y. (2001) *The Capacity to Govern: A Report to the Club of Rome*. London: Frank Cass.

Etkin, D. (2016*) Disaster Theory: An Interdisciplinary Approach to Concepts and Causes*. Waltham, MA: Butterworth-Heinemann.

Farazmand, A. (2007) "Learning from the Katrina Crisis: A Global and International Perspective with Implications for Future Crisis Management." *Public Administration Review*, December: 149–159.

Handy, C. (1998) *Beyond Certainty: The Changing Worlds of Organizations*. Cambridge, MA: Harvard University Press.

Hermann, C.F. (1969) *Crisis in Foreign Policy: A Simulation Analysis*. Indianapolis, IN: Bobbs-Merrill.

Lehmann, J.-P. (2007) "The Black Swan: Dealing Effectively with Improbable Events". Available at: www.imd.org/research/challenges/TC089–07.cfm

Schumacher, E.F. (1973) *Small is Beautiful: A Study of Economics as if People Mattered*. New York: Harper & Row.

Stacey, R.D. (1992) *Managing the Unknowable: Strategic Boundaries between Order and Chaos in Organizations*. San Francisco, CA: Jossey-Bass.

Taleb, N.N. (2010) *The Black Swan: The Impact of the Highly Improbable*. New York: Random House.

Urry, J. (2007) *Mobilities*. Cambridge: Polity Press.

12
EXPERIMENTAL APPLICATIONS OF EMERGING, ALTERNATIVE ENVIRONMENTAL MANAGEMENT

As we have discussed in the preceding chapters, the ecological crisis is a multifaceted problem – social, technical, political, philosophical and existential. The many dimensions of the challenge demand an equally broad conception of environmental management, which must involve experts and non-experts in collaborative governance. New and improved approaches to EM must build upon the history and existing strengths of the field. On the other hand, since we have argued that conventional approaches are insufficient, the future will need to be very different. In other words, the future of environmental management needs to feature both continuities and discontinuities – improvement to existing strengths as well as departures from current practice. In this chapter we discuss three interrelated components of emerging, alternative environmental management that would be considered departures or discontinuities, since they are hardly used at all at present: scenario development, weak signals and selected applications of concepts and frameworks derived from environmental sociology.

Scenario Development

Scenario development techniques have been used for many decades in fields that have historically had little to do with environment and sustainability: military and corporate. In those contexts, scenario development evolved mostly as a risk management tool, to help identify trends, threats and opportunities. At its most basic level, a scenario is simply a narrative – a story of a future that could happen. A good scenario needs at least three attributes. First, it needs to be *plausible*; if it is not considered plausible, no one will entertain it and it will be dismissed completely. Second, it needs to be *engaging*; if it is not interesting or intriguing, and fails to attract an audience, it is not useful. Third, it needs to be *relevant* – it needs to address issues and themes that resonate broadly enough. In practice, fulfilling all three criteria has proven to be an art form – no easy task. The relatively small body of literature pertaining to sustainability-focused scenarios (e.g. Carlsson-Kanyama et al., 2008; Myers and Kitsuse, 2000; Quist and Vergragt, 2006; Varum and Melo, 2010; Volkery et al., 2008; Mulvihill and Kramkowski, 2010) reflects a recurring inability to engage broad readership.

Why have mainstream audiences not paid attention to sustainability scenarios? Some of the reasons may be obvious enough – for example, they are seldom published in popular media and have not been promoted vigorously by publishers. They are often made available free of charge on websites. For example, the Global Scenarios Group makes its scenario reports easily available, but the pool of potential readers is no doubt predominantly made up of those who are already well initiated to environmental or sustainability literature through their work or studies. The Global Scenario Group's most notable work – *Great Transitions* – is exemplary in its creative and compelling use of sustainability scenarios (Raskin et al., 2002). In general, literature of this kind appeals to a specialized audience that is already well converted to the subject matter and the underlying premises. This means, in effect, that the broader potential readership for sustainability scenarios is virtually untapped and would need to be intrigued or engaged in new ways. To mainstream readers, it is an unfamiliar genre – not like the fiction or non-fiction that they may be accustomed to. We might wonder, why are so many readers willing to suspend their disbelief for science fiction, when many of the story elements of science fiction seem implausible or at least plausible only in the very long-term future? It must be remembered, however, that only the best science fiction resonates widely with readers, while the less engaging stories fail to connect. In the long run, the same will be true of sustainability scenarios. If they are engaging enough, audiences will read them. This was true in the earlier decades of the environmental movement, when seminal books such as *The Limits to Growth* crossed over into the mainstream imagination, and it could happen again if similarly provocative and compelling sustainability-focused scenarios are disseminated.

Explorative Scenarios and Deep Sustainability

There are generally three types of scenarios: *predictive* (concerning futures that are considered likely or probable, and often undesirable), *normative* (concerning futures that are considered desirable) and *explorative* (concerning futures that are not necessarily probable or desirable). It is primarily the third type of scenario – explorative – that we believe holds the most potential as a tool for alternative environmental management and the prospect of deeper sustainability. There are two main reasons for this. First, most of the experience with predictive pursuits (for example, weather forecasting, economic outlooks, risk assessment, conventional environmental impact assessment) confirms that there are significant and inherent limits to prediction. It is usually difficult or impossible to predict even relatively simple, short-term future events with a high degree of accuracy or reliability. The longer the time frame, and the more complex the future, the less useful and relevant predictions tend to be. There are many legitimate roles for the art of prediction, as long as its limitations are acknowledged and understood. We believe, however, that prediction can play only a limited role in the pursuit of deep, long-term sustainability, for reasons that were discussed in Chapter 2. Deep sustainability is a highly uncertain, complex prospect with countless variables and contingencies. For these reasons, it cannot be back-casted or reverse engineered, because too many unpredictable variables are beyond our collective control and influence. To be clear, it must be said that no one really knows how deep sustainability might be achieved. There is a considerable body of literature on sustainability plans and strategies, and we would be poorer without it, but it consists mostly of critiques, principles, criteria, visions and advocacy. But there is wide recognition that the pursuit of deep sustainability (once it begins in earnest) will be much more complex, complicated and serendipitous than might be imagined. It is, to a great extent, beyond the realms of prediction, planning and strategy. Deep sustainability would need to be a process of accelerated learning, experimentation and improvisation.

Even under ideal conditions and circumstances, the time frame needed to approach deep sustainability is unclear and highly debatable. It could be argued, optimistically, that it could happen within 30 or 40 years, if profound and revolutionary changes took place (for example, the normalization of no net losses of biodiversity, discontinued use of fossil fuels and other unsustainable trends, optimally efficient use of resources, sustainable livelihoods globally, etc.). But more than four decades have passed since the first Earth Day in 1969, and most would agree that progress since then towards deep sustainability has generally been only incremental. Indeed, it would be easy to argue that the overall trend has been negative and the world has become much more unsustainable since then. Therefore, we must assume that the pursuit of deep sustainability will be very long term and multigenerational, unless there are dramatic progressive breakthroughs resulting in greatly accelerated progress. In practice, if we view deep sustainability as a long-term prospect, it hardly matters whether the time frame might be 50, 100 or even 200 years, because the implications for environmental management might be the same for any of these time frames. That assumes, of course, that present generations have, and future generations will have the luxury of long-term time frames to address the ecological crisis. But clearly, the challenge implies a shift away from conventional, short-term, reactive approaches, and a shift towards alternative approaches.

The value of explorative scenarios (as opposed to predictive or normative) can be captured in a central point made by Peter Schwartz (1991), author of *The Art of the Long View*. Schwartz observes that the purpose of scenarios is to prepare us for what we think will *not happen* (Schwartz, 1991). This is a profound and profoundly counter-intuitive point. Schwartz and his colleagues used scenario development techniques for corporate strategy and risk management, but the applications have broadened considerably since the 1970s and 1980s, and there is now a considerable and growing literature concerning environmental and sustainability-focused applications of scenarios. A classic explorative scenario development exercise, adapted from the techniques used by Schwartz and others, would involve exploration and analysis of a combination of four components: (1) predetermined elements; (2) drivers; (3) critical uncertainties; and (4) weak signals (Schwartz, 1991). An explorative scenario thus consists of a combination of elements of different possible futures.

Examples of things that are already happening (predetermined elements)

- Demographic trends that are shaping social futures (aging populations in some countries; higher or lower fertility rates in other countries)
- Declining biodiversity, particularly in ecologically vulnerable regions
- Globalization
- Climate change

Examples of directions that seem likely to unfold or continue given current forces and trends (drivers)

- Increasing demand/supply of alternative energy systems
- Public pressure for corporate social responsibility
- Refugee migration
- Concerns about food security
- "Natural" and "unnatural" disasters
- Driverless vehicle technology

Examples of things that might or might not happen (critical uncertainties)

- Increasing or decreasing average life expectancy
- Medical and technological discoveries and breakthroughs
- Rapid transition to advanced renewable energy systems (e.g. hydrogen-based technologies)
- Collapse or recovery of ecological systems and resources (e.g. fisheries)
- Space travel/colonization of other planets

- Transition to more dematerialized economies
- Transition to less consumptive societies
- Reduction in the global fleet of vehicles resulting from automobile sharing

Examples of things that are happening now but are largely unnoticed (weak signals)

- Ecological collapse triggered by factors such as declining bee populations
- Ecological changes caused by invasive species
- Fledgling social movements that could gather momentum and eventually prove to be influential or transformative

There can be almost infinite debate about any single element of "the future" or different futures. What might be considered the key drivers of change over the long term? What are the key critical uncertainties impinging on the prospect of deep sustainability? What might be the weak signals of change, happening now right under our noses, but typically unnoticed or downplayed? It is interesting to note that not so long ago, many would have considered climate change to be an uncertainty, but now most people would agree that it is a predetermined element, at least for the foreseeable future. This shows how fluid the categories are; today's weak signal may be a driver or predetermined element tomorrow. More generally, which current environmental management policies and actions might make a critical difference over the long term, and which ones might not? Which international agreements and global governance arrangements are most likely to support deep sustainability? Explorative scenarios do not yield definitive answers, but they can provide a way of evaluating current strategies against different possible futures, and can generate valuable feedback.

When we consider a future narrative composed of some combination of the four elements, we can appreciate why it is beyond prediction and largely beyond our collective control. But this brings us to a central point: *we do not necessarily need to predict and control the future, nor could we, even if that were a goal.* We only need to imagine plausible futures well enough to guide and evaluate present-day actions. These present-day actions matter a great deal, because they can enhance or preclude prospects of substantive progress towards deep sustainability. In this sense, environmental management is the delicate art of choosing and refining actions that appear to be defensible under different scenarios. For example, we might manage freshwater resources differently if we believed that a scenario of greatly accelerated depletion and drought was plausible within the next generation. If, by the year 2050 global freshwater quantity and quality turned out to be the same as it was in 2015, no harm would have been done through the enhanced management measures. But if the more negative freshwater scenario came to pass, enhanced management in the present day might eventually make the difference between a manageable crisis and an unmanageable catastrophe. The same logic applies if we consider other plausible scenario elements or futures such as biodiversity collapse, loss of food security or various nightmare narratives driven by climate change. In every case, reactive environmental management measures will probably be too little and too late. Proactive measures, on the other hand, might make a big difference, even though the outcome might not be known until much later. In other words, if some futures are catastrophic enough that they could not be mitigated, the only sound strategy is to avoid them through present-day risk management measures.

Weak Signals

One of the most intriguing concepts in the scenario development repertoire is the idea of weak signals. The concept implies that a signal of some kind is present, though not necessarily noticed or received (Kuosa, 2010). In a world of information overload, there may be a deluge of signals at any given time, all competing for attention. Even strong signals may go unnoticed by some, or disregarded by others – for example, climate change seems to be an increasingly strong signal but many remain unmoved or impervious to its many manifestations. Weak signals pose difficulty not only because they go largely unnoticed or generate little concern, but also because they may or may not turn out to be significant. This compounds their subtlety and their counter-intuitiveness; they may or may not shape futures that, in any event, we think will not happen. But that also describes deep sustainability – *a long-term possible future that we are unfamiliar with, that might happen through a journey that we do not expect to take.* Guided by plausible future scenarios and weak signals, we can choose environmental management measures that seem sensible given current knowledge and understanding, can be adapted or revised, do no harm and might contribute to deep sustainability.

Weak signals are given little attention in environmental management at present. It may be more accurate to say that they are not used at all. What are the risks that we run by not considering weak signals? The history of environmental incidents and disasters, though incomplete and generally not well understood, often reveals that weak signals end up playing important roles in shaping events. The signals might be any kind of latent phenomena – social, cultural, ecological, political, institutional, etc. – that are present but largely dismissed. Once they become stronger signals, it may be too late in the life cycle of the disaster for effective intervention. Invasive species, for example, can be present but given little attention or low priority at first. Another example might be behavioral patterns that eventually result in a variety of "human errors" that are often identified as instrumental causes of events. Despite the obvious inherent uncertainty and imprecision of identifying weak signals and prescribing management measures for them, it is nevertheless possible to scan, imagine or brainstorm for weak signals. Since literally anything might be a weak signal, their subjectivity and ambiguity necessitate a sensibility that is uncommon in conventional environmental management. The objective is not to identify the "right" weak signals (which is difficult or impossible at any given time), but to broaden the scope of management to include their consideration. This might mean, in effect, that attention is paid to signals that turn out to be irrelevant. But, if one of the signals does become highly significant and it is perceived early enough to allow effective action, the exercise is worthwhile.

Linking Scenario Approaches and Environmental Sociology

Many of the concepts that we have discussed – scenarios, weak signals, black swan thinking, anticipatory surprise management, disaster incubation, etc. – have obvious links and interrelatedness. They share, to a considerable degree, similar underlying premises and philosophies. To a great extent, however, these and other related ideas have evolved separately, in different streams of literature and in different realms of practice. In some regards the organizational cultures in which the approaches evolved were radically different from one another: military, corporate, medical, non-government, academic, and so on. But as we discussed in Chapter 4, there is a tradition for the field of environmental management to borrow liberally from other fields; in its early days of improvisation, EM drew from health and safety practices. Now that the complexity of the challenges facing EM is increasingly appreciated, it is necessary for its theorists and practitioners to draw from a wide array of sources.

To the extent that EM becomes more influenced by fields such as sociology, it would fulfilling a longstanding goal of environmental practitioners – to become more holistic, integrated and interdisciplinary. The quest for interdisciplinary approaches dates back to the early days of environmental management in the 1970s, and was a cornerstone of the field, at least in aspirational terms. The reality of integrating theories and practices across the natural and social sciences has usually proved to be even more difficult than many imagined. The leap from cross-disciplinary to interdisciplinary requires time, and in hindsight the optimistic rhetoric of previous decades was probably premature. That is no longer so true; we see increasing evidence of a socio-ecological orientation in the social sciences, and we see clear signs that the newer generation of environmental practitioners operates across boundaries that were once less surmountable. Big changes are afoot in environmental management, as it expands and diversifies, using alternative approaches that were previously not on the radar. In the next, and final, chapter, we summarize the shapes of emerging, alternative EM and we discuss the "bridge" to the next stage of EM.

References

Carlsson-Kanyama, A., Dreborg, K.H., Moll, H.C., Padovan, D. (2008) "Participative Backcasting: A Tool for Involving Stakeholders in Local Sustainability Planning". *Futures* 40: 34–46.

Kuosa, T. (2010) "Futures Signals Sense-Making Framework (FSSF): A Start-up Tool to Analyse and Categorise Weak Signals, Wild Cards, Drivers, Trends and Other Types of Information". *Futures*, 42: 42–48.

Mulvihill, P.R. and Kramkowski, V. (2010) "Extending the Influence of Scenario Development in Sustainability Planning and Strategy". *Sustainability*, 2(8): 2449–2466.

Myers, D. and Kitsuse, A. (2000) "Constructing the Future in Planning: A Survey of Theories and Tools". *Journal of Planning Education and Research*, 19: 221–231.

Quist, J. and Vergragt, P. (2006) "Past and Future Back-Casting: The Shift to Stakeholder Participation and a Proposal for a Methodological Framework". *Futures*, 38: 1027–1045.

Raskin, P., Banuri, T., Gallopin, G., Gutman, P., Hammond, A., Kates, R. and Swart, R. 2002. *Great Transition: The Promise and Lure of the Times Ahead*. Stockholm Environment Institute, Global Scenario Group, Boston, MA.

Schwartz, P. (1991) *The Art of the Long View: Planning for the Future in an Uncertain World*. New York: Currency Doubleday.

Varum, C.A. and Melo, C. (2010) "Directions in Scenario Planning Literature – A Review of the Past Decades". *Futures*, 42: 355–369.

Volkery, A., Ribeiro, T., Henrichs, T. and Hoogeveen, Y. (2008) "Your Vision or My Model? Lessons from Participatory Land Use Scenario Development on a European Scale". *Systemic Practice and Action Research*, 21: 459–477.

13
CONCLUSION AND PROSPECTS FOR ALTERNATIVE ENVIRONMENTAL MANAGEMENT

In this book we have critiqued conventional environmental management and explored possible directions for better alternatives. EM, like everything else within the realm of "environment", is still a relatively new and evolving field. The field is in need of a much stronger theoretical foundation, informed by a much wider range of knowledge, including sources that have been largely ignored to date, such as environmental and disaster sociology. We need to go far beyond shallow analyses of environmental problems and sustainability challenges. Taking into account everything we have discussed in this book, we suggest eight principles for advanced, alternative environmental management.

Principle 1: Addressing the Ecological Crisis

We have argued throughout this book that the ecological crisis, unfolding globally and at all scales, is the ultimate context of alternative environmental management. This is not to say that other goals are unimportant – net zero, reducing footprint, social responsibility, etc. are all appropriate goals for EM. But it is important to be mindful of a bigger and more global picture. EM efforts and initiatives at all scales are necessary, but, in a context of climate change and other global ecological issues, the success of EM will ultimately be measured in terms of its ability to address the broader ecological crisis.

Principle 2: Addressing Deep Sustainability

Since the popularization of the concept of sustainable development in the 1980s and its subsequent mainstreaming in the current millennium, it has become increasingly evident that sustainability can be meaningful at times and meaningless at other times, depending on a wide variety of factors. Although evidence of shallower or deeper sustainability will usually be fluid, subjective and inconclusive, it is possible, at least in a normative sense, to aim for deep sustainability in EM. Aiming for shallow sustainability is self-defeating; aiming higher is more difficult and complicated but ultimately more meaningful. In this context, "deep sustainability" may be reflected in practices that are at the forefront of current understanding – for example, smallest possible footprint, carbon neutral, net zero impact, net positive effects of development or intergenerational equity.

Principle 3: Complexity, Uncertainty and Limits to Knowledge

The realities of environmental management (including complexity, irreducible uncertainty and gaps in baseline ecological knowledge) need to be acknowledged and embraced. We have argued that much of the history of conventional EM practice has unfolded largely in denial of complexity and uncertainty. Too often, EM has been practiced on shaky premises – for example, overconfidence in predictions, dismissal of rare events, obliviousness to weak signals, assumptions of high levels of ecological knowledge, etc. On the other hand, when complexity, irreducible uncertainty and limits to knowledge are assumed as preconditions, alternative approaches to EM have unfolded. A transition from the conventional to the alternative orientation in EM has begun slowly, but it may gather momentum as anecdotal evidence of the effectiveness of emerging approaches accumulates.

Principle 4: Transition to Governance

A shift towards alternative environmental management will require a greater degree of governance, as opposed to the pattern of less coordinated, less integrated and even adversarial dynamic that has predominated among government, industry and civil society. A governance-based approach will foster alternative EM in two ways. First, the emphasis on discourse in governance will draw attention to a wider array of options than might otherwise be considered. Second, EM measures that result from governance, with enhanced input from civil society, will tend to reflect a longer term, intergenerational perspective instead of the shorter term thinking that can prevail if only industry and governments are involved.

Principle 5: Addressing Long-Term Scenarios

We have argued that consideration of EM measures should be influenced not only by present-day knowledge, but also by plausible long-term scenarios that are revised continually. This requires a reorientation in how EM is conceived and evaluated. Instead of only asking "was the problem apparently addressed?", consideration of the possible long-term implications of an EM measure is equally important. The discipline of scenario development can help to distinguish actions that may be effective if certain long-term futures come to pass, but less so if other futures eventually play out. A quick fix measure might "solve" a short-term problem but lead to other problems or foreclose future options. Therefore, consideration of multiple time frames is necessary in EM, and scenario-based approaches can be helpful in addressing the inherent uncertainties of longer term futures.

Principle 6: Experimental Approaches

To a greater extent than ever before, we need to experiment now with measures that might help avoid unsustainable futures and disasters. The brief history of the modern environmental movement has been characterized by periods of innovation, but they have been more sporadic than continuous. The greater tendency has been for extended periods in which less experimentation and innovation have occurred. For example, after years of discussion and preparation, Environmental Management Systems began to be popularized and standardized – EMSs crossed over into mainstream practice in industrial sectors. EMS standardization prompted a great deal of conformity and catching up, and then a tendency to "wait for the next big thing". Meanwhile, alternative approaches to EM – aforementioned techniques such as scenario development, disaster incubation analysis, black swan thinking, etc. – remain largely on the fringe of EM practice. History suggests strongly that while many tend to wait for the "next big thing", many other unexpected things happen instead. Experimentation can lead to breakthroughs in understanding and the mainstreaming of alternative approaches.

Principle 7: The Value of Good EM Cannot be "Measured" in Standard Ways

As we have argued, there is often no way of determining, in the short term, whether or not environmental management measures are "effective" or "the right investment". There is seldom a definitive way to determine the financial return on investment of EM, although it sometimes becomes clear retrospectively, in the event of costly incidents or disasters, that relatively modest investments might have made a substantial difference. From a critical standpoint, the tendency to rely exclusively on financial metrics is untenable. In the absence of a reliable formula to evaluate "bang for the buck" of EM options before the fact, a broader perspective needs to prevail. The motivation to invest in good EM is a complicated matter, involving not only the avoidance of problems; it can also involve goodwill, stewardship, ethics and ideology.

Principle 8: Indicators of Good EM

A "good" environmental management measure is one that: (a) makes enough sense at present; (b) addresses a plausible long-term future scenario; (c) can be adapted, revised or discontinued; (d) does no harm; (e) might contribute to deep sustainability.

Bridging from Conventional to Alternative EM

The central argument made in this book concerns the need for a transition from conventional EM to a future in which alternative approaches to EM are common. We have discussed alternative approaches that are at the present time "fringe", in the sense that they are not common practice. EM involving scenarios, disaster incubation analysis, weak signals, black swan or other approaches from environmental sociology are clearly not part of the standard repertoire; they are used, at most, by a small segment of practitioners.

We have also argued that since environmental management is still, in both absolute and relative terms, a very young field (less than 50 years, or two generations), it is subject to evolution and transformation. It seems clear that the turn towards environmental governance, along with other forces of change that we have discussed, will stimulate change of various kinds in EM. It is unlikely that a sudden leap to alternative approaches will occur; it is more likely that gradual change will happen as a result of crises, experimentation and public pressure.

But it is easy to forget that very substantial changes have happened within the environmental movement over the past two generations. It is worth remembering that many terms and concepts that have become everyday household words were alternative not long ago. There are many examples. The word "footprint" had little or no ecological application a short time ago, but is now used widely in the environmental sector and in everyday language. "Organic" and "fair trade" were once only prevalent in alternative food circles, but are now very common. "Triple bottom line" had little or no currency at one time but is now normal language in many business settings. "LED" (light-emitting diode) was an unheard-of acronym not long ago but is now used automatically whenever lightbulbs are mentioned. And, of course, "sustainability" and "sustainable development" evolved from obscurity to mainstream use. It would be naive to assume that the normalization of alternative language in the environmental movement is only symbolic, trivial or token. When environmental consciousness and values crossed over and became normal, it could be argued that a new era began. Negative energy that was once directed at countering the environmental movement or denying climate change has largely dissipated. A much greater amount of energy is now being directed at finding sustainability solutions, and alternative EM will play a prominent role.

INDEX

Index uses italics for boxes and figures

actant 58
action-without-consciousness 58
actor-network theory (ANT) 58
Adams, Patricia 146
adaptation, adaptive capacity 99
Adorno, Theodor 48
age of exuberance 117
Alexander, D. 78
Ali, S.H. 109, 146
alternative environmental management: accounting for complexity 137; addressing limitations of 118–120; apolitical ecology of 124–125; bridging to 160; and citizens, ENGOs 41–42; and governments 42–43; in industry 39–41; principles for 157–160; value, indicators of 159; *see also* anticipatory surprise perspective; black swan perspective; environmental management (EM); post-normal science
Anderson, Ray, C. 39, 41
Anthropocene Era 63
anthropocentrism 53
anticipatory surprise perspective 131–132, *133*
anti-reflexivity movement 68–69
apolitical ecology position 124–125
Art of the Long View, The 151
astroturfing 73
Aven, T. 136

Barnett, J. 73
Barry, John 47, 48–49
baseline data, lack of 119
Beck, Ulrich 13–14, 20, 117, 129
bell curve, inadequacy of 138–139
Bermuda Triangle, of sustainability 37–38
Bhagwati, J. 116
biodiversity 144–145
black swan perspective: under-appreciation of 139; characteristics of 133–134; confining events 144; and disaster management 138–141; disconfirming instances 135; economic, social consequences of 143; greying of 141–143; increased event potential 137–138; narrative fallacy 135–136; in natural ecosystems 143–147; psychological bias 134; and uncertainty, unknowns 136–138; unknown knowns type 137; unknown unknowns type 136–137; unlikely event type 137; *see also* grey swan events
Black Swan: The Impact of the Highly Improbable, The 133
Brundtland Commission, The 8

Canadian Arctic 10
cap and trade systems 17–18
capitalism, role of 116–117
carbon, in atmosphere 65
carbon capitalism 72–73

Catton, William Jr. 52–53, 60n3
Chicago heatwave (1999) 89–90
civil society, and EM 41–42
climate change: catastrophist framing of 70–71; denial of, by elites 67–70; and disaster increase 91–92; economics imperialism in 71–72; feedback loops in 15, 70–71; gradualist framing of 70; greenhouse gases as cause 65; high stakes of decisions 123; and human intervention 14; overview of 64–65; reality of 153; significance of 63–64; social, psychological dimensions of 65–66; social framing for 66–71; as socio-ecological process 73; systems thinking for 71–74; urgency of 66; *see also* feedback loops
Climate Change and Society 77
co-constructionist theory 58–59
community involvement, in environmentalism 124, 126–127
complexity 9–11, 158
"Confessions of a Radical Industrialist" 39
confirmation bias 134–135
consciousness, in historical epochs 50
context sensitivity 74
corporate social responsibility (CSR) 32
critical theory, on EM 46–50
cultural rationality 126–128
Curry, J. 134
Cutter, Susan 96

Davidson, D.J. 19
decentralization 26–27
Derber, C. 66
Dessler, A. 65
Dialectic of Enlightenment 48
disaster management: and anticipatory surprise 132; and black swan events 138–142; convergence with environmental management (EM) 74, 78; core principles for 96, 100; cycle of 79–80; developing 102–103; HIRA as 98; *see also* environmental management (EM)
disaster research: narrowness of 84–86; natural vs social dimensions 87–89, 128; psychological responses to 89; on vulnerability and resistance 86
Disaster Research Center 83
disasters: Chicago heatwave (1999) 90–91; differing vulnerabilities to, 89–91; and the ecological crisis, 77–78; emulating wartime, 84; event-based limitations, 102–103; geographers' research on 81, 83; Hurricane Katrina (2005) 90–91; increase in 78; incubation of 104–106; management cycle of 79–80; organizational features of 104; process-based orientation for 103–104; research similarities to EM 80; September 11 (2001) 85–86; social context change through 91–92; technocratic approach to 80, 83; through terrorism 85–86; unnatural 13–15; worst-case designation 91; *see also* disease ecology
disaster sociology: beginnings of 83–84; narrowness of research 84–85; orienting toward hybrid emphasis 89; positive behaviors found 84; proposed link with environmental sociology 86; response similarity studies 84
disease ecology: *E. coli* outbreak 110–111; and globalization 146–147; outbreak examples 107–108; re-emergence of 106; *see also* Epidemiological Triad
diversity, in nature 144–145
Dunlap, Riley 52–53, 55–56, 68
Durkheim, Emile 50–51

Earth Day (1970) 29
ecological crisis: addressing 157; broader orientation needed 115–116; as social problem 45–46, 117; usefulness of term 7; ways of considering 8–9
ecological knowledge 12–15
economics, and climate change 71–72
ecosystems 9–12
environmental impact assessment (EIA) 24, 30
environmental justice 95, 101–102, 128
environmental management (EM): awareness of 15–16; bridging to alternatives 160; and capital projects 36–37; choosing actions for 153; compliance, due diligence, reputation 35–36; conventional 32–33; converging with disaster management 78; correction vs prevention 34–35; definitions for 3–6; and disaster management 74; drivers for 23–27; evolution, eras of 30–32; explorative scenarios, deep sustainability 150–153; Gaussian approaches in 140; governance in 19–21; limited vision of 36; need for mitigating disasters 91–92; origins of 29–30; political context of 16–19; pre-sustainability mode of 33; reactive orientation 34; scenario development

for 149–150; weak signal consideration 152, 153–154; *see also* alternative environmental management; climate change; disaster management; socio-ecological approach
environmental non-governmental organizations (ENGOs) 27, 33, 41–42
environmental sociology: actor-network theory (ANT) 58; beginnings of 54; biophysical roles, differences 56; co-constructionist theory 58–59; defined 56; differences between Europe, U.S. 60n5; linking biophysical, social worlds 59–60; linking scenario approaches to 154–155; panarchy theory 57; political ecology approach 56–57; recognized by sociologists 55; *see also* sociology
environmental studies 26–27
Environment Canada (Department of the Environment) 30
Epidemiological Triad 106–108, 107f
Erickson, Kai 88–89
Erlich, Paul 29
Etkin, D. 97, 98, 99, 144
Evans, J.P. 19
exemptionalist bias 53–54

Farazmand, Ali 132–133
Farmer, Paul 108–109
feedback loops: in climate change 15, 70–71; positive, negative 70–71, 73–74; recursive potential of 138
Fischer, Frank 125–127, 128
foresight failure 104
Frankfurt School environmental critique 48, 59
Freudenburg, W. 56
Frickel, S. 19
Functowicz, S. 120, 121–122, 124
future discounting 65, 99

Garcia, S.M. 19
Gaussian thinking 138–139, 140, 142, 147n1
Geographic determinism 51–52
Global Biosphere Reserve 10
globalization: and disease spread 146–147; as EM driver 23–24; interlocking relationships 143, 146; as negative force 38; as trend 152
Global Scenarios Group 150
global warming 65; *see also* climate change
governance: cultural rationality in 127–128; as EM driver 19–21, 25; growth of 32; in post-positivism 125–126; technocratic vs post-positivism 128–129; transitioning to 158
governments, and EM 42–43
Grainger, M. 19
Great Transitions 150
green business 40–41
greenhouse gases 65; *see also* climate change
greenwashing 73
grey swan events 141–143
Gunderson, Lance 57

Hajer, M. 19
Hannigan, John 66
Hansen, James 69
Hazards Identification and Risk Assessment (HIRA): black swan reasoning for 141, 142; in Ontario 80, 81b–82b; resilience thinking in 98
Hermann, Charles 132
Holling, C.S. 57
homelessness, and disease 108–109
Hooke's Law 97
Horkheimer, Max 48, 49
Huntington, Ellsworth 51–52
Hurricane Katrina (2005) 90–91

incubation, of disasters 104–106
industry, and EM 39–41
institutional cycling 109
instrumentalism, instrumental rationality 48–49
interactive complexity 112n1
Interface, Ltd. 39
Intergovernmental Panel on Climate Change (IPCC) 25, 69, 72
irreducible uncertainty 11, 13

Kay, J.J. 10
Keil, R. 146
Klinenberg, Eric 89–90
knowledge limits, of EM 158
Kuhn, Thomas 121

"Last Call" 7–8
Latour, Bruno 58
Lawrence, D.P. 10
Lehmann, J.P. 136
Limits to Growth, The 7–8

Mandelbrotian randomness 142
Martell, Luke 55
Marx, Marxism 46–50, 50, 60n2
matrix, socio-ecological 109f
McCright, A.M. 68

McMichael, A.J. 106, 107
Millennium Ecosystem Assessment (2005) 12
Mitigation 98–99
Mol, Arthur, 54–55 60n4
Murdoch, J. 56

narrative fallacy 135–136
National Environmental Protection Act (1969) 12, 24
National Science Foundation 83, 84
natural ecosystems 144–147
neoliberalism 16–18
Neo-Marxism 47
Networked Disease: Emerging Infections in the Global City 146
New Ecological Paradigm (NEP) 53
Newell, Peter 116
Niagara Escarpment 10–11
non-linearities 137–138
Normal Accident theory 112n1

Oliver-Smith, A. 86, 100, 101
O'Neill, S. 73
Our Common Future (1987) 40

panarchy theory 57, 59
Parson, E. 65
Perrow, Charles 112n1
Picou, J.S. 91
polar ice caps, 15; *see also* climate change
political ecology theory 56–57, 59
post-normal science: bridging social and natural 124–125, 128; and community involvement 124, 129; and complex systems 120–121; post-positivism 125; quality control in 124; vs traditional science 120–123, *122*
post-positivism 125, 126–128, 129
psychological bias 134
psychological resilience 97–98

Raskin, P. 150
Ravetz, J.R. 120, 121–122, 124
redundancy, in nature 144
resilience 96–97, 99
resource management 12
risk society 13–14, 87, 117, 129
Robbins, Paul 124–125

scale-free networks 139–140
scenario development 149–150, 158–159
scenarios, explorative 150–155
Schneider, E.D. 10
Schumacher, E.F. 145

Schwartz, Peter 151–152
September 11 (2001) 85–86
Small is Beautiful: A Study of Economics as if People Mattered 145
social constructionist approach 60n6
Social Darwinism 51
social science 44–45, 46–50
socio-ecological approach: adaptation, adaptive capacity 99; baseline data lack 119; to disaster incubation 105–106; to disease outbreaks 106–111; expanding focus with vulnerability perspective 100–101; institutional cycling hampering 109; matrix approach for 109–111, 109f; mitigation 98–99; overview of 95–96; psychological resilience 97–98; reorientation for 118–119; resilience in 97, 99; uses of 112; *see also* vulnerability
socio-ecological matrix 109–111
sociology: and biophysical environment 50–52; as carbon-blind 66; of environmental issues 55; environmental subdivision of 52–54; resistance to use of essentialism 51; *see also* environmental sociology
specificity, historical 50
Stern Review (2006) 72
sustainability, sustainable development: concept developed 31; deep 8, 150–153, 157–158; mainstreaming of, for EM 25–26; negative forces in 37–38; positive forces needed 37; terms popularized 8; and time-scales 11
systems thinking logic 71–74

Taleb, Naseem 133–134, 137–139, 141, 142, 143–147
terrorist attacks 85–86
Tierney, Kathleen 84–85, 86, 100
time-scales 11
toxic effects, of disasters 89
tragedy of the commons 17–18
Turner, Barry 104

uncertainty 11–12, 158
United Nations International Strategy for Disaster Reduction (UNISDR) 96, 98
Urry, John 71–72, 73, 77–78, 86
U.S. Army Corps of Engineers 80, 87
U.S. Department of Homeland Security 85–86

vulnerability: analysis proposed 96–97; defined 95; differing 89–91; to disease outbreaks 108–109; and environmental justice 101–102; research on 86; vs resilience 99

Walkerton, Ontario 110–111
Wall, E. 124
Waltner-Toews, D. 124
weak signals 152, 153–154

Weber, Max 47, 48, 50
White, Gilbert F. 83
Wisner, B. 100–101
World Commission on Environment and Development 8

Young, Nathan 56, 58–59, 69, 116, 125
Youngman, Nicole 98, 99

Taylor & Francis eBooks

Helping you to choose the right eBooks for your Library

Add Routledge titles to your library's digital collection today. Taylor and Francis ebooks contains over 50,000 titles in the Humanities, Social Sciences, Behavioural Sciences, Built Environment and Law.

Choose from a range of subject packages or create your own!

Benefits for you
- Free MARC records
- COUNTER-compliant usage statistics
- Flexible purchase and pricing options
- All titles DRM-free.

Benefits for your user
- Off-site, anytime access via Athens or referring URL
- Print or copy pages or chapters
- Full content search
- Bookmark, highlight and annotate text
- Access to thousands of pages of quality research at the click of a button.

REQUEST YOUR FREE INSTITUTIONAL TRIAL TODAY

Free Trials Available
We offer free trials to qualifying academic, corporate and government customers.

eCollections – Choose from over 30 subject eCollections, including:

Archaeology	Language Learning
Architecture	Law
Asian Studies	Literature
Business & Management	Media & Communication
Classical Studies	Middle East Studies
Construction	Music
Creative & Media Arts	Philosophy
Criminology & Criminal Justice	Planning
Economics	Politics
Education	Psychology & Mental Health
Energy	Religion
Engineering	Security
English Language & Linguistics	Social Work
Environment & Sustainability	Sociology
Geography	Sport
Health Studies	Theatre & Performance
History	Tourism, Hospitality & Events

For more information, pricing enquiries or to order a free trial, please contact your local sales team:
www.tandfebooks.com/page/sales

Routledge — Taylor & Francis Group
The home of Routledge books

www.tandfebooks.com